D1540110

"Bad" Shakespeare

179048

"Bad" Shakespeare

Revaluations of the Shakespeare Canon

Edited by
Maurice Charney

822.33
G1b
Y6

Rutherford ● Madison ● Teaneck
Fairleigh Dickinson University Press
London and Toronto: Associated University Presses

Alverno College
Library Media Center
Milwaukee, Wisconsin

© 1988 by Associated University Presses, Inc.

All rights reserved. Authorization to photocopy items for internal or personal use, or the internal or personal use of specific clients, is granted by the copyright owner, provided that a base fee of $10.00, plus eight cents per page, per copy is paid directly to the Copyright Clearance Center, 27 Congress Street, Salem, Massachusetts 01970. [0-8386-3310-2/88 $10.00 + 8¢ pp, pc.]

Associated University Presses
440 Forsgate Drive
Cranbury, NJ 08512

Associated University Presses
25 Sicilian Avenue
London WC1A 2QH, England

Associated University Presses
P.O. Box 488, Port Credit
Mississauga, Ontario
Canada L5G 4M2

The paper used in this publication meets the requirements of the American National Standard for Permanence of Paper for Printed Library Materials Z39.48-1984.

Library of Congress Cataloging-in-Publication Data

"Bad" Shakespeare.

"Grew out of a seminar at the meeting of the Shakespeare Association of America in Montreal on 28 March 1986"—Acknowl.
   Includes bibliographies and index.
   1. Shakespeare, William, 1564–1616—Criticism and interpretation.   2. Canon (Literature)   I. Charney, Maurice.   II. Shakespeare Association of America.
III. Title: Revaluations of the Shakespeare canon.
PR2976.B225   1988   822.3'3   87-45773
ISBN 0-8386-3310-2 (alk. paper)

PRINTED IN THE UNITED STATES OF AMERICA

Contents

PART IV. *Questions of Text*

Acknowledgments

THE ESSAYS IN *"Bad" Shakespeare* grew out of a seminar at the meeting of the Shakespeare Association of America in Montreal on 28 March 1986. Ten of our contributors offered papers on that occasion, which are now printed in a much revised and expanded form.

The paper of Terence Hawkes is used by permission of Cambridge University Press, which printed part of the present essay elsewhere. The cartoon that illustrates Harriett Hawkins's essay is used by permission of the cartoonist, Rick Mayrowitz.

Introduction

MAURICE CHARNEY

"BAD" SHAKESPEARE raises the teasing question: Can any of Shakespeare be bad? "Bad" in what sense? After the Bible, Shakespeare's works are our primary canonized text. This makes it difficult to approach the plays and poems with any sense of comparative values or the relation of Shakespeare to his fellow dramatists. By their status as canonical texts, Shakespeare's works are set apart from a living tradition, especially from what was actually going on in the theater. This position obscures the fact that Shakespeare was not only an imitator of other playwrights but that he also tried to surpass his models. The set of attitudes conveniently classified as Bardolatry prevents us from understanding Shakespeare as a working dramatist and poet rather than The Bard, before whom all others are as chaff. Bardolatrous critics have discovered ingenious ways of defending everything that seems bad in Shakespeare. Like moral evil, badness in literature is illusory; judicious and searching critics will reveal the excellence that lies behind seeming badness. What we object to is one set of standards for Shakespeare and another for all other dramatists of his age. Shakespeare's texts have been so overedited and so overcriticized that they have lost their relation to other works written in the late sixteenth and early seventeenth centuries.

"Bad" Shakespeare also addresses itself to Shakespeare's reputation, to the hierarchy of plays and poems that have been ruled good, better, and best. Our authors are eager to question the established Shakespeare canon insofar as it places a higher value on works that seem more "Shakespearean" than others. One conventional way to deal with plays that do not seem Shakespearean at all is to demonstrate that they lack authority and that they are therefore not authored by Shakespeare or show his hand only in the superior bits. Our project proposes criteria for what is Shakespearean and speculates about the range of possibilities in Shakespeare's style. Canonical thinking tends to be extremely rigid and zealous—a kind of Shakespeare fundamentalism. We cannot be sensitive to changes in taste and sensibility and also be faithful to the orthodox demands of canon. The best criticism has always questioned the assumptions of the established canon.

9

Within genres, for example, how do we go about setting up criteria for judgment, and between genres how do we determine comparative values? Are dark comedies better (meaning worthier of our attention) than farces? This value judgment grows out of the common assumption among critics that comedy improves as it approaches the domain of tragedy. In this way of thinking, for comedy to become more "serious" and less "frivolous" is a good in itself. In the same vein, do the late romances represent a higher order of dramatic achievement than the early romances? Are they more philosophic? Can Shakespearean tragedy be studied in relation to normative criteria derived from Aristotle's *Poetics?* This almost immediately means that revenge tragedy is downrated in relation to tragedy with more clearly defined ethical criteria. In addition, it would explain the tragic primacy of *King Lear* in our time as opposed to *Hamlet* the revenge play. If we object to this set of priorities, we are obliged to attack the prevailing orthodoxy in the Shakespeare canon. We need to say a good deal about the relation of Shakespeare's revenge tragedies to other revenge plays of the period and their common problems, traditions, and aspirations.

There are obviously historical fashions in Shakespeare's reputation, and plays that once stood low in esteem, like *Antony and Cleopatra* and *Coriolanus,* now stand exceedingly high. Perhaps even *Titus Andronicus,* which T. S. Eliot called "one of the stupidest and most uninspired plays ever written, a play in which it is incredible that Shakespeare had any hand at all, a play in which the best passages would be too highly honoured by the signature of Peele," perhaps even this play, through the whirligig of time and taste, will rise high in our critical judgment. Eliot's dismissive remarks, from "Seneca in Elizabethan Translation" (1927), already seem woefully old-fashioned and beside the point. In relation to other Roman plays of the period, *Titus Andronicus* is one of the freshest and most lyrical examples, as well as being an extraordinary imitation of Ovid. Our critics thus engage in the subversive task of unfixing the canon, or at least of refusing to accept it as generally constituted. Readers can expect some surprises in *"Bad" Shakespeare,* including attacks on such well-established plays as *The Tempest* and *Romeo and Juliet.*

Another large purpose of this volume is to defend plays that stand low in the canon, such as *The Comedy of Errors, The Taming of the Shrew, All's Well that Ends Well,* and *Henry VIII,* or at least to offer arguments that raise their status. Some of our contributors grapple with the implied question: What is Shakespearean about Shakespeare? As a matter of fact, some plays—much neglected by criticism, of course—seem very uncharacteristic of Shakespeare. *The Merry Wives of Windsor* is certainly an odd play, not very comfortably established in the Shakespeare canon, although it is striking how good the play seems in performance. What are we to make of it as a Shakespearean product? The inability to compare if effectively with other Shakespearean comedies makes the act of criticism difficult. We are forced to go outside the Shakespeare canon to other plays about life in London and its environs.

The Taming of the Shrew is the only play with two essays devoted to it, but there could have been many more. How shall we deal with the patriarchal assumptions of this play? Does the play's misogyny seem more irritating and less acceptable now than it did to its original audiences, who came to the theater with different assumptions about the role of women? Is there a way out of the difficulty by playing *The Shrew* as if Kate and Petruchio really love each other, and the taming is only another indication that the course of true love never did run smooth? I am putting the issues of this book in the form of questions because the issues are deeply problematic. There is no settled opinion at this moment, for example, on whether *The Comedy of Errors* is a minor masterpiece in the much neglected genre of farce, or whether farce is by definition in the lowest category in our hypothetical hierarchy of genres. These questions are meant as a sampling of the troubling issues our authors raise. One of the purposes of *"Bad" Shakespeare* is to unsettle our fixed notions about the Shakespeare canon.

Performance raises a special problem. Can bad Shakespeare be converted into good Shakespeare in the theater? This was a question hotly debated in the seminar, and it enters strongly into the articles in this book. What is the relation of specific productions to the playtexts we read? There was general agreement that performance must grow out of the script that Shakespeare wrote, that it can not be something autonomous, a product of free-floating creativity for which the written text is only a pretext. Certain plays have had a much more distinguished stage history than their status in Shakespeare criticism would seem to warrant. *Coriolanus* has one of the principal women's parts in Shakespeare, and Timon has always seemed a more attractive role when acted than reading the play would suggest. Ford in *The Merry Wives of Windsor* overshadows Falstaff in the theater, although on the page the jealous husband seems a stereotyped comic conception. Perhaps we cannot fathom the tremendous energy that playing the part releases. Once performance is introduced as a criterion, the issue of good and bad Shakespeare becomes more complicated. We certainly do not want the sort of classic, school Shakespeare that characterized the early productions of the BBC-TV series.

I have included a long essay on Shakespeare's text because I think that bad quartos and corrupt texts raise the same issues as bad Shakespeare in general. We desire a final, perfected text for plays that are fluid and constantly changing as human values change, and for which our criteria are generally irrelevant. The whole science, or pseudoscience, of textual study has paid very little attention to the theatrical nature of Shakespeare's texts. We may well ask: How bad are the bad quartos? The implication is that they are bad in some normative sense—that they are unworthy of the great Shakespeare. One possibility is that the bad quartos represent early versions of well-known plays, and that they are not as bad as we think they are. They certainly are full of interesting and perhaps contemporary stage directions and stage usages.

"*Bad*" *Shakespeare* is divided into four large sections. We begin with the essays of Levin and Hawkins, expressing a more or less conservative position, which are set against the more radical essays of Hawkes and Dawson. Revaluations of comedies are contrasted with revaluations of tragedies and histories. In the comedy section we have three plays that are not very high in status: *The Comedy of Errors, The Taming of the Shrew,* and *All's Well that Ends Well.* The section on tragedies and histories also takes up plays that have fallen in reputation, especially *Hamlet,* or risen sharply like *King Lear. Romeo and Juliet, Timon of Athens,* and *Henry VIII* are all works that have a problem in genre and cannot be considered exemplary. The section on text raises questions about what constitutes the authentic script of a Shakespearean play.

We open with a piece by Richard Levin, the author of *New Readings vs. Old Plays: Trends in the Reinterpretation of English Reniassance Drama* (University of Chicago Press, 1979), a book that is closely related to the present study. In "Shakespearean Defects and Shakespeareans' Defenses," Levin argues that our attempts to save Shakespeare from loose ends, minor inconsistencies, and other defects often involve critics in absurd misreadings that are based on false ironic and thematic assumptions. Levin's six examples are relatively innocuous compared with the arguments that have been mounted in their defense. Levin proposes three general principles to guard against our alarming tendency to defend everything that Shakespeare ever wrote: (1) we should know when to give up on ingenious defenses that violate good sense; (2) we should recognize, with Ralph Rader, that some of Shakespeare's positive constructive intentions bring with them unintended and unavoidable negative consequences, especially in relation to minor characters and loose endings; and (3) we should be aware that some of the difficulties of readers and audiences have a longstanding, historical basis, like the problem with Bertram in *All's Well.* Another dangerous fallacy is to think of performance as a way of correcting bad Shakespeare, as if what worked on stage were the only criterion of excellence no matter what distortions of the playscript were needed to make it work. It is refreshing to see that Richard Levin goes so far as to attack the other Richard Levin to make his point.

Harriett Hawkins objects to the depoeticizing and deromanticizing of Shakespeare in her essay, "From *King Lear* to *King Kong* and Back: Shakespeare and Popular Modern Genres." She is allied with Levin in objecting to the rationalizing of Shakespeare, as if his roots in popular genres must be destroyed in order to maintain the pure Shakespeare of fashionable criticism. Hawkins makes much of the air of mystery and mystification in Shakespeare as this energizes the plays. It is no small leap from Lon Chaney, Jr., as he is involuntarily converted into a werewolf at full moon, to Macbeth, whose own anxious imaginings are translated into the stage action. We therefore need real witches and real ghosts in Shakespeare in order not to lose the romantic appeal of the plays. Although Hawkins does not deal directly with bad Shakespeare, she seems to be saying that what we popularly think of as bad Shakespeare—his connection with popular literature and strong and direct emotions—is the very force that gives the plays their vitality. This force may be crude and vulgar, but the mingling and cross-fertilization of high art and low art is a source of dramatic power. *King Lear* needs *King Kong* (and vice versa) to complete its meaning.

Terence Hawkes stands at an opposite pole from Levin and Hawkins in his essay, "Wittgenstein's Bad Shakespeare." Through some remarks of Ludwig Wittgenstein, he presents a Shakespeare radically open to all possible interpretations. Hawkes's nominalism is boldly formulated: "Shakespeare's plays have no essential qualities," and " 'Our' Shakespeare is our invention: to read him is to write him." Thus we can imagine a Nazi version of *Henry V* meant to counter the Laurence Olivier version supported by the British War Office. In essence Hawkes is restating objections expressed elsewhere to Shakespeare as a cultural institution and the hegemonic property of the genteel classes. Bad Shakespeare becomes a political construct of how Shakespeare can be processed to assert the authority of the state. It is not surprising, therefore, that Wittgenstein as an alienated Jewish refugee in England should express such strong feelings about the "badness" of Shakespeare, who represents the values of a society from which he feels excluded.

Anthony Dawson writes specifically on *The Tempest* in "*Tempest* in a Teapot: Critics, Evaluation, Ideology," but his essay has a wider purpose similar to Hawkes's, to whose political position Dawson is strongly attracted. The idealist version of the play casts Frye and Kermode in the role of Prospero, whereas the revisionist, third-world play features Caliban and the powerful argument against colonialist discourse. Everyone is so agitated about *The Tempest* because it is the central Oxbridge text; to attack it is part of an attempt to wrest the definition of "English" from its

Oxbridge bastion. Dawson has somewhat ambiguous feelings about the political positions he presents so vividly, but he is looking for a way to rescue a boring, unactable play from its boring and no longer tenable critical underpinnings. It is interesting that both Hawkins and Dawson give such importance to this play. Dawson makes some acerbic comments on the theory of the last plays as climactic in Shakespeare's career, and he includes a mischievous little playlet called "The Sense of an Ending: or Mandatory Retirement," featuring Shakespeare and Heminges and Condell.

Our central section of revaluations of comedies, tragedies, and histories is more concerned with particular plays than with dramatic theory, but all of our contributors make certain assumptions about Shakespeare, most notably that Shakespeare wrote mixed plays. It is not the critic's purpose to praise Shakespeare's canonical text, like fundamentalists defending the literal truth and excellence of the Bible, but rather to evaluate what Shakespeare actually wrote. The texts lie open to interpretation, and we can either praise what no one has deemed worthy before or fault obvious inconsistencies between our own ideology and the sensitivities of Shakespeare's time. The historical argument forces us to make judgments and to erect a hierarchy of our own values. Shakespeare does not stand as an untouchable monument for all time; rather, his plays keep changing according to our perceptions of value at any particular moment. Nothing can be guaranteed, not even the primacy of *King Lear* among the tragedies. We may be returning to the *Hamlet* mood that dominated the nineteenth century.

In the revaluations, we proceed more or less chronologically, beginning with Russ McDonald's spirited defense of *The Comedy of Errors* and the genre of farce in "Fear of Farce." McDonald attacks the generic snobbery that would downrate farce, and in this sense he is like Hawkins in his defense of popular theater and entertainment. *The Comedy of Errors* must be judged for its own virtues and not as an anticipation of different kinds of comedy, or even tragedy. Much of this criticism is absurd in its strenuous effort to show that comedy is "no laughing matter" (in Levin's apt phrase). McDonald is both witty and practical in his claims for the play. It is strongly commercial and businesslike in its insistence on the importance of theatrical properties. There is a Lacanian ring to McDonald's assertion that the puns are a linguistic equivalent of twinship and that, at the heart of the action, is a struggle for control of the slippery meanings of words. If *The Comedy of Errors* is a bad play or a minor play, as has usually been thought, it is one we can all wholeheartedly delight in. McDonald's essay raises important questions about the hierarchy of genres, in which farce is usually placed at the very bottom of the heap. As the author puts it, "That the author of *King Lear* was capable of writing *The Comedy of Errors* should be a source of wonder, not embarrassment."

Peter Berek also takes up the status of farce in his essay, "Text, Gender, and Genre in *The Taming of the Shrew*," but he is less welcoming than McDonald. Farce is a genre that displays aggression and hostility, as in Barbara Freedman's psychoanalytic theories, but *The Taming of the Shrew* does not resolve its conflicts. In this sense, it prepares us for the expansion of gender roles in Shakespeare's later comedies. Berek does not try to justify the play; rather, he argues that if it is bad Shakespeare, it is better than we usually think. In relation to *The Taming of a Shrew*, the bad quarto of 1594, *The Shrew* mollifies its antifeminism and makes Katherine more sympathetic. Perhaps *A Shrew* is a crude and vulgar rewriting of *The Shrew* as it appeared on stage in the early 1590s.

In *"The Taming of the Shrew:* Inside or Outside of the Joke?" Shirley Nelson Garner's reactions to the play are more violent than Berek's. She is outraged by its sexist and patriarchal assumptions, by its violence and aggression. She does not see anything witty or ironic in Kate, nor does she appreciate Petruchio's "game." Unlike Berek, she feels herself outside the community for whom the joke is intended and therefore unable to participate in its humor. All the males in the play applaud the conversion of the angry, assertive woman that Kate is before her taming into the silent woman of male mythology. "Taming" in itself is an assertion of male values. Garner argues relentlessly against the play from a feminist perspective. Simply put, *The Taming of the Shrew* is bad Shakespeare because it is offensive to women. We cannot distort our basic values in deference to Shakespeare's reputation. In this sense, Garner remains a "resisting" reader or audience.

Dolora Cunningham takes up problems in *All's Well that Ends Well*, especially the conception of Helena, in "Conflicting Images of the Comic Heroine." Helena is set against Portia in *The Merchant of Venice* and both Hero and Beatrice in *Much Ado* (with some attention to Hermione and Perdita in *The Winter's Tale*). Some of the contradictions in Helena are resolved in *Much Ado* by using a pair of sharply contrasted women. At some points in *All's Well*, Helena appears strongly assertive and a woman-in-charge, but at others she is remarkably submissive. This contrast is never worked out. As Helena pursues Bertram, *All's Well* seems like *The Taming of the Shrew* in reverse, and we feel that Shakespeare is experimenting with a different kind of heroine. That the experiment is not entirely successful should not blind us to the novelty and originality of Helena as a dramatic character. Cunningham does not exaggerate the virtues of *All's Well*, and she mounts a fascinating comparative evaluation.

The revaluations of tragedies and histories also use a comparative method, setting early or late plays against acknowledged masterpieces. Avraham Oz, in "What's in a Good Name?: The Case of *Romeo and Juliet* as a Bad Tragedy," faults the play for its failure to explore its own tragic assumptions. Everyone is too ready to accept the feud without probing it. The lovers, particularly, never struggle against the feud, but seem to welcome their role as fortune's fools. Their suffering is therefore pathetic or melodramatic but not tragic. *Romeo and Juliet* seems like a naive version of *Antony and Cleopatra,* in which the love themes are worked out with more satisfying assurance. There is no myth of history, in Jacques Ellul's sense, in *Romeo and Juliet* as there is in *Antony and Cleopatra.* Oz thinks there is some natural correspondence between bad Shakespeare and bad criticism, which rushes to the rescue of a tragedy that is not up to the mark. Overpraising *Romeo and Juliet* may harm our judgment of the mature tragedies.

Alex Newell's paper, "The Etiology of Horatio's Inconsistencies," is an ingenious account of a problem in *Hamlet* that has been noticed before but never pursued. The issue itself is like those flaws, loose ends, and defects enumerated by Richard Levin. Briefly stated, Horatio appears to be a resident military officer in the opening scene, but then for the rest of the play he is a student on a visit from the University of Wittenberg, as are Hamlet and Rosencrantz and Guildenstern. How to account for this glaring inconsistency? Newell offers a clever theory involving the strangely garbled version of *Hamlet* that appears in the play *Der Bestrafte Brudermord* ("Fratricide Punished") in 1781 based on a manuscript from 1710 that no longer survives. *Der Bestrafte Brudermord* is probably a version in German of a *Hamlet* seen on stage before the publication of the First Quarto in 1603. In the German play Horatio is an entirely consistent figure as an officer of the watch, and Hamlet is the only student. Newell conjectures that *Der Bestrafte Brudermord* reflects conceptions in the lost *Ur-Hamlet* that preceded Shakespeare's play. Thus it is important for Shakespeare to develop the theme of students in his *Hamlet,* even though the representation of Horatio is not entirely consistent. In tracking down Shakespeare's defects, we seem to see lost sources reemerging from obscurity.

In "The Worst of Shakespeare in the Theater: The Cuts in the Last Scene of *King Lear,*" John Russell Brown raises some teasing questions about performance. Theatrical practice can offer its own verdict on bad Shakespeare because it can simply change or cut whatever it does not like. Using four promptbooks of *King Lear* from the Shakespeare Centre in Stratford—Peter Brook's (1962), Trevor Nunn's (1968, 1972), and Adrian Noble's (1982)—John Russell Brown considers the numerous cuts in the last scene and tries to explore their origin. It is surprising how much unanimity there is among directors about what lines of Shakespeare are unplayable. Brown does not go beyond some speculations on theatrical practice and the text of the play, but he suggests that directors may be obscuring a complexity and an acute sense of crisis and chaos that are essential to our understanding of *King Lear*.

"Wormwood in the Wood Outside Athens: *Timon* and the Problem for the Audience," by Ninian Mellamphy, returns us to one of the questions with which we began: Can bad Shakespeare be improved by good performance? Mellamphy seems to answer a resounding no, at least in relation to the excellent production of *Timon* by the Grand Theatre Company, directed by Robin Phillips and presented in London, Ontario, in September 1983. William Hutt played Timon. There is a deep paradox in the fact that "the production exposed the play's defects even as it embodied the play's vision." One problem, of course, is that Mellamphy was already convinced that *Timon* was bad Shakespeare before he saw the Robin Phillips version, so that nothing short of a theatrical conversion could shake his prejudgments. Another way to consider the argument is to assume that the author puts tremendous emphasis on the playtext as the basis for an authentic performance. No amount of tampering with the playtext could basically change this conception of a weak Shakespearean play. As Mellamphy puts it, "no felicitous inventions of director and player can remedy the text while honestly interpreting it."

The only essay on the history plays is Iska Alter's " 'To Reform and Make Fitt': *Henry VIII* and the Making of Bad Shakespeare." Alter raises the interesting question of what sort of history play audiences want. *Henry VIII* is an odd example of the genre and also a very late product of Shakespeare's invention (and that of his collaborator, if there was one). The search for a second author is partly a product of Bardolatry, since one can conveniently fob off on the collaborator passages and scenes that seem un-Shakespearean. This has also been done with *Timon*. Dual authorship is partly a fantasy for critics who believe that Shakespeare should be paradigmatic. The stage history of *Henry VIII* has tended to emphasize pageantry and spectacle and the star roles of Wolsey and Katharine rather than the complex interweaving of themes. We need to reconnect this play with other late romances of its period rather than with much earlier history plays. We seem to be caught in a genre problem. Once we accept *Henry VIII* in its own context, the play seems to improve in quality.

The essay on Shakespeare's text plays on our notions of Bardolatry, since the very designation "bad" quarto seems to desecrate and profane the Shakespeare we all know and love. The bad quartos are thought to be bad in some puzzling moral sense, as if they also needed to be driven out of existence. As a practical matter, it is much easier to consult the bad or dubious sources than the bad quartos to which the good plays are so closely related. These are among the many points raised in Steven Urkowitz's rich and wide-ranging paper, "Good News about 'Bad' Quartos." Urkowitz boldly takes issue with the methods and techniques of the New Bibliographers, especially Greg, Alexander, and Hart, and he strongly attempts to explode the notion of "memorial reconstruction," so essential to the low status of the bad quartos. Is the bad quarto of *Hamlet* pirated by the actor of Marcellus and Voltemand? The evidence on which this well-accepted theory is based is extremely dubious. Urkowitz would explain the bad quartos as earlier versions of plays that were later revised. Whether or not we agree with this explanation, we should certainly start reading the bad quartos for their own intrinsic merits.

Our enterprise has tried to establish a "bad" Shakespeare in the teeth of Shakespeare Bardolatry in order to encourage the belief that Shakespeare was a living author who took chances, tried out things, and experimented with types of plays and varieties of characters that did not always work. If he did some things well, he did other things even better, and some few things superlatively well. Shakespeare has some meaningful relation to other playwrights of his own time, whom he imitated and tried to surpass. He never outdid Marlowe or Jonson in what they did best, although Shakespeare certainly tried hard to compete. He never wrote comedies of London life as good as Middleton's or Dekker's, and his wit and satirical skill could never match the concentrated eloquence of Webster, which does not mean that, on the whole, his theatrical art did not basically exceed theirs. We should think of Shakespeare in relation to the achievements of his fellow dramatists and not as an isolated but enduring monument.

"Bad" Shakespeare encourages our own evaluation and the setting up of our own Shakespeare hierarchy. If there is already an established canon, many of our authors do not agree with its rankings, and in their papers they present their own heterodox views. Bad Shakespeare assumes automatically the existence of good Shakespeare, which is equally our focus. We are trying to dispose of the idea that Shakespeare could do no wrong and that everything he wrote is equally inspired. In its simplistic or subtle forms, Bardolatry is the real enemy of our endeavors. We need to see Shakespeare, steadily and whole, in his own dramatic context and in ours.

"Bad" Shakespeare

PART I
Positions

1

Shakespearean Defects and Shakespeareans' Defenses

RICHARD LEVIN

OUR SUBJECT OF "bad Shakespeare"—that is, of negative evaluations of his artistry—really breaks down into two separate problems, since such evaluations can be made of an entire play, or of certain parts or aspects within a play. Both of these operations now seem well on their way to becoming lost arts. Most of the great Shakespeare critics of the past were not at all reticent about voicing their objections to any play, or any portion of a play, that they felt was defective, for they believed that one of the responsibilities of a critic was to criticize. Today, however, it is usually assumed that the duty of a Shakespeare critic is to defend every play he discusses from every criticism that has been levied against it. I will return to this point later; but I mention it now to acknowledge our indebtedness to the program committee and our chairman for their courage in challenging the current trend by bringing forth in this conference a seminar dedicated to restoring to respectability the proposition that all authors are created fallible.

It seems clear that the first problem of "bad Shakespeare," involving adverse judgments of an entire play, is considerably more complex than the second, because any evaluation—positive or negative—of a work of art is always comparative, even when this is not explicit, and therefore always raises the question: compared to what? The answer, of course, is that the work should be judged relative to others of the same kind, but there are many ways of defining that kind. Should *Titus Andronicus*, for instance, be evaluated in comparison to all other plays, or to all other plays based on Roman history, or to all other tragedies, or only to other plays or Roman plays or tragedies written during the same period (which itself can be defined in various ways), or only to other plays or Roman plays or tragedies by Shakespeare, or to some other group of works? Moreover, the criteria for evaluation will vary according to what each critic values most in drama: the ideas, the morality, the emotional effect, the structure, the characters, the verse, and so on. And a third variable is introduced by the fact that plays may be subjected to either "literary" or "theatrical" evaluations.

I have decided instead to focus on the second problem—the adverse judgment of parts or aspects within a play—because it is simpler and therefore easier to handle in a short paper. But it is certainly not simple, and all I can do here is to make a beginning by looking at a few examples of different kinds of defects in the plays, along with the arguments that have been advanced to defend them, in order to arrive at some tentative general principles for dealing with the problem. My first example is the discrepancy in *Measure for Measure* between Claudio's complaint that the laws against fornication have not been enforced for "nineteen zodiacs" (1.2.168) and the Duke's statement that he has let them sleep "for this fourteen years" (1.3.21).[1] Although this may seem trivial, it is representative of a large class of similar minor inconsistencies appearing in almost all the plays, and the issues raised by the attempt to defend it are of some significance. In fact Alfred Harbage, in his incisive essay on "The Myth of Perfection" (which might well serve as the text that this paper is annotating), cites such an attempt by Edmond Malone as one of the earliest instances of Bardolatry: according to Malone, "Claudio would naturally represent the period during which the law had not been put in practice greater than it was."[2]

The second example, on an ascending scale of complexity and importance, is the disposition (or rather, lack of disposition) of Antonio at the conclusion of *Twelfth Night*, where he is left languishing in a legal limbo. It is also representative of a large class of these loose ends, usually involving minor characters, that are found in the closing scenes of many of the plays; and it has also elicited a defense, although a much more recent one, in an essay by J. Dennis Huston that argues that the failure to free Antonio contributes to Shakespeare's ironic undercutting of the apparently happy resolution and especially of the marriage of Orsino and Viola:

> Perhaps as testimony to the precariousness of this union, to the violence that can at any moment transform Orsino's totalitarian commitment from love to hate, is the figure of Antonio, whose faithful, vigorous love has not, like Viola's, been at last rewarded by Orsino's grace. Antonio's fate, we know, can become hers.[3]

My next example is Prospero's lengthy lecture to Miranda in *The Tempest* (1.2.36–186), which can be taken to represent the class of awkward and undramatic expositions in some of Shakespeare's opening scenes (a much smaller class in this case, including *The Comedy of Errors*, *Cymbeline*, *The Winter's Tale*, and a few other plays). It too has found a recent defender in John Cutts, who explains that it is designed to comment ironically on the reprehensible character of the speaker:

> The long tedious second scene of the play, in which Prospero outlines in detail what the initial situation had been in Milan . . . [is attributable] quite simply to the fact that [he] is tediously striving to justify his actions to himself, to Miranda, and to the audience, and in so doing he metaphorically puts us to sleep. His oration would cure deafness if it were really persuasive, would automatically gain rather than command attention if it were indeed worthy.[4]

The fourth example is the role of the Clown in *Othello*, who appears in two very brief episodes in 3.1.1–30 and 3.4.1–22. These also belong to a class of similar scenes of what used to be called "comic relief" in some of the tragedies; but this Clown's banter, unlike that of the Gravediggers in *Hamlet* or the Porter in *Macbeth* or the Clown with the asp in *Antony and Cleopatra*, does not seem to have any direct bearing on the main action and is not even funny, so he is usually regarded (by those who think of him at all) as the most irrelevant and most forgettable character of this class in Shakespeare. But even he has his defenders, invariably of the thematic persuasion. One of them is Robert Watts, who finds that "both of his brief appearances reflect Shakespeare's most subtle use of comic scenes as thematic microcosm," and thus are "integral parts of the structure" and "serve an important function in the overall thematic scheme" by "focusing the major themes of the tragedy," these being "the theme of music" and "the dichotomy of reason and passion which permeates the play."[5]

The fifth example on this ascending scale is the striking alteration of Cassius's character in *Julius Caesar*. In the opening scenes he is presented as a cynical hypocrite who manipulates Brutus to serve his own ends, as he himself tells us in one of those typical soliloquies of self-revelation so dear to the stage Machiavellian ("Well, Brutus, thou art noble. . . . / If I were Brutus now and he were Cassius, / He should not humor me" [1.2.308–15]); but in acts 4 and 5 he has become a much nobler man, whose devotion to Brutus now appears to be completely sincere. The defenses of this change that I have seen are always thematic, although they always employ different themes. A number of critics find that any inconsistency in Cassius simply disappears once we realize that he and all the other major characters are supposed to represent "the tragic limitation of human perception," or the "irreconcilable contradiction" between politics and ethics, or the inexorable power of the "historical process," or whatever abstraction they claim the play is really about; and Mildred Hartsock makes this inconsistency itself the central theme, arguing that "*Julius Caesar* is a dramatic statement about the relative nature of truth," since it is "a play about a problem: the difficulty—perhaps the impossibility—of knowing the truth of men and of history," and that the disparity "between Cassius the schemer and Cassius the suffering man and doughty Roman" is therefore consciously designed by Shakespeare as part of the play's "*demonstration* that the truth of character cannot be known."[6]

My final example is the portrayal of Bertram in *All's Well That Ends Well,* which is highest on this scale because of its crucial effect upon the overall structure of the play and upon our response. The difficulty here, I believe, lies not in some inconsistency in his character but in its inappropriateness to his role in the resolution, because up to his last-minute conversion he is made so unsympathetic, primarily by his callous treatment of Helena and Diana, that he does not seem worthy of Helena's love, and, consequently, her winning him at the end does not seem to merit the kind of rejoicing that the resolution calls for. There have been several different defenses of this portrayal in our day, but most of them can be grouped around two basic interpretations that are diametrically opposed. One is the theologically oriented thematic reading, exemplified by Robert Grams Hunter, who claims that Bertram is deliberately debased to emphasize the play's positive judgment of Helena by showing that she has "served as the instrument of God's grace" in bringing about his spiritual "regeneration"; the other is the ironic reading, exemplified by Richard Levin, who claims that Bertram is deliberately debased to emphasize the play's negative judgment of Helena by giving her "the husband she deserves," and thus undermining the apparently happy ending (and the title), wherein all may seem to end well but really does not.[7]

Now I believe that all six of my examples are "bad Shakespeare"—that is, real defects in the plays—which means that I do not believe any of these defenses. And when I try to account for this, I find that I am relying upon a fundamental principle of interpretation that most of us employ all the time, but which I have never seen stated: the principle of Knowing When to Give Up. When we confront a play (or any other literary work) for the first time, we usually begin with an assumption that is the exact opposite of the proposition I endorsed at the outset. We assume, as a kind of working hypothesis, that its author is *not* fallible, that he has composed a flawless play whose various parts, if properly interpreted, will all be seen to cohere perfectly in a unified artistic whole. Therefore, when we come upon a part that seems to be defective in some way—inconsistent or inappropriate or disproportionate or ineffective—we assume, to paraphrase Cassius, that the fault is probably not in the work but in ourselves, and so we try another interpretation. And if that one also fails to justify or "make sense" of the part in question, we try others. But at some point in this process, when we seem to have exhausted all of the reasonable justifications, we should decide to give up our search and conclude that the fault probably does not lie in our interpretation of the part but in the part itself—that it really is defective.

It is of course much easier to enunciate this principle than to apply it, because everything depends upon determining the location of that point where we should give up. Since its location will differ with each individual case, this determination will always be largely a matter of critical tact or judgment, for which there can be no certain rules. In every case presented to us we will have to judge, not only the probability that the proposed justification of the part is correct, but also the probability that the part is defective, and that in turn will necessarily involve our estimation of the author's artistic ability in general and in each stage of his career. Thus, for instance, we ought to give up more quickly and more easily if the part in question is in a play by Heywood rather than by Shakespeare, or if it is in an early play of Shakespeare's rather than one from his mature period. But I would still maintain that there always is a point when we should give up, even when we are dealing with the greatest plays of our greatest playwright. For we have not actually contradicted the proposition with which I began—and to which this seminar is dedicated—that all authors are fallible. We only hold it in abeyance temporarily when we adopt, as a working hypothesis, the assumption that every part of the play can be justified. And since this is only a working hypothesis, we must be prepared to abandon it when we are unable to find a reasonable justification of the part, by invoking the principle of Knowing When to Give Up. I believe it is the failure to observe this principle that is responsible for the defenses of the six examples we have just surveyed, and for many other similar misreadings of Shakespeare by critics who apparently regard it as their duty to "save" every part of the play at any cost.

The application of this principle in each case, I said, will involve a weighing of the probability of the proposed justification of the part against the probability that the part is defective. And the weight we give to each justification will of course take into account the mode of criticism that it employs. It is no coincidence, I believe (in fact I know, since I selected them), that every one of the defenses cited earlier derives from either the thematic or the ironic approach, because these two recent approaches can be used to explain away *any* artistic defect, and so are primarily responsible for the virtual disappearance of "bad Shakespeare" in our day.[8] The thematists accomplish this by finding an abstraction that will encompass and therefore justify the defective part, which is always easy to do. No matter what the Clown says in *Othello*, his remarks can be related to some idea in the play that will then make them "integral parts of the structure"; no matter how inconsistent Cassius's actions are, they can be subsumed under some theme of this sort (and if all else fails, the inconsistency itself can become the central theme of the play, as we saw); and no matter how despicable Bertram seems, his union with Helena can be vindicated in terms of some thematic idea that it represents. These last two examples also point to another way in which this approach eliminates defects in the plays: since it operates on such a high level of abstraction, the critic can readily pass over (or perhaps not even notice) any difficulties on the mundane level of characterization or emotional effect, which are not relevant to the thematic structure he is erecting above them.

The ironic approach works in a different manner, but is just as effective in eliminating artistic defects, because it typically finds that each defect is not to be blamed on the author but on the character, so that it is really not a defect after all. Perhaps we should not associate Edmond Malone with this approach, since he lived long before it became prominent on the critical scene, yet that is the method he uses in our first example to justify the discrepancy in *Measure for Measure*, which turns out to be Claudio's misrepresentation rather than Shakespeare's error. (I have not encountered any recent treatments of this problem by the ironic critics, but they would presumably place the onus on Duke Vincentio, who is one of their favorite targets, by claiming that Claudio is telling the truth and the Duke is lying either to Friar Thomas or to himself.) Essentially the same kind of argument is adopted in the second and third examples, where the defenses assert that we are not to blame Shakespeare for the dangling loose end in *Twelfth Night*, or the clumsy exposition in *The Tempest*, but are instead to blame Orsino's totalitarianism and Prospero's need to justify himself. And in the sixth example the fault in the resolution of *All's Well* is not Shakespeare's but Helena's; rather than his giving her an unworthy husband, she gets "the husband she deserves." One can easily see how this kind of defense could be applied to a great many other defects in the plays, and that is equally true of the thematic defense. Indeed, it is very difficult to think of any defect that could not be justified by at least one of these two approaches, and sometimes (as we saw in the example from *All's Well*) they can both be used for this purpose. That does not mean, of course, that ironic or thematic defenses must necessarily be rejected in any particular case, but it will certainly affect the weight we give to them.

This weight will be affected by a third factor as well, for in applying our general principle of Knowing When to Give Up, we must not only judge the probability of these proposed justifications of a part against the probability of its being defective, but must also consider any other possible ways to explain the part in question. In every one of our examples—and, I believe, in most other cases of the same sort—we can find another kind of explanation of the part that does not justify it but does account for its defectiveness, and that seems more probable than these justifications. In the first example that explanation is perfectly obvious: the discrepancy in *Measure for Measure* could have been an oversight of Shakespeare's (if it was not caused by the compositor's confusion of *xiv* and *xix* or of *14* and *19* in the manuscript, as many editors suggest). I think most of us would agree that it is much more likely that he simply forgot than that he was making some very subtle point about Claudio's state of mind. In fact, the justification proposed by Malone seems so improbable that we would not even consider it unless we believed that Shakespeare could *not* forget, which would mean that we believed in his infallibility. (It is interesting to observe the deployment of a similar logic to justify discrepancies in our other infallible text: a biblical scholar has recently argued that the inconsistency in naming the mountain where Moses received the commandments, which is called Sinai in Exodus and Horeb in Deuteronomy, "is intentional . . . [because] the authors did not want future generations to know where God revealed himself."[9]) And the same sort of authorial oversight could also account for our second example, the failure to free Antonio at the conclusion of *Twelfth Night*.

There is, however, still another kind of explanation of this failure, and of most of the remaining examples, which introduces what I would regard as the second basic principle for dealing with defective Shakespeare—Ralph Rader's conception of "the unintended and unavoidable negative consequence of the artist's positive constructive intention."[10] This refers to the situation where an author, in order to secure some important intended effect, may have to admit into the work some less important defect that is "unintended" in the sense that he would have avoided it if he could, and did not mean to have it affect his audience's response. And such a defect, Rader cautions us, "if its genesis as an unintended consequence were not perceived, could be used plausibly to support serious misinterpretation." This might apply to the resolution of *Twelfth Night*, since the absence of any reference to Antonio in the final lines may well be the result, not of Shakespeare's oversight, but of his conscious decision to exclude anything that would dilute our concentration upon the fates of his main characters; so Huston's attempt to derive an intentional irony from this "unintended consequence" would then be just the kind of misinterpretation that Rader warns us against. The same explanation can be applied to Prospero's exposition at the beginning of *The Tempest*, although this is a little more complex. Shakespeare's "positive constructive intention" here, presumably, is not only to preserve the unity of time, as many critics have noted,[11] but also to ensure that we are aware from the start of all the relevant past history, so that we can grasp the full significance of the action as it is unfolding. Therefore he must begin with these lengthy, static speeches by Prospero, the only character who knows the entire story, rather than have the information come out more dramatically in smaller units during the course of the action. The speeches do indeed seem tedious and self-justifying, but that is only the "unavoidable negative consequence" of Shakespeare's solution of his expository problem, and thus the ironic reading that Cutts builds upon this "unintended" effect represents essentially the same type of misinterpretation as Huston's.

The application of this principle to our fifth example, the inconsistency in the characterization of Cassius in *Julius Caesar*, is still more complicated and will probably seem less convincing to many, because it depends upon the interpretation of the tragedy, on which there has been considerable disagreement. It seems to me, however, that the change in Cassius can be explained as the "unintended consequence" of Shakespeare's primary "constructive intention" to make Brutus a sympathetic and admirable tragic hero. In the opening scenes Cassius is portrayed as a Machiavellian manipulator of Brutus in order to establish a contrast with Brutus's much more honorable motives for joining the conspiracy and to emphasize his essential innocence. But in the last two acts, when their fates are inextricably linked, Cassius must become a nobler man, especially in the depth and sincerity of his love for Brutus, in order to validate Brutus's own feelings for their friendship and thus to enhance our tragic empathy with him, as can be seen very clearly in their poignant parting before the battle (5.1) and in his reaction to Cassius's death (5.3). This is of course an oversimplified account, which would have to be demonstrated in much greater detail, but I think it provides a consistent explanation of Cassius's inconsistency.[12] And if it is correct, then Hartsock's use of this inconsistency as evidence that the play is making a thematic "statement about the relative nature of truth" would be another instance of the kind of misinterpretation that Rader is referring to.

Since our sixth example, the portrayal of Bertram in *All's Well*, involves the basic plot of that play, the application of Rader's principle will be even more complex and again can only be sketched in briefly. The plot derives from the folklore motif of the "fulfilling of the tasks," which presents Shakespeare with a very difficult problem. In order for these tasks to be imposed on Helena, Bertram must reject her; and in order for her to fulfill them, he must try to seduce another woman; and in order for these actions of his to seem probable, he must be depicted as the kind of man who would reject her and seduce Diana, which in turn makes him the kind of man who does not seem worthy of her love. Of course, Shakespeare attempts to mitigate this by emphasizing his youth, and by having many characters in the play blame his dreadful behavior on Parolles,[13] but it still must be an unsympathetic portrait. In fact, our sympathy for Helena depends to a considerable extent upon our antipathy to Bertram, since the plot makes them adversaries. It would appear, then, that the unworthiness of Bertram is another one of Rader's "unavoidable negative consequences," and therefore that the defenses of this portrayal cited above are, once again, misinterpretations resulting from the failure to perceive its genesis. Thus all five of these examples follow the same general pattern: in each case the most probable explanation seems to be that it is an *unintended* defect, caused either by Shakespeare's oversight or by his "constructive intention"; and in each case the defenders, bound by the dogma of Shakespearean infallibility, insist that it is *intended*, and therefore must resort to some improbable thematic or ironic interpretation in order to prove that it is really not a defect. (My impression is that in this operation the ironic approach tends to produce the more serious misreadings, since the thematists are usually content to exonerate the defect, while the ironists try to convert it into a positive virtue by making it undermine the resolution or score some point against the character they have targeted.)

We have not yet accounted, however, for the fourth example, the Clown scenes in *Othello*, which can scarcely be oversights and do not seem to be the unavoidable consequences of any constructive intention that I can imagine. For them we must consider another kind of explanation that I call "extra-artistic," since it involves those causes which are external to the authorial constructive intention as conceived by Rader. It is admittedly a grab bag classification that requires further refinement, but we need it because not all of the factors affecting the composition of a play can be traced to the playwright's artistic purposes. I suppose that to be consistent we should place Shakespeare's oversights in this category, for they presumably had some cause—a headache, or a distracting interruption, or the pressure to meet a playhouse deadline. It is this last kind of cause—the theatrical conditions under which he worked, and specifically the need to keep his acting company and his audience happy—that was most frequently invoked by critics of the past to explain apparent defects in the plays. Such explanations have now gone out of fashion, and with good reason, since they were often used to avoid coming to grips with the artistic problem, but that does not mean they are always wrong. Some years ago, for instance, Thomas Marc Parrott suggested that Shakespeare wrote the Clown into *Othello* because Robert Armin demanded a part in the play,[14] and I cannot think of a better explanation. Of course, similar pressures may lie behind the Gravediggers in *Hamlet* or the Porter in *Macbeth*, and it is even possible that the actor playing Cassius in *Julius Caesar* told Shakespeare that he was tired of being the villain and wanted a sympathetic death scene. Extra-artistic causes of this sort, even if we could prove them, would not cancel out the artistic explanations of those roles; they would simply show that Shakespeare was usually able to reconcile the demands of his art and these external demands. It is only when they are *not* reconciled successfully that we become aware of a defect that has to be explained in these extra-artistic terms, which seems true of the Clown scenes. It is, in other words, an explanation of last resort, when no probable artistic cause can be found. And it is not a justification; it does not make the scenes any less defective but only accounts for their defectiveness, as I said earlier of all these explanations. In the realm of aesthetics, to understand all is not to forgive all.

In many of these cases there is another general principle that can assist us in our task of weighing the probability of the proposed justifications of a part against the probability that the part is defective. It is based upon the actual responses that the play has evoked down through the centuries. For if we can assume that Shakespeare usually succeeded in communicating his intended meaning, then whenever these responses form a consensus on the interpretation of a play (which of course does not always happen), it greatly enhances the probability that this interpretation corresponds to his intended meaning, and that opposing interpretations do not. I think this principle applies to three of our examples, and in all three it works against the quoted justifications of the part in question (and therefore in favor of my contention that the part really is defective), because, so far as we can ascertain, the overwhelming majority of spectators and readers have *not* felt that the union of Orsino and Viola is supposed to seem precarious, or that Prospero is supposed to be unsympathetic, or that Helena's final victory is supposed to be regarded either as a divine miracle or as an empty mockery. Therefore, if these defenses were correct, we would have to conclude that Shakespeare was incapable of communicating his meaning to the audience, which seems rather ironic when we remember that they are meant to be defenses of his infallibility.

I believe that this principle can also be employed in certain cases where the historical response involves a judgment of the play or of the part itself. We are of course less likely to find a consensus in these judgments than in interpretations, because of the changes in sensibility over the years, but when we do have one it certainly constitutes evidence that should enter into our weighing of the probabilities. This would apply to our fourth and sixth examples, since almost all of the commentators on *Othello* and *All's Well*, from the earliest recorded reactions down to the present, have either condemned the Clown or ignored him (which implies a negative judgment), and have objected to Bertram.

These include both viewers of performances and readers of the texts, and people of very different aesthetic persuasions living in periods dominated by very different tastes and fashions, so that all such variables tend to cancel out. To adapt a famous dictum promulgated by Samuel Johnson (who was himself one of Bertram's severest critics), no part of a play can displease many, and displease long, unless there is something seriously wrong with it—something that cannot be set right by appeals to "the dichotomy of reason and passion" or "God's grace" or "irony," or by any of the other defensive maneuvers we have been surveying.[15]

There remains, finally, one other principle that is frequently invoked in discussions of "bad Shakespeare," but that I think is much more problematic: the test of performance. We are often told that some part or aspect of a play that appears to be defective really is not because "it works on the stage," or at least "goes better" there. The argument has an obvious appeal, since these plays were after all designed for the theater, but the trouble is that it can mean several different things. On the simplest level, it may merely be claiming that some minor defect would probably not be noticed in a performance. That presumably is what Kenneth Muir had in mind when he said recently that "things invisible to an audience should not be regarded as flaws."[16] This clearly applies to our first two examples from *Measure for Measure* and *Twelfth Night* (and to the classes they represent), which would ordinarily be "invisible" in this sense—unless, of course, the performance deliberately called attention to them.[17] But I do not believe this proves that they are not defects, since it still would have been better if Claudio and Duke Vincentio had agreed on their chronology, and Orsino had pardoned Antonio; it only proves that they are even less significant than they might appear during a reading of these plays.

Serious problems arise, however, when we are dealing with more important defects, and the claim is advanced that performance does not simply have the negative effect of making them inconspicuous, but functions in a positive manner by making them "work," so that they should be judged more favorably. I have never heard this said of our third example, Prospero's expository speeches in *The Tempest*, and I have never seen them really "work on the stage" (although they undoubtedly do "go better" in a good performance than on the printed page); but I recall a production of *The Comedy of Errors* where the equally clumsy exposition was made to "work" very effectively. They played Aegeon's long account of his family history for laughs: he was portrayed as a doddering old bore, and Duke Solinus and his courtiers ostentatiously displayed their growing exasperation as he droned on and on, and kept trying to shut him up, to the great delight of the audience. Thus the scene "worked," but at considerable expense, since the audience necessarily missed some of the information needed to understand the ensuing action, as well as the threat of death that hangs over it.[18] This is obviously an extreme example (though I can think of many others of the same kind), yet it serves to raise the question of what exactly is meant by the assertion that an apparently defective episode is not actually a defect because it will "work on the stage." If it means, as in this instance, that the episode can be performed in such a way as to secure a purely "local" success that sacrifices the larger concerns of the play, then that certainly does not prove it is not defective. In fact it proves the opposite, for if such expedients are required to overcome it and make it "work on the stage," then it must be a defect.

I suppose that a good comedian could even milk a few laughs out of the Clown scenes in *Othello*, our fourth example, but I have never seen one do it because almost all performances solve the problem that these scenes present by simply omitting them, without any apparent loss, which—like the failure of almost all commentators on the play to take note of them—is pretty good evidence that they cannot be "integral parts of the structure," as Watts claims, but are in fact defects. I have been fortunate enough to see some fine Cassiuses (our fifth example) who were able to create the impression of a fairly consistent character, although they had to work against very stiff odds. However, it is to the sixth example from *All's Well* that this theatrical defense is most often applied. A number of critics have argued that the problem of Bertram, and especially of his last-minute conversion, disappears on the stage, because there he can be made to appear more sympathetic, and his reformation more convincing.[19] That of course would not involve the sort of desperate expedient adopted to make a part "work on the stage" that we just discussed, but it raises other kinds of questions about this line of argument. It is true that a talented actor can do a lot with Bertram's role, even with that limp final couplet he has to speak. Indeed, if Shakespeare had not given him any lines at all to express his conversion, the actor might be able to mime it quite persuasively. I am not sure what this proves, however, since we still have to acknowledge, as in the three preceding examples, that the part presents a real difficulty that the performance must strive to *overcome*, which means that we would still have to regard it as a defect. Moreover, the rationale behind this theatrical defense, if carried to its logical conclusion, would thrust us into a major dilemma, because *any* part of a play will always "go better" in an effective performance, so if that in itself made the part better, we would then have no defective parts of plays. In fact, we would then have no defective plays, because any play, no matter how inferior, could undergo a similar improvement on the stage.[20] Thus both of the forms of "bad Shakespeare" that I distinguished at the outset would disappear, and our seminar would be left without a subject.

Notes

1. *The Riverside Shakespeare*, ed. G. Blakemore Evans (Boston: Houghton Mifflin, 1974), has been used for all quotations and citations of Shakespeare's plays. Parenthetical text references are to act, scene, and line.

2. Alfred Harbage, "The Myth of Perfection," *Conceptions of Shakespeare* (Cambridge: Harvard University Press, 1966), 25–27 (reprinted from *Shakespeare 400*, ed. James McManaway [New York: Holt, Rinehart and Winston, 1964]). The justification (quoted from Harbage) is attributed to Malone in the 1793 edition of *The Plays of William Shakespeare* (4:205) and in subsequent "variorum" editions.

3. J. Dennis Huston, " 'When I Came to Man's Estate': *Twelfth Night* and the Problem of Identity," *Modern Language Quarterly* 33 (1972): 287–88.

4. John Cutts, *Rich and Strange: A Study of Shakespeare's Last Plays* (Pullman: Washington State University Press, 1968), 88.

5. Robert Watts, "The Comic Scenes in *Othello*," *Shakespeare Quarterly* 19 (1968): 349–54; see also Harold Goddard, *The Meaning of Shakespeare* (1951; Chicago: University of Chicago Press, 1960), 2:99–100, and Lawrence Ross, "Shakespeare's 'Dull Clown' and Symbolic Music," *Shakespeare Quarterly* 17 (1966): 107–28.

6. Julian Rice, "*Julius Caesar* and the Judgment of the Senses," *Studies in English Literature* 13 (1973): 239–43, 254; Moody Prior, "The Search for a Hero in *Julius Caesar*," *Renaissance Drama* 2 (1969): 90–93; Norman Rabkin, *Shakespeare and the Common Understanding* (New York: Free Press, 1967), 117–18; Mildred Hartsock, "The Complexity of *Julius Caesar*," *PMLA* 81 (1966): 60–62.

7. Robert Grams Hunter, *Shakespeare and the Comedy of Forgiveness* (New York: Columbia University Press, 1965), 112, 128–31; Richard Levin, "*All's Well That Ends Well*, and 'All Seems Well,' " *Shakespeare Studies* 13 (1980): 131, 141–42.

8. I discuss this point at greater length and with other examples in *New Readings vs. Old Plays* (Chicago: University of Chicago Press, 1979), 65, 125–32.

9. Yehuda Radday, "A Bible Scholar Looks at *BAR*'s Coverage of the Exodus," *Biblical Archaeology Review* 8 (1982): 69.

10. Ralph Rader, "Fact, Theory, and Literary Explanation," *Critical Inquiry* 1 (1974): 253.

11. This is the only other explanation that Cutts considers (*Rich and Strange*, 88).

12. On some of these points I am indebted to a dissertation by Douglas Friedlander, "Shakespeare's Functional Characters" (State University of New York at Stony Brook, 1985), chap. 2.

13. The Countess in 3.2, Diana and Mariana in 3.5, the first Lord in 4.3, and Lafew in 4.5. Both Hunter (pp. 119–21) and Levin (p. 142) observe, correctly, that these accusations are not borne out by the action.

14. Thomas Marc Parrott, *Shakespearean Comedy* (1949; New York: Russell and Russell, 1962), 291. Unfortunately he doesn't quit while he's still ahead, but goes on to give us an object lesson in the abuse of this mode of explanation by arguing that "Shakespeare was obliged to create parts" for "every full member of the company" and so invented the Duke, Brabantio, Roderigo, Montano, Gratiano, Lodovico, and Bianca "to accommodate his fellow-actors."

15. Samuel Johnson, "Preface to Shakespeare" (1765), in *The Works of Samuel Johnson*, vol. 7, ed. Arthur Sherbo (New Haven: Yale University Press, 1968), p. 61. For his view of Bertram, see pp. 400, 401, and 404.

16. Kenneth Muir, *Shakespeare: Contrasts and Controversies* (Norman: University of Oklahoma Press, 1985), 3.

17. There are ironic directors who, like ironic critics, focus on the loose ends in order to subvert the happy ending. Some go to even greater lengths; in a recent production of *Twelfth Night* by the American Shakespeare Repertory in New York, directed by Janet Farrow, Antonio was beheaded at the end during Feste's song (see Naomi Liebler's review, *Shakespeare Bulletin* 4 [1986]: 15).

18. Compare Hamlet's objection to clowns who invent stage business "to set on some quantity of barren spectators to laugh too, though in the mean time some necessary question of the play be then to be consider'd" (3.2.41–43). See also Alan Dessen's perceptive comments on "short-term gain[s] at the expense of some long-term effect" in "Price-tags and Trade-offs: Chivalry and the Shakespearean Hero in 1985," *Shakespeare Quarterly* 37 (1986): 102–6.

19. J. L. Styan quotes several of them in *Shakespeare in Performance: "All's Well That Ends Well"* (Manchester: Manchester University Press, 1984), 114–15.

20. For a striking example of how this kind of argument can be employed to transform an inferior play into what he calls "a work of great art," see Homer Swander, "The Rediscovery of *Henry VI*," *Shakespeare Quarterly* 29 (1978): 146–63.

2

From *King Lear* to *King Kong* and Back

Shakespeare and Popular Modern Genres

HARRIETT HAWKINS

There is nothing either good or bad, but thinking makes it so.
> —*Hamlet*

Troilus. What's aught but as 'tis valued?
Hector. But value dwells not in particular will:
  It holds its estimate and dignity
  As well wherein 'tis precious of itself
  As in the prizer.

> —*Troilus and Cressida*

TO WHAT DEGREE is great literature—or bad literature—an artificial category? Are there any good—or bad—reasons why most societies have given high status to certain works of art and not to others? Could Hamlet be right in concluding that there is *nothing* either good or bad but thinking—or critical or ideological discourse—makes it so? Or are certain works of art so precious, so magnificent—or so trashy—that they obviously ought to be included in the canon or expelled from the classroom? So far as I know, there is not now any sign of a critical consensus on the correct answer to these questions either in England or in the United States.[1]

In England there are, on the one hand, eloquent cases for the defense of the value of traditional literary studies, like Dame Helen Gardner's last book, *In Defence of the Imagination*.[2] On the other hand, there are critical arguments insisting that what really counts is not what you read, but the way that you read it. You might as well study *King Kong* as *King Lear,* because what matters is not the script involved, but the critical or ideological virtues manifested in your own "reading" of whatever it is that you are reading. Reviewing a controversial book entitled *Re-Reading*

37

"I thought you said King Lear..."

English, the poet Tom Paulin gives the following account of the issues involved in the debate:

> The contributors are collectively of the opinion that English literature is a dying subject and they argue that it can be revived by adopting a "socialist pedagogy" and introducing into the syllabus "other forms of writing and cultural production than the canon of literature" . . . it is now time to challenge "hierarchical" and "elitist" conceptions of literature and to demolish the bourgeois ideology which has been "naturalised" as literary value. . . . They wish to develop "a politics of reading" and to redefine the term "text" in order to admit newspaper reports, songs, and even mass demonstrations as subjects for tutorial discussion. Texts no longer have to be books: indeed, "it may be more democratic to study *Coronation Street* [England's most popular soap opera] than *Middlemarch.*"[3]

However one looks at these arguments, it seems indisputably true that the issues involved are of paramount critical, pedagogical, and social importance. There are, however, any number of different ways to look at the various arguments. So far as I am, professionally, concerned, they raise the central question, "Why should any of us still study, or teach, Shakespeare's plays (or *Paradise Lost* or *The Canterbury Tales*)?" After all, there are quite enough films, plays, novels, and poems being produced today (to say nothing of all those "other forms of writing," including literary criticism, that are clamoring for our attention) to satisfy anyone interested in high literature, or popular genres, or any form of "cultural production" whatsoever. They also raise the obviously reflexive question: "Assuming that all traditionally 'canonized' works were eliminated, overnight, from the syllabus of every English department in the world, would not comparable problems of priority, value, elitism, ideological pressure, authoritarianism, and arbitrariness almost(?) immediately arise with reference to *whatever* works—of whatsoever kind and nature— were substituted for them?"

If, say, the place on the syllabus currently assigned to *King Lear* were reassigned to *King Kong,* those of us currently debating the relative merits of the Quarto, the Folio, or a conflated version of *King Lear* would, *mutatis mutandis,* have to decide whether to concentrate classroom attention on the "classic" version of *King Kong,* originally produced in 1933, or to focus on the 1974 remake (which by now has many ardent admirers of its own). Although classroom time might not allow the inclusion of both, a decision to exclude either version might well seem arbitrary or authoritarian and so give rise to grumbles about the "canon." Moreover, comparable questions of "canonization" might well arise with reference to other films excluded from a syllabus that included either version (or both versions) of *King Kong.* For example: Why assign class time to *King*

Kong and not to (say) *Slave Girls of the White Rhinoceros?*[4] Who, if any, of
us has the right to decide whether *King Lear* or *King Kong* or the *Slave
Girls* should, or should not, be included on, or excluded from, the
syllabus? And can the decision to include, or exclude, any one of them
be made, by any one of us, on any grounds whatsoever that do *not* have
to do with comparative merit, or comparative value judgments, or with
special interests—that is, with the aesthetic or ideological priorities,
preferences, and prejudices of the assigners of positions on whatever
syllabus there is? And insofar as most, if not all, of our judgments and
preferences are comparative, are they not, inevitably, hierarchical?

Is there, in fact, any form of endeavor or accomplishment known to
the human race—from sport to ballet to jazz to cooking—wherein comparative standards of excellence comparable to certain "hierarchical" and
"elitist" conceptions of literature are nonexistent? Even bad-film buffs
find certain bad films more gloriously bad than others. And, perhaps
significantly given its comparatively short lifetime, the avant-garde cinema has, by now, produced snobs to rival the most elitist literary critic
who ever lived, such as the one who thus puts down a friend who likes
ordinary Hollywood films:

> Ah that's all right for you, I know the sort you are, but give me a
> private job that's shot on faded sepia sixteen millimetre stock with
> non-professional actors . . . no story and dialogue in French *any day of
> the week.*[5]

What is striking about this snob's assumption is how characteristic it is of
a long tradition of critical elitism that has consistently sneered at popular
genres (e.g., romance fiction, soap operas, horror films, westerns, etc.)
that are tainted by the profit motive and so tend to "give the public what
it wants" in the way of sentimentality, sensationalism, sex, violence,
romanticism, and the like. Critically speaking, one point of the rest of
this paper is to stress the obvious fact that Shakespeare's art can be
categorized as "bad"—or as "good"—in the same ways, and for the same
reasons, that a film of enduring popularity like *King Kong*, can be categorized as "good" or as "bad" (in comparison with that "private job" shot
on faded sepia sixteen-millimeter stock). I should also add that my own
tentative answers to the critical questions raised above are based on
personal, but I suspect rather typical, experiences, resulting *not* in a
conflict between "high art" and popular genres, but in synergistic inter-
actions between them that have positively, and continually, enhanced
my enjoyment of both.

* * *

Biographically speaking, the foundation of my subsequent career as a
teacher and critic of Shakespearian drama was a childhood spent watch-

ing practically every movie shown in the small town where I grew up. In terms of personal chronology, this paper would be most accurately entitled "From *King Kong* to *King Lear* and Back," since I loved, and wept while watching, the majestic and terrifying African King enchained and humiliated, then defying the airplanes and trying to save the little heroine, years before I had ever heard of Lear, King of Britain. Yet it was upon watching the original film of *King Kong* that I first felt that I was seeing "A sight most pitiful in the meanest wretch, / Past speaking of in a King!"[6] And that was not the worst way for a ten-year-old to experience, firsthand, what Aristotle meant when he described the combined emotions of pity and terror characteristic of the highest tragic impact. By now, I cannot remember the original film of *King Kong* without thinking of *King Lear* ("Howl, howl, howl, howl"). And today, I cannot think of either King without thinking of the connection Karen Blixen made between Shakespeare's tragedy and the real-life tragedy of the natives and animals she described in *Out of Africa:*

> All my life I have held that you can class people according to how they may be imagined behaving to King Lear. You could not reason with King Lear, any more than with an old Kikuyu, and from the first he demanded too much of everybody; but he was a king. It is true that the African Native has not handed over his country to the white man in a magnificent gesture, so that the case is in some ways different from that of the old king and his daughters; the white men took over the country as a Protectorate. But I bore in mind that not very long ago, at a time that could still be remembered, the Natives of the country had held their land undisputed, and had never heard of the white men and their laws. . . . Some of them were carried off by the slave-traders and were sold at slave-markets but some of them always remained. . . . The old dark clear-eyed Native of Africa, and the old dark clear-eyed Elephant,—they are alike. . . . Either one of the two might find himself quite perplexed by the sight of the great changes that are going on all round him, and might ask you where he was, and you would have to answer him in the words of Kent: "In your own kingdom, Sir."[7]

The insights that works deemed "high art" (like *King Lear*) or popular films (like *King Kong*) or memoirs (like *Out of Africa*) give us into other works of art would seem to fade to insignificance in comparison with their extensions of our sympathies, or the insights they afford us into life. But they can, also, illuminate each other. It is not the artistic tradition but the critical tradition that has erected barriers between "high art" and popular genres, even as it has erected barricades between art and life. The artistic tradition (popular as well as exalted) tends to break all such barriers down.

For instance, in the middle of Cole Porter's *Kiss Me, Kate,* a couple of tap-dancing gangsters stop the show to give the following advice to the audience:

> Brush up your Shakespeare,
> Start quoting him now.
> Brush up your Shakespeare
> And the ladies you will wow.

Cole Porter's hoods clearly see "high literature" as eminently practical equipment for living, and theirs is a view with which Shakespeare himself would certainly concur: "Learning is but an adjunct to ourself, / And where we are our learning likewise is" (*Love's Labour's Lost*, 4.3.310–11).[8] But so far as both "high art" and popular genres are concerned, what is especially interesting here is that the advice, "Brush up your Shakespeare," seems equally applicable to anyone who wants to "wow" the ladies (even as Richard III wowed Lady Anne) and to someone who wants to wow an audience at a Broadway musical.Cole Porter, for instance, obviously took his own advice. He not only brushed up his Shakespeare in the writing of his Broadway version of *The Taming of the Shrew*; he started quoting him at the outset, in the title, *Kiss Me, Kate*. And, of course, the same kind of quoting, and brushing up, of Shakespeare occurs throughout the Bernstein-Robbins-Sondheim *West Side Story* of *Romeo and Juliet*, wherein their teenage heroine derives her best-known lyric "Tonight, tonight, I'll see my love tonight," from Juliet's own most lyrical lines, "Come night, come Romeo . . . come loving, black-browed night." The same feelings are felt, and communicated, in both—and so is the same rhythmical heartbeat.

As Leonard Bernstein observed (in a television interview some years ago), the pulse of the mightiest lines of English verse—the iambic pentameter of Marlowe, Shakespeare, and Milton, also throbs through Dixieland jazz (as well as the song from *West Side Story*). *Any* regular iambic pentameter line can be set to "St. Louis Blues":

> I hate to see the ev'ning sun go down.
> Tonight, tonight, I'll see my love tonight.
> Come night, come Romeo, come thou day in night.

T. S. Eliot, of course, caught the jazz connection in his own line, "O O O O that Shakespeherean Rag."[9] Walt Disney, along with Michael Jackson and Vincent Price (in "The Thriller Rap"), apparently preferred the four-beat line that Shakespeare had, for once and for all, rhythmically associated with magical incantations:

> When shall we three meet again?
> In thunder, lightning, or in rain?

> (*Macbeth*, 1.1.1–2)

And grizzly ghosts from every tomb
Are closing in to seal your doom.

("The Thriller Rap")

When his love he doth espy,
Let her shine as gloriously
As the Venus of the sky.

(*A Midsummer Night's Dream*, 3.2.105–7)

Mirror, mirror on the wall,
Who's the fairest of us all?
Her lips like blood,
Her hair like night,
Her skin like snow,
Her name, Snow White.

(*Snow White*)[10]

Nothing could be easier than to demonstrate, on the basis of these—and countless other examples—that neither popular genres, as we know them, nor numerous subsequent works of "high literature," would exist—as we know them—if Shakespeare had never written; even as it is possible to argue that Shakespeare's works would not have lived long enough to come down to us if he had based them on Renaissance academic theories about what high art ought to be like, rather than on the most popular theatrical and literary genres of his time.

I have cited the most obvious examples of the way Shakespeare has been successfully brushed up and quoted in Broadway musicals, and will give further examples from science fiction and horror movies, as well as works by Tom Stoppard, John Fowles, and Woody Allen, in order to argue that it ought to be—although nowadays it often tends not to be—taken for granted that a firsthand knowledge of Shakespearian drama in particular (and, indeed, of "high art" generally) might prove the best of all possible foundations for a commercially successful career as a popular novelist, or playwright, or lyricist, or film producer; and that, by exactly the same token, a knowledge of popular plays and films and novels will inevitably enhance one's understanding and enjoyment of Shakespearian drama. For the fact is that the forces and energies and impacts that account for the status, and indeed the survival, of an "immortal" masterpiece are pretty much the same forces and energies and impacts that assure commercial success at the box office in any age.

For that matter, the legendary producer-director, Cecil B. De Mille, looked at the Old and New Testaments themselves as ready-made script factories. "Give me any couple of pages from the Bible," said C. B., "and I'll give you a picture." Thus De Mille gave due credit to the most distinguished, and by all odds the holiest, of all his ghost writers.[11] Of course, the Book of Judges may still be reverently read long after De

Mille's film version of the story of Sampson and Delilah is forgotten. But the fact remains that the most—if by no means the only—significant difference between what is revered as a work of high, and even holy, literature, and the latest best-seller or blockbuster hit at the box office, is, surely, that the work deemed a classic of its kind has proved to be continuously, or sporadically, popular with and meaningful to readers or audiences for centuries rather than for weeks, months, or years, even as the comedies and tragedies of Shakespeare have, so far so successfully, stood and passed the acid test of time: they have been liked better than their competitors by the kind of people who like that kind of thing (audiences, actors, directors, subsequent playwrights, etc.). The same would hold true of a "classic" jazz recording, or country-and-western recording, or a ballet performance.[12] Whatever its kind, any work of art has to compete in an ongoing popularity contest in which its very survival, as well as its status, must finally depend on the quantity and quality of admirers that it can attract, and keep on attracting.

One can, therefore, predict with as much certainty as one can predict anything, that if—for instance—the works of Woody Allen prove comparably popular with audiences and inspiring to other artists over four hundred years, the works of Woody Allen will, inevitably, be ranked as classics and studied alongside the works of William Shakespeare by our great-great-great-grandchildren's grandchildren (assuming, of course, that anyone is then around to study any art at all). Conversely, if or when Shakespeare's comedies and tragedies ever cease to appeal to audiences and readers and artists, they will, finally, cease to be reprinted or staged, and so they will perish; or perhaps be rediscovered and reclassified as "of historical, or academic, interest only" to the kind of scholar who, in the year 3000, might publish a learned note on "The Influence of A Little-Known Comedy by William Shakespeare on Woody Allen's *A Midsummer Night's Sex Comedy*." In short, Shakespeare's works will be divested of their current status as formula-one masterpieces precisely insofar as they cease to exert any popular appeal in their own right, and thus prove unable to stand up to, or win out against, or to outlast, their competitors.

This is why it seemed to me to be insufferably patronizing, as well as demonstrably erroneous, when, at the Congress of the International Shakespeare Association (held at Stratford-upon-Avon in 1981) that was devoted to Shakespeare as a "Man of the Theater," several directors and academics insisted, as if it were truth beyond controversy, that because audiences nowadays are far too sophisticated to believe in ghosts, witches, spirits, and fairies, modern productions must, necessarily, send up or put down or demystify or otherwise update Shakespeare's supernatural beings in order to make them acceptable to modern theatergoers.

For surely the idea that modern audiences are incapable of crediting or enjoying imaginative portrayals of witches, ghosts, demons, spirits, and magic can be proved false by a glance at lists of film hits—from *Rosemary's Baby* to *The Omen* and *The Return of the Jedi*—which would seem to suggest that, far from being put off by them, modern audiences are starved for mystery, for magic, for the paranormal, for demonic and benevolent beings from elsewhere, and, today as yesterday, will willingly spend their hard-earned money at the box office in order to watch supernatural beings not a whit any less difficult to believe in than the Ghost in *Hamlet,* the witches in *Macbeth,* or Oberon, Ariel, or Caliban.

There are, of course, lots of people who read best sellers and enjoy modern horror and science fiction films who do not read Shakespeare's plays and do not go to see Shakespeare productions, because they do not have the chance, or because they find the language difficult, or because they loathed having *Julius Caesar* force-fed to them in high school. But the reason why certain people, nowadays, may not want to see or to read, say, *Macbeth,* or *Hamlet,* or *A Midsummer Night's Dream,* or *The Tempest,* surely have little, if anything, to do with the fact that these particular plays have supernatural beings in them, since virtually identical types of creatures abound in films that they do go to see and, perhaps most significantly, take their children to see.

Indeed, by now the odds are very good that, regardless of their education, their age, or their class, most people who make up the audiences at any performances of Shakespeare's plays and at modern films alike have, so far as their enjoyment of the drama is concerned, cut their teeth on horror films and science fiction films, from the original *King Kong* and the Bela Lugosi *Dracula* on through *Star Wars* and *E. T.* By now there are whole cohorts of thoroughly modern playgoers and cinemagoers who spent their childhoods watching "Star Trek" in America, and glued to "Dr. Who" on British television, and heaven only knows how many episodes of both these popular series were directly or indirectly derived from Shakespeare's *The Tempest,* along with other equally fantastical classics of imaginative literature, like Swift's *Gulliver's Travels* and Milton's *Paradise Lost.* The ultrarational Mr. Spock in "Star Trek" is the Vulcanian counterpart of a Swiftian Houyhnhnm lord, just as surely as Darth Vader is a direct descendant of Milton's Satan, who was, after all, the one who started—and for all we know may yet win—the most crucial of all "star wars." Shakespeare's "spirits of a gentler sort," like Puck and Ariel, have most recently been reincarnated as R2D2 and C-3PO, even as Prospero is the prototype of Obie-Wan-Kenobie—"The Force" is with them both.

So far as popular modern fiction is concerned, John Fowles's magus,

Maurice Conchis, explicitly compares himself to his Shakespearean pre-
cursor: "Prospero will show you his domaine," says Maurice to Fowles's
antihero, Nicholas Urfe. "Prospero had a daughter," observes Nicholas
hopefully. "Prospero had many things," replies Maurice. "And not all
young and beautiful, Mr. Urfe."[13] Thus, differing works of differing
genres tend, either directly or indirectly, to derive from and pay homage
to each other. In cases like these, all competition ceases and various
works of art successfully cooperate with each other in enchanting or
enlightening or amusing their audience. Thus, appreciation and understanding of either one will tend to enhance appreciation and understanding of what is going on in the other. And this holds true no matter
which one was written first, and no matter which one was seen or read
first. Whichever way one looks at them, it is equally easy to trace the
relationships between, say, Woody Allen's *A Midsummer Night's Sex Comedy*, Ingmar Bergman's *Smiles of a Summer Night* (or its musical version, *A
Little Night Music*), and Shakespeare's *A Midsummer Night's Dream*.

The ordering of my title, "From *King Lear* to *King Kong* and Back," was
nevertheless mandated by the fact that in so many differing forms of
dramatic construction, character types, and comic and tragic effects,
Shakespeare was the one who got there first. Thus, his most sympathetic
of monsters, Caliban (who had dreams so beautiful that when he woke,
he wept to dream again), can be seen as the dramatic prototype of
countless beauty-loving monsters, including the Hunchback of Notre
Dame, the Phantom of the Opera, and the Creature from the Black
Lagoon, as well as Kong, the king of all the beasts that beauty killed. The
fairy-tale, mythical, archetypal, fantastical elements in Shakespearean
drama contribute to, rather than detract from, their enduring appeal. So
does the treatment of sheer villainy. Shakespeare's Richard III, who can
smile, and murder while he smiles, and set the murderous Machiavel to
school, is clearly the direct ancestor of J. R. Ewing, whose seductions
and connings of his wife, his brother Cliff Barnes, and practically everybody else in "Dallas" are directly analogous to the seductions and connings of Lady Anne, Clarence, and the various other losers in *Richard III*.
So far as Shakespeare's most gruesome portrayals of cruelty are concerned, there is no moral or critical attack on the most horrendous
portrayals of sadism, mutilation, and violence in X-rated films that could
not be leveled against *Titus Andronicus*, which (it could go without
saying) was extremely popular in its heyday.

One could argue on the basis of these and countless other examples
that Shakespeare's plays would have to be "required reading" for practically any course in "popular modern genres." For that matter, some of
Shakespeare's methods have proved of far more use to popular, than to

elitist, writers. For although he never appears to have been inhibited by any considerations of due decorum and good taste, Shakespeare invariably knew a sure-fire dramatic situation when he saw one. "Come to my bed," says Angelo to Isabella, "or I'll have your brother killed." "Come to *my* bed," says J. R. to Sue Ellen in "Dallas," "or I'll have your young lover jailed on a drug charge."

The modern American soap opera, as Julie Burchill has reminded us, is the *nouveau riche* relation of high drama,[14] and anyone familiar with *Measure for Measure* will know that nothing could be easier than to chart the cliffhanging, mission-impossible, how-will-the-characters-get-out-of-*this*-mess format of questions raised in (shall we say?) the continuing saga of "Vienna." Episode 1: Will Isabella yield her body up to Angelo? If not, will Claudio die? Episode 2: Will the bed-trick played on Angelo succeed? If so, will Angelo pardon Claudio? Episode 3: Since Angelo breaks his word, and refuses to pardon Claudio, how will the Duke save poor Claudio from the executioner's axe? Will he allow Barnardine to die? Episode 4: When will the Duke make his power known? Will Isabella pardon Angelo for Mariana's sake? Will the Duke really have Lucio whipped and hanged? Will Isabella accept the Duke's proposal? Will Isabella find true happiness as a Duchess? Will Mariana find true happiness with Angelo? Although the action of *Measure for Measure* is condensed into three hours, and that of a soap opera can be extended ad infinitum, it is probably best to play each episode, and each character, in *Measure for Measure* for maximum dramatic impact as they would be portrayed in a soap opera. After all, its dramatic life may depend as much on its sensational, lurid, cliffhanging qualities as the success of a popular soap opera, or the success of the kind of episodic novel ("Will little Nell die?") from which the structure of the soap opera descended. It thus could be argued that the affinities—not the lack of affinities—between Shakespeare's plays and popular genres like romances, revenge plays, novels, and soap operas account for their primary appeal to any audience. But, of course, Shakespeare's greatest plays have other qualities as well.

* * *

As I believe a brief account of the obvious similarities and the most significant differences between *Macbeth* and a justifiably famous horror film can serve to illustrate, whatever differences there are between a masterpiece that will live on for centuries to come, and a TV potboiler whose impact will not outlast the night on which one watched it, those differences must, necessarily, have to do with the quality and validity of the insights they contain and communicate to the audience. For the differences clearly have nothing whatsoever to do with their genre, their origins, or their raw materials—or their subject matter—all of which may be virtually identical.

The second time that I, personally, experienced Aristotelian pity and terror was while watching the original werewolf movie, starring Lon Chaney, Jr., as a man who had been attacked by what appeared to be a wolf. Soon afterward, we in the audience, along with the horrified hero, were informed by an old, witchlike gypsy that ever after, when the moon was full, he would inevitably turn into a werewolf. As the moon rose we—and he—watched with horror as the mutation began, and the wolf fur started to grow on his hands and face. The force compelling the mutation was indeed inexorable, and subsequently drove him to commit murder after murder. The only way the werewolf himself could be killed was with a silver-tipped cane displaying the head of a wolf and the design of a pentagon.

This is essentially the same movement that occurs in *Macbeth*. On hearing the prophecies of the witches, Macbeth is, as it were, bitten by the werewolf of ambition. Subsequently driven to commit murder after murder, Macbeth—like the hero-victim-villain of the werewolf movie— looks on himself as if he were contemplating an alien creature:

> What hands are here? Ha! they pluck out mine eyes.
> . . . .
> To know my deed, 'twere best not know myself.
> . . . .
> Had I but died an hour before this chance,
> I had lived a blessed time.
> . . . .
>   Better be with the dead,
> Whom we, to gain our peace, have sent to peace,
> Than on the torture of the mind to lie,
> In restless ecstasy.
>   (*Macbeth*, 2.2.59, 73; 2.3.89–90; 3.2.19–22)

Macbeth thus describes the "fate worse than death" familiar to all of us from countless horror movies depicting the state of the "undead." Macbeth cannot be killed save by the Shakespearean equivalents of a silver-tipped cane displaying the head of a wolf and the design of a pentagon. Macbeth cannot die until Birnam Wood comes to Dunsinane; only a man who was "not of woman born" can kill Macbeth.

Like the werewolf movie, *Macbeth* can be seen as a nightmare image of the way human beings may be victimized, infected, altered, and doomed by forces outside their control. Yet *Macbeth*, unlike the werewolf film, can also be seen in moral terms, as a Dostoevskian portrayal of crime and punishment. Moreoever, Macbeth's tragedy has to do with natural, as well as supernatural, forces—with historical, social, sexual, and domestic pressures—as well as with the psychological proclivities of the individual that interact to determine all our destinies. The word "if" occurs countless times within the play,[15] and the conditional frame of reference sometimes seems to imply that things could have gone in an entirely different way. Without the influence exerted on him by his wife, Macbeth might not have acted on the promptings of the witches (Banquo did not); and if fate would crown Macbeth, then fate might have made him king, as it made him Thane of Cawdor, without his stir. Thus *Macbeth* affords us, as the werewolf movie does not, a comprehensive account of the complex interaction between psychological, moral, social, historical, and domestic pressures and circumstances that, in real life, determine the way human beings actually do live and die. It also allows us to observe the way that prophecies and imaginings may play a part in bringing about their own fulfillment insofar as they incite us to act upon them. What we imagine or are told that we are destined to be—or not to be—may influence the way we behave, and thus determine the future we actually get, which may turn out not to be the kind of future we really wanted at all.[16] There is no more powerful reminder than the way things turn out for Macbeth of the cruel ironies with which fate may keep the word of promise to our ear, and break it to our hope.

Yet there is one sure way to kill *Macbeth*, for once and for all, both on the stage and in the classroom. And that is to divest it of the very qualities that made both it, and the original werewolf movie, unforgettable to audiences in the first place. I have never been more bored, nor have I ever seen an audience so bored as the captive audience of tourists at the Royal Shakespeare Company production of *Macbeth*, directed by Howard Davies in 1982, wherein (1) the witches were not witches—they were three perfectly ordinary young women innocuously passing a piece of cloth back and forth; (2) Macbeth was costumed like a hard hat and played as a very stupid one at that; and (3) the poetry was delivered in a flat monotone and at a snail's pace. Strip either the werewolf movie or *Macbeth* of their metaphysical ramifications; take away their most dramatic "instruments of darkness"; hold the tragic hero victim-villain in contempt; divest the poetry or the cinematography or the soundtrack of any emotional impact, and you will assure that the audience spends a very boring time in the theater. Brechtian alienation is alien to the spirit of Shakespearean tragedy in that, as in the werewolf movie or the original *King Kong*, tragedy depends on evoking primal terror and pity, and therefore engages our emotions by every means at its disposal, including sentimentality, sensationalism, and special effects.

Because recent productions, including the generally boring BBC television productions, have tended to desentimentalize, desensationalize, depoeticize, and deromanticize Shakespeare's plays in accordance with the interpretations imposed upon them by critics and directors, it is immensely refreshing to have a popular playwright's perspectives on the issues here involved. In a lecture with a title well worth pondering—"Is It True What They Say About Shakespeare?"—Tom Stoppard raises some good questions about certain performances that have disputed Shakespeare's claim to fame as the author of a theatrical event, and not merely a text for critical or directorial commentaries. Here is Stoppard's account of the Royal Court Theater's London production of *Hamlet*, which de-externalized and updated the Ghost by having its lines come from Hamlet himself:

> In this Royal Court production . . . what happens is that, at the moment where he is brought to the pitch of confronting the Ghost of his father, and at the moment where Shakespeare was ready for the Ghost to utter, Hamlet sinks to his knees and appears to be about to be sick, and an awful retching noise starts coming from his stomach, and lo! the retching becomes the words "Mark me!" The duologue takes place between the actor playing Hamlet and a voice, his own distorted voice, being wrenched out of his guts. . . . One might reasonably ask: if the Ghost of Hamlet's father is being wrenched up from Hamlet's stomach, what happens to the scene where the ghost is first seen by Horatio, Marcellus and Bernardo? The answer is perfectly simple in this case: the scene is simply cut and the production begins with the second scene of the play. But this needs to be looked at slightly more carefully. You all recall that first scene: there is a real theatrical excitement about the way the play just kicks off, it goes off like a motor-bike: "Who's there?"—"Nay, answer me!" "Stand, and unfold yourself!" "Long live the King!"—the whole thing is so fast. . . . "What! Has this thing appeared again tonight?" and, what thing?, we all say, what thing, what thing? But without that scene, we begin with a gathering together of the court, and there is Claudius saying: "Though yet of Hamlet our dear brother's death / The memory be green," and so on. The scene misses that retroactive glance at what we have been shown and . . . I must say I was not surprised to read at least one commentator say that without the first scene the production gets off to a slightly tedious start.[17]

Samuel Taylor Coleridge saw the first characteristic of Shakespearean drama as a preference for "expectation" over "surprise."[18] Years later, Alfred Hitchcock made the same distinction between cinematic surprise and suspense. "Surprise," said Hitchcock, "is when you show a group of men playing poker in a cellar and a bomb suddenly goes off. Suspense is when you show the audience the bomb ticking away before you show the men sitting down to play poker." "There is no terror in a bang," said Hitchcock. "Only in the anticipation of it."[19] Shakespeare's usual method is suspense: in effect, he shows the audience the bomb that will go off by having the witches meet the audience before they meet Macbeth, and by having the audience, as well as the soldiers, see the Ghost on the parapet at Elsinore before Hamlet does and so (as the song goes) sets up that "Shakespearian scene" where "A Ghost and a Prince meet / And everything ends up mincemeat" ("That's Entertainment!").

Here, to illustrate some of these points, is Kenneth Burke's brilliant account of the way the master combines suspense with surprise in the dramatic crescendo that climaxes in Hamlet's confrontation with the Ghost:

> It is not until the fourth scene of the first act that Hamlet confronts the ghost of his father. As soon as the situation has been made clear, the audience has been, consciously or unconsciously, waiting for this ghost to appear, while in the fourth scene this moment has been definitely promised. . . . Hamlet has arranged to come to the platform at night with Horatio to meet the ghost, and it is now night, he is with Horatio and Marcellus, and they are standing on the platform. Hamlet asks Horatio the hour.
>
> *Horatio.* I think it lacks of twelve.
> *Marcellus.* No, it is struck.
> *Horatio.* Indeed? I heard it not. It then draws near the season
>   Wherein the spirit held his wont to walk.
>
> Promptly hereafter there is a sound off-stage. Hamlet's friends have established the hour as twelve. It is time for the ghost. Sounds off-stage, and of course it is not the ghost. It is, rather, the sound of the king's carousal. . . . A tricky, and useful, detail. We have been waiting for a ghost, and get, startlingly, a blare of trumpets. . . . But the trumpets announcing a carousal have suggested a subject of conversation. In the darkness Hamlet discusses the excessive drinking of his countrymen. He points out that it tends to harm their reputation abroad, since, he argues, this one showy vice makes their virtues "in the general censure take corruption." And for this reason, although he is himself a native of the place, he does not approve of the custom. Indeed, there in the gloom he is talking very intelligently on these matters, and Horatio answers, "Look, my Lord, it comes." All this time we had been waiting for a ghost, and it comes at the one moment which was not pointing towards it. This ghost, so assiduously prepared for, is yet a surprise.[20]

To return to the alterations made to *Hamlet* at the Royal Court Theater, the point here is that whatever consistency and power that version of the confrontation might have claimed, its impact on an audience had to be altogether different from the Shakespearian fusion of suspense and surprise in that every single one of the special effects described by Tom Stoppard and Kenneth Burke would be lost. For there is no way that an audience could ask "What thing?" "What thing?" during the opening scene, or that Horatio could announce that it "draws near the season / Wherein the spirit held his wont to walk" immediately before the cannon fires and those trumpets sound in the fourth scene, if the only spirit in the play is confined to Hamlet's belly.

Discussing the technical problems involved in producing successful film adaptations of popular novels and Broadway hits, the Hollywood producer, David O. Selznick, said that he took it for granted that the audience knew the conventions of the cinema and would accept the cuts and revisions necessary for a film adaptation of a well-known novel like *Rebecca* or *Gone With the Wind*. But he warned his scriptwriters against tampering with what he called the "chemicals" of a popular play or novel being adapted for the screen, on the principle that "the same elements that drew people to a classic or a Broadway hit or a best-selling novel would attract them to the movie." He therefore vetoed major alterations to the original structure or characterization, on the grounds that "No one can certainly pick out the chemicals which contribute to the making of a classic. And there is always the danger that by tampering, you may destroy the essential chemical."[21]

Certain successful works of high, and popular, art alike—whether by design or by a chance combination of chemicals—do, somehow, achieve the alchemical change that transforms, or transmutes, an audience from witnesses to participants in the tragic or comic recognition, even as these works transmute their raw materials, which may be hackneyed old saws, into the pure gold of art. As Tom Stoppard observed, the transformation of an audience from spectators to participants was once achieved quite by accident in a production of *Hamlet,* wherein "the Ghost was supposed to be a bright light shining from the back of the auditorium, and on the night I was there, some member of the audience unfortunately having to leave the theater at that point, got in the way of this light—and a shadow passed over the audience; and my blood, and I think everybody's blood, went cold."[22]

It is critical and directorial efforts to turn Shakespeare into some kind of nonpopular, nonsentimental, nonsensational, antiheroical, antiromantic moralist or ideologue that have tampered with, to the point of destroying, the essential chemistry of the Shakespearian properties they are dealing with. By the same token, one could destroy the original *King Kong,* or the werewolf movie, or a song by the Beatles, or practically any popular work, if one divested it of the rhythm, the special effects, the poetry, the pity, or the terror that made it popular to begin with. For, as Yeats reminds us in a poem appropriately entitled "The Circus Animals'

Desertion," it is a fatal mistake to assume that even the most masterful images of art have their origins in, or make their primary impact on, "pure mind," or that they can long survive independently of their energy sources in, and their power lines leading up from and down to the place where all artistic ladders start, in the "foul rag-and-bone shop of the heart." Moreover, as Karl Marx observed, it is not at all difficult to see any work of art as the product of a given social, historical, and technological stage of development, or in terms of a reigning ideology. What Marx himself believed it was far more difficult—and more important—to account for, was why Greek art and Shakespearean drama had continued to give succeeding generations such great pleasure, and, to ages in very different stages of social and technological development, "still prevail as standards and models beyond attainment."[23]

Notes

1. This paper grew out of a symposium on "High Literature and Popular Genres" that was held at Oberlin College in 1984. I have previously discussed some of the issues here involved, in differing critical contexts, in *The Devil's Party: Critical Counter-Interpretations of Shakespearian Drama* (Oxford: Clarendon Press, 1985), and in *Measure for Measure: A Critical Introduction* (forthcoming at the Harvester Press).

2. See Helen Gardner, *In Defence of the Imagination* (Oxford: Clarendon Press, 1982).

3. See Tom Paulin's review of *Re-Reading English*, ed. Peter Widdowson (London: Methuen, 1982), in *The London Review of Books*, 17–30 June 1982.

4. See Harry and Michael Medved's compilation of "the best of the worst in motion pictures," *Son of Golden Turkey Awards* (London: Angus & Robertson, 1986), 164: "*Slave Girls of the White Rhinoceros* (1967). In a civilization dominated by sadistic brunettes, all blondes (whether bleached or natural) become the helpless Slave Girls of the White Rhinoceros." The Medved brothers did not, finally, award the *Slave Girls* a Golden Turkey as the "Worst Male-Chauvinist Fantasy" ever put on film, but it *was* a front-line contender for that prize. According to its *auteur*, however, the "tragic" conflict between blondes and brunettes was intended as an allegorical commentary on "the futility of racism."

5. See *The Best of Myles*, ed. K. O'Nolan, as quoted by Jasper Griffen in the *Small Oxford Book of Snobs* (Oxford: Oxford University Press, 1982).

6. See *King Lear*, 4.6.204–5. All subsequent references to Shakespeare's plays, which include act, scene, and line, are to *The Complete Works of Shakespeare*, ed. Peter Alexander, rev. ed. (London, 1981). On the critical points here posited, see also Gore Vidal's essay on "The Oz Books" in *The Second American Revolution and Other Stories* (1976–1980) (New York: Random House, 1982), 57: "After all, those books (films, television, too . . .) first encountered in childhood do more to shape the imagination and its style than all the later calculated readings of acknowledged masters. Scientists are often more candid in their admiration (our attempts to find life elsewhere in the universe is known as Operation Ozma). Lack of proper acknowledgment perhaps explains the extent to which Baum has been ignored by . . . English departments, by . . . As I write these words, a sense of dread. Is it possible that Baum's survival is due to the fact that he is *not* . . . officially, Literature? If so, one must be careful not to murder Oz with exegesis."

7. See Karen Blixen, *Out of Africa* (London: Jonathan Cape, 1964), 404–5.

8. See also *The Two Gentlemen of Verona*, 3.1.104–5: "That man that hath a tongue, I say, is no man / If with his tongue he cannot win a woman.'"

9. For further discussion, see Terence Hawkes, "That Shakespeherean Rag," in *Shakespeare's More Than Words Can Witness*, ed. Sidney Homan (Lewisburg: Bucknell University Press, 1980), 63: "The work of the almost eponymous team of Gene Buck and Herman Ruby (words) and Dave Stamper (music), *That Shakespearean Rag*, with its chorus

That Shakespearean Rag
Most intelligent, very elegant,
That old classical drag,
Has the proper stuff, the line, 'Lay on Macduff'

was one of the hit numbers of 1912." Eliot, of course, interpolated the extra syllable in "Shakespeherean." I am indebted to Hawkes's essay—it is reprinted in his *That Shakespeherean Rag: Essays on a Critical Process* (London: Methuen, 1986)—throughout this paper.

10. Another connection between Shakespeare and Walt Disney is pointed to in Laurence Olivier's book, *On Acting* (London: Weidenfeld and Nicolson, 1986), 85. For the film *Richard III*, Olivier based his makeup on an American theater director called Jed Harris, "the most loathsome man I'd ever met." Harris was "apparently equally loathed" by the man who used him as the model for the Big Bad Wolf in the Disney cartoon of *The Three Little Pigs*. Thus, Olivier's Richard bears an uncanny resemblance to the Big Bad Wolf—and vice versa—and so the loathsome Jed Harris has achieved a kind of immortality in art.

11. See Leslie Halliwell, *Halliwell's Filmgoer's Book of "Quotes"* (London: Granada, 1978), 89. De Mille took neither credit nor blame for his themes: "I didn't write the Bible and didn't invent sin" (p. 90).

12. Like sports, all arts can be seen as "democratic" insofar as artistic talent, like athletic ability, knows no class distinctions. On the other hand, sports and arts alike can be seen as profoundly elitist—as hereditary aristocracies—insofar as some people are born with great talent, or athletic ability, and others are not. No amount of effort, or training, or wealth, could make Florence Foster Jenkins sound like Kiri Te Kanawa. Looked at from this angle, it is hard to see how "great literature" is any more, or less, of an artificially imposed category than the superstar status accorded by the people who enjoy the kind of thing they do, to certain athletes and composers and artists (like Hank Williams or Miles Davis or Elvis Presley or Loretta Lynn). And what about the canonization of certain critical theorists? Arguments objecting to the canonization of Shakespeare, and to the tyranny of "author-ity," often contain appeals to the authority of names intoned like those of saints: Roland Barthes, Michael Foucault, Louis Althusser, Antonio Gramsci, Pierre Machery, and Jacques Lacan. Comparable degrees of connoisseurship are involved in the ranking accorded to jazz performers by jazz buffs, critical theorists by theory buffs, Country-and-Western singers by their fans, etc., etc., even as successive audiences, actors, playwrights, directors, etc. have acclaimed Shakespeare above the authors of *Gorboduc* and successive musicians, conductors, and audiences have preferred the works of Mozart to those of Salieri. The questions of why certain works of art should, or should not, be forced on our students cannot really be answered by flinging charges of elitism back and forth. So far as the "canon" is concerned, it could be argued that the surest way to destroy the popular status of any given work of literature would be to put it on the syllabus, thus forcing students to read and reread it and worry it to death for new meanings in paper after paper. The true distinction between "popular" art forms and academically canonized works could be that people who are fans of popular art and artists engage in their connoisseurship, scholarship, etc. voluntarily, and not in school. But the same energies go into the journals, *Elvisly Yours* and *Downbeat*, that go into works devoted to the most beloved authors in the canon, as labors of love.

13. See John Fowles, *The Magus* (London: Jonathan Cape, 1966), 73. *The Tempest* seems the most influential of Shakespeare's plays on twentieth-century art forms, high and low

alike. See also John Fowles, *The Collector;* Aldous Huxley, *Brave New World;* Rachel Inglis, "Mrs. Caliban"; W. H. Auden, *The Sea and the Mirror;* Teiresias's lines in T. S Eliot's *The Waste Land;* John Cassavetes' updated film version; Derek Jarman's art-film version (ending with a magnificent rendition of "Stormy Weather"); the science fiction film, *The Forbidden Planet,* and so on and so forth.

14. See Julie Burchill, *Girls on Film* (London: Virgin Books, 1986).

15. See Marvin Rosenberg, "Shakespeare's Tragic World of '*If,*'" *Deutsche Shakespeare-Gesellschaft West,* Jahrbuch 1980, 109–17.

16. See Loren Eiseley, "Instruments of Darkness," in *The Night Country* (New York: Scribner, 1971), 47–55.

17. See Tom Stoppard, "Is It True What They Say About Shakespeare?" *International Shakespeare Association Occasional Paper No. 2* (Oxford: Oxford University Press, 1982), 5, 8–9.

18. See Coleridge, "Recapitulation and Summary of the Characteristics of Shakespeare's Dramas," in *Shakespeare Criticism: A Selection, 1623–1840,* ed. D. Nichol Smith (London: Oxford University Press, 1923), 236: "As the feeling with which we startle at a shooting star, compared with that of watching the sunrise at the pre-established moment, such and so low is surprise compared with expectation."

19. See Hitchcock in *Halliwell's Filmgoer's Book,* 140. See also (on the same page) the anecdote about how Hitchcock caused consternation by muttering the following paraphrase of Lady Macbeth's famous lines (*Macbeth* 5.1.38) very audibly to a friend in a crowded elevator: "I didn't think the old man would bleed so much."

20. See Kenneth Burke, "Psychology and Form," in *Perspectives by Incongruity by Kenneth Burke,* ed. Stanley Edgar Hyman (Bloomington: Indiana University Press, 1964), 20–21.

21. See Selznick, as quoted by Roland Flamini, in *Scarlett, Rhett, and a Cast of Thousands* (New York: Collier Books, 1975), 197–99.

22. See Stoppard, "Is It True What They Say," 4–5.

23. See Marx, *Grundrisse,* in *Karl Marx: Selected Writings,* ed. David McLellan (Oxford: Oxford University Press, 1977), 360. As Kenneth Muir has demonstrated, Marx himself was a card-carrying Shakespearean—see Muir's essay on "*Timon of Athens* and the Cash-Nexus," in *The Singularity of Shakespeare and Other Essays* (Liverpool: Liverpool University Press, 1977), 56–75.

3

Wittgenstein's Shakespeare

TERENCE HAWKES

THE PHILOSOPHER Ludwig Wittgenstein found Shakespeare's poetry "bad" and made no bones about it:

> Shakespeare's similes are, *in the ordinary sense*, bad. So if they are all the same good—and I don't know whether they are or not—they must be a law to themselves.[1]

By this he seems to have meant that both the equivalences proposed by Shakespeare's poetic devices and those apparently proposed by the plays at large (to push his word *Gleichnisse* to its broadest reach) fail to match reality "in the ordinary sense" as he perceived it. That they therefore rank as "bad" (he uses the uncompromising German word *schlecht*) strikes him as an obvious conclusion, and the only surprising thing about it is that it does not appear to be shared by everybody. In fact, as he points out, large numbers of people unaccountably share an opposite conviction, that Shakespeare's work, despite the evidence, is *"dennoch gut."* This generates an obvious dilemma for him, which he finds difficulty in resolving:

> It is remarkable how hard we find it to believe something that we do not see the truth of for ourselves. When, for instance, I hear the expression of admiration for Shakespeare by distinguished men in the course of several centuries, I can never rid myself of the suspicion that praising him has been the conventional thing to do; though I have to tell myself that this is not how it is. It takes the authority of a Milton really to convince me. I take it for granted that he was incorruptible.— But I don't of course mean by this that I don't believe an enormous amount of praise to have been, and still to be, lavished on Shakespeare without understanding and for the wrong reasons by a thousand professors of literature. (48e)

Wittgenstein's solution lies in his suggestion that in Shakespeare's case "truth to life" perhaps is not relevant: "You just have to accept him as he

56

is if you are going to be able to admire him properly, in the way you accept nature, a piece of scenery for example, just as it is" (49e).

This clearly helps. If we take that position and wish to admire Shakespeare properly we must cease to regard him as a man trying to communicate with his fellows, and start to think of him more as a natural phenomenon, like a mountain, or a piece of scenery, something that is just *there*. His quite evident "badness" (and Wittgenstein to his credit never abandons that judgment) needn't bother us, any more than the fact that he is frequently just plain wrong into the bargain:

> Shakespeare and dreams. A dream is all wrong *(unrichtig)*, absurd, composite *(zusammengesetzt)*, and yet at the same time it is completely right: put together in *this* strange way it makes an impression. Why? I don't know. And if Shakespeare is great, as he is said to be, then it must be possible to say of him: it's all wrong *(falsch)*, things *aren't like that*—and yet at the same time it's quite right according to a law of its own. (83e)

If we accept this, we can forget about the distinction between right and wrong, good and bad. Shakespeare can be wrong *and* right, bad *and* good—or, to put it less contentiously, we can drain away these values and content ourselves with staring "in wonder" (84e) at the Bard as if at a "spectacular natural phenomenon" rather than a "human being" (85e).

It is important of course to place Wittgenstein's remarks in context, and when we do so this apparently rather odd view of Shakespeare takes on a special significance. Most of the comments I have quoted come from notes made just after the war during the years 1946–50, when Wittgenstein was living in Britain, either at Cambridge or in places where he had been engaged in war work as a hospital porter. It was a time when, in the company of many others, he could hardly have helped thinking of himself as a refugee from events that had all too recently taken place in those parts of the world where he perhaps had felt originally at home. As a Jew, as a former citizen of Vienna, and as a native speaker of German, he would have had a sense of the full horror of those years that few of his Cambridge colleagues could have appreciated. Indeed, as a Jew, an Austrian, and a German speaker, it was precisely his world, more than any other, that had been shattered by the events of 1939–45.

Wittgenstein's alienation was by then virtually total. For we must add to the above the evidence that the issue of his own sexuality was a cause of some personal difficulty, and that he was of course fully estranged by this time from the fundamental precepts of his earlier philosophy. In this sense, he appears as a man to whom all available languages are foreign. This rather daunting reality—its full extent only beginning to emerge in the years 1945–50—is surely part of what he finds Shakespeare's plays inadequate to match, and his irritation at the "thousand professors of literature" (many of them presumably German) who thought otherwise is at least understandable. At the very least, Wittgenstein's position offers an opportunity for us to reflect on what sort of reality Shakespeare did appear to be adequate to in Britain at that time. If Wittgenstein's fierce intelligence found his work *schlecht*, how could lesser minds find otherwise?

And yet we know that they did. In fact, far from finding Shakespeare a neutral "piece of scenery," neither right nor wrong, good nor bad, the evident conclusion of the British government was that his plays were perfectly good and absolutely right in respect of a particular version of reality.

To be specific, it had clearly become vital in the last years of the war that the flagging spirits of the British people should be raised in advance of the final assault on Europe that would begin on D-day. As a prolegomenon to that event, the government financed, as is well known, a major piece of propaganda: the film of Shakespeare's *Henry V,* starring Laurence Olivier, who was released from other war duties for the purpose. Dedicated to the Airborne Division, this complex vehicle was charged with the simplest of objectives: to show (in the face of a good deal of evidence to the contrary) that a British military force was capable of mounting and sustaining a successful campaign against a corrupt and effete enemy in northern France. Shakespeare was clearly considered to be "good" for this purpose, not simply because of his standing as a British cultural hero, the repository and symbol of all that is finest in the national character and way of life and thus the focus of social and political unity. His play also evidently was ranked as "good" on exactly the grounds that concerned Wittgenstein: it could be proved "true to life" in the simplest and most obvious sense, as the Normandy campaign unfolded.

An obvious conclusion to emerge from this must be that "goodness" and "badness" are not qualities of Shakespeare's plays themselves in any sense. If *Henry V* were objectively "good," then we can assume Wittgenstein would have registered that. His value to us lies precisely in his alienated vision: in the fact that he does not. And that supports the conclusion that ultimately—that is, to the objective, uninvolved, alienated eye—the plays offer us no values that exist as essential features of themselves. They are not essentially good, or essentially bad, or essentially anything. They are, to take up Wittgenstein's metaphor, far more like natural phenomena—mountain ranges, pieces of scenery—to which we may attribute features in accordance with our various purposes. In other words, Shakespeare's plays have no essential qualities. They are not transparent entities yielding immediate access to single, coherent, preordained meanings. As complex and inherently plural structures, they must be open to manifold readings, numbers of them contradictory. Like words themselves, in short, they have no essential meanings, only uses.

If this is true, then it must follow that even a play like *Henry V* can be put to different uses: that it could, to take up a debating position, have been equally well used by the opposing German forces as a propaganda exercise *against* the Normandy campaign. If that were so, then Wittgenstein's point (or the point I have wished upon him) would be made: an evidently "bad" Shakespearean play would appear where once an obviously "good" one stood.

The German production would of course be dedicated to the Wehrmacht. It would focus on the English, their nature and purpose. It would show how the English king could, by means of chopped logic and patriarchal bonhomie, persuade his people of the justice of his fanatical cause. It would stress the way in which "Englishness" is tyrannically imposed on those quite distinct cultures which make up the British way of life. It would show how the representatives of Wales, Ireland, and Scotland could be persuaded to join forces under an alien English and Englishing flag (even to the extent that Henry is seen cannily to exploit his own Welsh connections in the enlistment of such as Fluellen). It would show how he craftily sidesteps the genuine moral issues generated by his own men, for instance on the eve of the battle of Agincourt. And it would show how, steamrollering across France, Henry cruelly "Englishes" everything in his path (the parallels with the methods adopted in the development of the British Empire would not be lost) until finally, in his encounter with the French princess, he forces her to abandon her native tongue and to treat with him in English. In short, from the German standpoint, the play would expose the English (and by now the American) project to force the civilized world to speak their language, and accordingly to accept their values, their politics, their domination. Against this project the heroic German forces would pit their might as part of a cultural battle that had raged since 1914 between the rival claims of English and German to be the dominant world language and the repository of all that is civilized and admirable in human affairs.[2]

My case is a simple one. If Shakespeare can be made to support causes as opposed as those above, then his plays are neither good nor bad in themselves, and beyond the various readings to which they may be subjected there lies no final, authoritative, coherent, or essential meaning to which we can ultimately and gratefully turn. Any party can lay claim to Shakespeare; any camp can make him "ours" (German references to *"unser Shakespeare"* are not unknown). But "our" Shakespeare is our invention: to read him is to write him. And as only one instance of this we might refer to the dispute in the pages of *Scrutiny* in 1942 in which F. R. Leavis strenuously wrests *Measure for Measure* from the grasp of a recalcitrant L. C. Knights, who has found the play woefully ambiguous. For Leavis, any suggestion that that play may be "bad" is wholly insupportable. In his reading it becomes "one of the very greatest of the plays, and most consummate and convincing of Shakespeare's achievements." It might even have been this rather surprising assessment of a play that was, after all, set in his own native Vienna that prompted Wittgenstein—able perhaps on this occasion to judge acutely the inaccuracy of its *gleichnisse*—to urge Leavis to "give up literary criticism."[3]

No doubt Wittgenstein's alienated position as a German-speaking Viennese Jew living in Britain urged—even required—him (whether or not at a conscious level) to see Shakespeare as he did. His position scarcely encouraged him to voice his disquiet, but his notebooks indicate that he felt it. And in the word *schlecht* he expresses a sense of the disjunction that only an alien can fully perceive between the claimed "truths" of an ideology, and those constructions which are deemed innocently and transparently to make them manifest. Immediately after the war, another philosopher would see in the same disjunction the lineaments of a similar attitude that he was prepared to condemn, no less trenchantly, as "bad" faith.

Notes

1. Ludwig Wittgenstein, *Culture and Value (Vermischte Bemerkungen)*, ed. G. H. von Wright and Heikki Nyman, trans. Peter Winch (Oxford University Press, 1980), p. 49e. Subsequent quotations from Wittgenstein are from this volume; page numbers are given in parentheses in the text. For an illuminating commentary on this material see George Steiner, *Reading Against Shakespeare* (The W. P. Ker Lecture, 1986, Glasgow University Press, 1987).

2. I have developed this point in *That Shakespeherian Rag* (London and New York: Methuen, 1986), 51–71.

3. For details see my "Take Me to Your Leda," *Shakespeare Survey 40* (Cambridge University Press, 1988), 21–32.

4

Tempest in a Teapot
Critics, Evaluation, Ideology
ANTHONY B. DAWSON

Making Ends Meet

I THINK *The Tempest* is Shakespeare's most consistently overrated play. Its appeal to modern critical method, whether constructive or deconstructive, conservative or radical, has been almost irresistible. And I need hardly say that whatever text serves to open the vein of critical discourse will invariably be evaluated upward. Texts are good insofar as they generate commentary, and *The Tempest*'s inviting allegory has done that in spades. Allowing myself to think this way leads me almost inevitably to Lytton Strachey, perhaps the last critic to say directly that *The Tempest* is not a very good play.[1]

Strachey was as well one of the first critics to recognize the importance of chronology in the assessment of Shakespeare's plays—the fact that *The Tempest* comes at the end of Shakespeare's career means that it will be read retrospectively, as climactic. Strachey mounts his famous attack on the last plays by self-consciously adopting the assumptions of the allegorizers (Furnivall, Dowden, and the rest) that Shakespeare's mental state can be deduced from the plays. His predecessors had celebrated the final plays as the climax of Shakespeare's career, seeing them as the mellow fruit of a prolonged ripening process. But Strachey seizes on boredom rather than serenity, withdrawal rather than transcendence, as the referents of the romances' malleable signs. In doing so he redefines the shape of Shakespeare's career as anticlimactic rather than conclusively triumphant, thus rather wickedly suggesting that interpretation is as much a matter of desire as of analysis. In developing this critique, however, Strachey leaves behind the insight with which he begins—that the achievement of nineteenth-century scholarship in establishing the chronology of Shakespeare's plays has enabled a brand of evaluative interpretation based on the place of a particular play in the canon. This point actually works against Strachey's account, since his strategy depends on reversng the evaluation while retaining the method.

But what if we were irreverently to pursue the question of chronology a little further? How many unexpected virtues would suddenly appear in *Two Gentlemen of Verona* if it were proven to date from, say, 1597 or *(pace Palladis Tamia)* 1603?[2] Its reliance on duologues and soliloquy, for example, no longer a mark of immaturity, might emerge rather as a strategically disintegrative gesture functioning as a check on conventional romantic momentum. The abruptness of its ending, especially Proteus's change of heart and Valentine's notorious offer of his beloved to his perfidious friend, might now be seen as a parody of the extended denouement of its companion plays, *All's Well* and *Measure for Measure;* and the callous handing around of Silvia could be seen in the harsh light of the sexual exchanges in other "middle" plays. That, admittedly, is a rather fanciful example—few readers of Shakespeare would want to redate *Two Gentlemen,* even if Meres had not provided evidence of its existence before 1598. But *All's Well* could easily be moved forward to 1608–10 and Bertram be exonerated by a simple gesture of last-plays "forgiveness"; indeed, the uncertainty surrounding the evaluation of *All's Well* is, I think, related to uncertainty about its date. *Cymbeline,* to choose another example, might be moved backward and descend, like our hypothetical *Two Gents,* into the muddle of a problem play. *Cymbeline's* final scene, described by Pelican editor Robert Heilman as "one of the most skillful in all drama,"[3] might then be seen more clearly as the cranked-up job it is. As Strachey reminded us, there is no reason to assume that a particular chronological slot guarantees artistic success or failure.

In the case of *Cymbeline,* to reverse gears on that play for a moment, critics have often suggested that its vagaries of plot and structure, its deus ex machina, its overly elaborate final scene, its crabbed language, mark it out as apprentice work in comparison with *The Winter's Tale* and *The Tempest;* so it is seen usually as written earlier than they, pointing toward them as *Two Gentlemen* points to *As You Like It* and *Twelfth Night.* I can detect in the continuing power of this assumption the spirit of Furnivall and Dowden—we do not like to imagine *Cymbeline* as Shakespeare's last complete play. Who would want to end a carefully constructed Shakespeare course with *Cymbeline,* giving to the blockhead British king instead of the shrewd and authoritative Italian magician the last (bathetic and syntactically tangled) word: "Never was a war did cease, / Ere bloody hands be washed, with such a peace"? But what real impediment is there to maintaining that *Cymbeline* was written after *The Tempest* rather than before? What is wrong with imagining Shakespeare's career trailing off, going from bad to worse, from *The Tempest* to *Cymbeline* and parts of *Henry VIII*, before being judiciously terminated by his worried partners in The King's Men, who perhaps asked young Fletcher to do what he could to make the old master's new texts acceptable to their increasingly perplexed audiences? Well, we all *know* what is wrong with thinking this way—we have too great an investment (personal, academic, and ideological) to make it desirable.

Perhaps it is time, though, to reassess our stock and make at least a gesture of divestment. In that spirit, permit me to offer the following dialogue, recently discovered among John Payne Collier's papers, and said to be transcribed from an original manuscript, now lost:[4]

The Sense of an Ending: or Mandatory Retirement

Scene 1

Henry Condell *discovered, seated at a table, reading a manuscript. He jumps up, slaps the paper on the table. Walks. Sits down again and takes up paper.*

Cond. Damn! *(reading laboriously)* "The two kings, Equal in lustre, were now best, now worst, As presence did present them: him in eye Still him in praise." (Repeats this last phrase.)

(Enter John Heminges.)

Cond. Well, John, thank God you've come. Take a look at this.

Hem. (reading) "Him in eye Still him in praise; and being present both, 'Twas said they saw but one, and no discerner Durst wag his tongue in censure." Good lord, it's getting worse isn't it?

Cond. How are we going to handle this? We can't just cashier the dear fellow, can we?

Hem. I've talked to Fletcher—he's willing to work with him. That might keep him straight. How much of this has he done?

Cond. Only a few scenes. I think he's had it, really. He's bored, lost his zest, but he won't admit it.

Hem. Well look, if we can convince him to work with Fletcher, we can at least get a workable plot—and maybe some of this stuff can be slipped in without anyone noticing.

Cond. Remember those lines of Leontes?—"Thou mayst co-join with something; and thou dost and that beyond commission"—and I thought *they* were obscure! *(Blackout)*

Scene 2

Shakespeare, Condell, Heminges. Evening, storm.

Shake. Fletcher! But I taught the wretch everything he knows, and all he can do is pisspot imitations and flights of sentiment. You must be kidding.

Cond. Well, Will . . . he can handle a plot fairly adroitly, don't you think? What about—

Shake. Who cares about plot? I've been getting away with the most outrageous stuff for five or six years now—and most of it I swiped from him.

Hem. But that's just the point, Will.

Shake. What d'you mean?

Hem. Well, you've got to admit that things got a little out of hand in your last play—not even Fletcher would go that far—there were more surprises in that last scene than there were people left in the theater.

Shake. Fletcher's the one that loves surprises. I keep the audience informed—even wrote that wooden soliloquy for Belarius (at *your* insistence) to tell them who was who.

Cond. (aside to Heminges) See, I told you. Now what do we do?

Shake. (half to himself) But what the hell, maybe you're right. My heart's not in it any more— guess I should take a bit of a rest. Let Fletcher finish it. He's been working on that Chaucer piece—a big yawn, I can tell you. What if I throw in a few scenes to spice that up while he's doctoring my Henry? *(Pause)* And after that, I'll come roaring back with something new—what about a good revenge tragedy? *(Thunder)*

Hem. Look Will, that's just the point—we were thinking—well, we considered all the great stuff you'd written and, uh . . .

Cond. Also, we remembered that lovely place you'd bought yourself back in Stratford, and then there's Susanna, and we thought that, well . . .

Hem. We'd like to collect your plays together, keep them safe, you know—maybe publish them someday, ha, ha—that would be a joke on old Ben, eh?

Cond. Anyway, we thought maybe you ought to retire back up to New Place—bask in a little well-deserved glory, you know?

Hem. Yeah, and of course keep a hand in here as well, write some scenes for Fletcher, spice things up a bit, as you said.

Shake. Pension myself off with the promise of a folio, is that it? Good God—I never thought I'd see the day when I'd be treated like one of my own characters. *(Storm still)* I'll be revenged on the whole pack of you, I'm tempted to shout, but that's not it. *(Increasingly to himself)* You've simply killed my heart . . . my occupation's gone . . . but I have yet a daughter . . . *(Thunder gradually transforming to the sound of viols)* yes . . . most heavenly music! It nips me into listening, and thick slumber Hangs upon mine eyes. Let me rest . . .

(Light fades.)

The Tempest and Its Readings

The established view of *The Tempest*, as outlined in Frank Kermode's New Arden introduction and innumerable articles and books in the wake of Knight, Frye, and others, needs no reiteration here.[5] We all know about reconciliation, harmony, the spirits of earth and air, art and nature; and we know as well that the mighty concerto can contain within it some few unharmonious or irascible notes, but only enough to add a shadow or two to the bright future, a touch of irony to the brave new world, a boundary of temporariness to the vision of perfection. They do not intrude on the essential grace. Let Frye's magisterial summing up speak for all the bedazzled allegorizing that *The Tempest* has engendered over the years:

> [In] the great romances . . . Shakespeare seems to have distilled the essence of all his work in tragedy, comedy, and history, and to have reached the very bedrock of drama itself. . . . In these plays the central structural principles of drama emerge with great clarity, and we become aware of the affinity between the happy endings of comedy and the rituals marking the great rising rhythms of life: marriage, springtime, harvest, dawn, and rebirth. In *The Tempest* there is also an emphasis on moral and spiritual rebirth which suggests rituals of initiation . . . we may come to the play on any level, as a fairytale with unusually lifelike characters, or as an inexhaustibly profound drama. . . . *The Tempest* is a play not simply to be read or seen or even studied, but possessed.[6]

Frye's possession of *The Tempest* rests on its representation of generic structure; one therefore surmises that the play is to be valued because it serves his system, illustrating the very principles that he derives from it (even though that system is supposed to be free of evaluative judgments); it links what he wants to say about structure with what he wants to say about archetypes. But to make the point, Frye has to leave a lot out—Sycorax, for example, and Caliban. He admits that "it is a little puzzling" that "New World imagery should be so prominent when the play really has nothing to do with the New World" except, he goes on to say, for a vague resemblance "between the relation of Caliban to the other characters and that of the American Indians to the colonizers and drunken sailors who came to exterminate or enslave them."[7] It is extraordinary that Frye thus alludes to and at the same time marginalizes what the various revisionist readings of the play put at the center. There is a disturbance in the smooth surface of Frye's text here (marked by words like "exterminate" and "enslave") akin to the disturbance that Caliban causes in *The Tempest* itself. But it is just a brief bubble. For Frye to allow the full implications of what he has said about Caliban to invade his text would mean he would have to abandon his normally lofty stance; he would have to admit that the play might actually have some relation to the real world. Furthermore, he would have to surrender what in his eyes makes the play great—its generic inclusiveness. To see Caliban as a repressed element rather than an included one would mean too far-reaching a readjustment of his categories. But he is too good a critic not to notice Caliban's disturbance, and too honest a one not to mention it. Thus in Frye's text we have a replay of Shakespeare's; in both cases, it is impossible to admit Caliban and impossible to keep him out.

Suppressing Caliban pays off, since it allows for the critical construction of an idealist *Tempest*, a strategy that allows us all to talk about universal significance, grandiose themes that immersion in literature gives us magic access to; and this of course confers significance on us. We are its priests.[8] One form such readings have taken is an identification of Shakespeare with Prospero, a device that goes way back to Dowden and the sentimental fiction, still strongly felt, of Shakespeare, through his theatrical magus, bidding farewell to his art. But this is not a necessary feature of idealizing readings—as we have seen more recently, many critics have emphasized Prospero's irascibility and harshness, his punitive attitude toward premarital sex, or his weary sense of mortality, while retaining a view of the play committed to reconciliation, harmony, and the like. This last move actually offers the critic the advantage of complexity: he can stress the play's inclusive awareness of discontinuity and thus praise it all the more highly.

It is noteworthy that writers from colonized nations, especially black ones, have also read *The Tempest* as an allegory, but not one of beatitude and grace. In opposition to Frye and the others, they have sided with Caliban, not Prospero, seeing him as the brutalized victim of European expansion and oppression—his land taken away, his way of life destroyed, and his desires harnessed to fit the image that the white colonialist seeks to give him. The historical irony here centers on "our language," which Trinculo is astonished to hear Caliban speak.[9] For writers like George Lamming, Aimé Césaire, and Edward Braithwaite, the dilemma is neatly posed by Caliban's "You taught me language and my profit on't / Is, I know how to curse." Their predicament is that of "the writing Caliban whose subject is the liberated Caliban but whose medium is Prospero's language."[10] The ideological need and strategy at the basis of such a reading is clear enough, as is the fact that it challenges the hegemony of both mother tongue and mother country as ways of defining meaning.

Meanwhile the theater too has been busy displacing the benevolent Prospero. Jonathan Miller's celebrated production in 1970, in which both Ariel and Caliban were black, emphasized the imperialist reach of the play; seven years earlier, in a more thoroughly deconstructive gesture, Peter Brook and Clifford Williams put together a production in which they felt impelled (though they backed off at the last minute) to lift all the scenery at the end and put all the characters in clown suits in order to "underline the derisory nature of the play's 'resolution.' "[11] Brook himself later wrote of the play that as a plot it is uninteresting, as a pretext for fancy costumes and special effects it is hardly worth reviving, and "as a potpourri of knockabout and pretty writing it can at best please a few matinee-goers."[12] Although there is often some gap between the theater's and the academy's ways with Shakespeare's plays, in the case of *The Tempest*, the gap is unusually wide—for two reasons. One is that the persistent allegorizing and idealizing of mainline academic criticism are almost impossible to play, and the other is that as a straight acting text the play is boring. And to try to play the allegory is likely to make it all the more so. (A tacit recognition of this second point may indeed be behind the academic impulse to overpraise it.) Thus directors and actors have sought ways, understandably, to liven the thing up.

An obvious problem with producing the play is that actors swaying and lurching on an adamantly stationary stage floor are unlikely to persuade us of the storm at sea—despite the help of gauze and scrim, creaking rigging, or screaming winds over which the actors have to shout their inconsequential and usually inaudible lines. And the same goes for the other spectacles of the play—the disappearing banquet, the wedding masque, even the "discovery" of Miranda and Ferdinand—it is all so disconcertingly stagy. What Lamb said about *King Lear* seems more precisely applicable to *The Tempest*, that the "contemptible machinery by which they mimic the storm" and, we could add, the banquet, masque, and the rest, is no more adequate "to represent the horrors of the real elements [or the wonder of magic], than any actor can be to represent" Ariel, Juno, Ceres, or the other inhuman figures that people the isle.[13] Besides these problems, there are the "dreary puns and interminable conspiracies" of the noblemen, of which Strachey justly complained, and the wearisome antics of Trinculo and Stephano, who along with Launcelot Gobbo are surely Shakespeare's least funny clowns. Onstage, and this may indeed be the bottom line, the play usually fails to engage the audience in a fully satisfying way.

The quick comeback to the point just made, one that its proponents think will simply knock me dead, is "I've seen a *great* production of the play and that *proves* that it works." This is what I call the "so there" method of argumentation, and my answer is equivocal: well, yes and no. It is, of course, possible to have a very good production of a not very good play (*Titus Andronicus* comes to mind). With *The Tempest* in particular, I may be tempted to respond—"You thought the production was great because it fulfilled your ideas (probably idealized and universalized), about the play" or "You have so much invested in the play that you can't afford to see its difficulties as a stage piece." This kind of argument goes around in circles and proves nothing. All I know is that of all Shakespeare's acknowledged "major" plays, *The Tempest* is the only one that a large number of respectable scholars and teachers of Shakespeare will privately admit is not very effective theatrically, although they will often go on to say that it is important for other reasons etc. etc. (I have only done a very informal survey on this point, one that has been

deliberately, indeed provocatively, unscientific, but I have been surprised at the near unanimity of the results.) In any event, the issue here
is not primarily one of "taste"; I am in fact more interested in why *The
Tempest* is valued as it is. What, that is, are the ideological bases of
evaluation?

No account of revisionist responses to *The Tempest* would be complete
without some reference to the "new orthodoxy" (a term that I have been
prating about in corridors for some time now, but that has also, I was
surprised to learn, recently gained notorious currency in the pages of *PN
Review*).[14] I mean in particular that group of critics (they refer to themselves as "cultural materialists") who seem at some point to have clus-
tered around Terry Eagleton and who are best represented in the pages
of the Methuen New Accents series. Unlike the idealist critics, with their
hidden class biases and their supposed commitment to lofty Arnoldian
disinterest, these writers are explicit about their ideological position and
pugnacious in their encounter with tradition. The extent of their pug-
nacity is demonstrated by a recent letter to the *London Review of Books*
from Terence Hawkes, the general editor of New Accents (and a contrib-
utor to the present volume). He attacks Graham Hough for failing to
recognize that the appeal of critical theory in "some institutions" (i.e.,
the "new" universities and polytechnical institutes that employ most of
these critics) is connected to underfunded libraries and other depriva-
tions:

> Posh institutions, such as the one graced by Mr. Hough [Oxford] . . .
> offer their members plenty of books to read, and I dare say no end of
> time and opportunity for the purpose. But there is an academic world
> elsewhere. . . . The broadly-allusive, finely-tuned, widely-learned
> mode isn't for the likes of us. How could it be? Theoretical and
> analytic work . . . genuinely matches our resources. . . . Tell him it
> has its own integrity. . . . Tell him its existence in places like Cardiff
> might even be the price he and his pals have to pay for their quite
> different concerns elsewhere. Then tell him to piss off.[15]

Hawkes's Calibanic virulence is surprising to an innocent North American like myself, but it reveals the class consciousness and hostility
beneath some of the theoretical work being done in Britain today, and
helps to explain the revaluation of central Oxbridge texts like *The Tempest*.

The volume *Alternative Shakespeares*, part of the New Accents series,
neatly illustrates the situation. It is concerned far more with critical than
with literary texts, and views "Shakespeare" less as a writer than as a
cultural and ideological construction. Major critical eminences of the
past loom large. Johnson, Sir Walter Raleigh, Eliot, and Leavis are

displaced, their implicit ideologies and their role as purveyors of "English" made manifest. Leavis especially is to these critics the tyrannical father who must be killed off, whose iron grip on the definition of "English" must be pried loose in order to make room for his impatient and rebellious progeny (this is particularly clear in the volume *Re-Reading English*). What Hawkes makes explicit in his letter is implicit in many of these essays—that critical theory in Britain is a grab for power, a way of wresting the reins of academic hegemony from the Prosperos of Oxbridge. (Here *The Tempest* becomes an allegory in which the chief characters are all critics!)

It is interesting that of the plays discussed in *Alternative Shakespeares*, the only one to be represented twice is *The Tempest*. That may be a coincidence, but it shows that the play is as useful for the opposition as it has been for the Establishment. Like the black and Québecois writers and like many theatrical producers, the cultural materialists seize on Caliban to make their argument. An essay by Peter Hulme and Francis Barker, "Nymphs and Reapers Heavily Vanish: The Discursive Con-texts of *The Tempest*," is a case in point.[16] In it, they seek to show "how much of *The Tempest*'s complexity comes from its *staging* of the distinctive moves and figures of colonialist discourse."[17] Kermode's introduction to the New Arden edition serves them as a model of the idealist reading, complicit with colonial power, a "production of a site for *The Tempest*'s meaning"[18] that "occludes" both Caliban's political claims and the actual intrusion into the text of the "con-texts" of colonial expansion. (The hyphenated coinage in their subtitle refers to the texts that constitute the discourse of colonialism.) For these critics, the play is most notably disturbed at the moment referred to in the essay's title, when Prospero suddenly remembers the foul conspiracy of the beast Caliban, and what is revealed is the "text's own anxiety about the threat posed to its decorum by its New World materials." That this threat is contained, and the text ends with reconciliation, "may then be read as the quelling of a fundamental disquiet concerning its own function within the projects of colonialist discourse."[19] (We saw above how Frye's reading of the play uses a similar maneuver.) The moment of disturbance also drives a wedge between Prospero's play and Shakespeare's, differentiating them clearly, thus enabling the present reading by demystifying Prospero's colonialist rule over the text as well as over Caliban. The fact that the gap is later closed only confirms the reading, since the larger play accedes to Prospero's version of history by containing the conspirators in the safely comic mode; thus the containment as well as the eruption indicates the text's anxieties.

Another, similar, materialist essay, Paul Brown's " 'This Thing of Darkness I Acknowledge Mine': *The Tempest* and the Discourse of Colonialism," insists also on the gaps in the play, which register "if only momentarily, a radical ambivalence at the heart of colonialist discourse."[20] Shakespeare's text, for Brown, oscillates—but then so does his own, since he shuttles between demystification of The Tempest's colonialist moves and admiration for its representation of the "characteristic operations of colonialist discourse" that are here "driven into contradiction and disruption."[21] He asks whether the final distancing of Prospero from his narrative, his abandonment of both magical and political mastery, is "an unravelling of his project" or merely a "courtly euphemisation of power" (i.e., power effacing its own operations), and he concludes that it is both.[22] The text's rifts support its claim to privileged status. But at the same time there is a disconcerting tendency to fault Shakespeare and/or his text for not being up to the ideological mark. The Tempest is complicit with colonialism, and is indeed a central text in the web of colonialist discourse; as such as it is bad. But wittingly or no, it also reveals the contradictions of colonialism, and as such it is good. Like the play itself, Brown's evaluation is split. More to our point here, however, we should notice a special privileging of the critical text over the text being analyzed, based on the claim that the former is not complicit, not benighted—it seeks only to expose, and hence escape from, the mechanisms of power. But its very presence in the book Political Shakespeare tells a different story. There is here a bid for power directed not only against critical Prosperos, though that is clearly in the background, but against "Shakespeare" himself—his power is up for grabs.

In the kind of readings just sketched, there is a curious reversal of traditional strategies of evaluation. (To see this age! A text is but a chev'ril glove to a good wit. How quickly the wrong side may be turned outward!) As Richard Levin has shown, a common critical gambit has been to produce a reading through which elements of a text previously thought to be irrelevant or incoherent are shown to be harmoniously related to the whole;[23] the critical act becomes then a demonstration that the text is more conspicuously unified than people thought, and hence better. In the present instance, and indeed in a lot of deconstructive and neo-Marxist criticism, the text shows itself to be better because of its disunity rather than its unity. That both the idealizing critical act that unifies and the materialist or deconstructive act that disunifies are political is stressed by the "new orthodox" critics themselves, who argue that their project is an explicit, even revolutionary, exposure of the political bad faith of their forebears. What is "occluded," however, is the fact that their project is part of a critical campaign to wrest the definition of "English" with all that implies from its Oxbridge bastion. Thus when Brown or Hulme and Barker demystify The Tempest's collusion with colonialism, something that colonial writers and theatrical producers have been doing for years, the act of decentering and disrupting the text can be seen as analogous to the bid for the decentralizing of academic power. Their "re-valuation" of the text is necessary since it constitutes the ground of their "contestation" of social and academic hegemony.

In Hulme and Barker's reading, Frank Kermode becomes implicitly identified with Prospero—he constructs a meaning exactly parallel to Prospero's construction; displacing the one will therefore displace the other. This leaves room for "Shakespeare" to re-enter (Shakespeare's *Tempest* is distinct from "Prospero's play"), identified for the moment with Caliban rather than Prospero, and with these critics rather than, say, Kermode. A reversal of the standard meaning of the play is thus effected, where the critics' victory enables Caliban's—but the latter's is only temporary, as they argue, since the gap in the text is closed by the authoritative ending, and Prospero's play becomes again indistinguishable from Shakespeare's. Ultimately, though, *The Tempest*'s "complexity," and hence its value, comes from its staging of colonialist moves, so that the argument finally ends up, like Kermode's (or Frye's), sacrificing Caliban in order to establish its own, and Shakespeare's, victory. The complexity of the text consists of its openness to rifts, but its ultimate valuation depends on an identification (of "Shakespeare" with the critic) that is as old as the hills and that functions mainly to empower the critical position, particularly in opposition to Prospero-Kermode and the hegemony of academic colonialism.[24]

Brown's case is a little more complex. Critical identification with Shakespeare is put to the side only to reappear from the wings. To adopt a metaphor the play itself provides, Brown seeks to check, or even mate, the White King (i.e., "Shakespeare" as the critical grandmasters have constructed him). A knight move seems to do the trick, but as we study the configuration, it looks as if Brown's text is hooked by the same "radical ambivalence" he traces in Shakespeare's. He seems uncertain whether to bury Shakespeare or to praise him. This is an honest position insofar as it registers the dilemma posed by this kind of criticism, but an uneasy one in that it promotes a kind of ideological condescension. Brown can't help but be ambivalent, since his text wrestles both *for* Shakespeare's power and *against* it.

My own position is, I am afraid, as ambivalent as Brown's. I sympathize with the way "materialist" critics expose the hidden biases of traditional criticism, but I feel that they fall into some of the same traps, particularly in the vexed area of evaluation and the ideological assumptions that the act of evaluating often makes plain. If the "grounds of evaluation are historical and ideological,"[25] as Eagleton I think rightly claims, then why do Caliban-critics value the play as much as Prospero-critics? That is the question I have been trying to answer and it is one that, despite their alertness to the ground of Kermode's evaluation, I do not think these critics have fully attended to in themselves. To value the play as they do, the Caliban-critics have ironically to leave the "historical" Caliban behind and insert themselves in his place. This does not necessarily invalidate their critique, any more than their situating Kermode invalidates his. But it does call into question the ideology of their evaluation.

I am not finally convinced that the play is any better for its reversibility, though I have to admit that Prospero's island is more interesting as a battleground than as a land of pure enchantment. But the play still faces the central problem that it so frequently displays in the theater: neither its allegory nor its textual "anxiety" can be adequately played. Strachey, to close where I began, remarks that in *The Tempest* "unreality has reached its apotheosis."[26] His insistence on realistic criteria may seem dated now and hopelessly naive in the wake of poststructuralism. But engagement with figures whose humanity is somehow recognizable and important still seems to be something we look for in the theater, regardless of our critical predispositions. And if for that reason it is Caliban who most fully commands our theatrical attention, as has been the case in many modern productions, then the text's aims (from either critical point of view) have demonstrably failed. If Strachey's statement seems untenable today, I think that is less because of its critical assumptions, however we may decry them in theory, and more because of our habitual refusal to disengage ourselves from the symbolic overlay that the text's "unreality" has generated. It may indeed be that the emperor-text has clothes that I am unable to see, but if what I have said carries any weight at all, then the critical tailoring that has dressed up *The Tempest* may be its most elaborate "con"-text.

Notes

1. See Strachey's notorious essay, "Shakespeare's Final Period," first published in 1904, reprinted in *Literary Essays* (London: Chatto & Windus, 1948), 1–15.

2. Francis Meres mentions the play in his famous list in *Palladis Tamia* published in 1598.

3. Robert Heilman, Introduction to *Cymbeline*, in *The Complete Pelican Shakespeare* (Baltimore, 1969), 1292.

4. I owe the basic idea for this dialogue to an irreverent conversation with my colleague, Joel Kaplan, to whom I am therefore ambiguously grateful.

5. G. Wilson Knight, one of the most thoroughgoing allegorizers of them all, wrote in 1929 (that fateful year) that *The Tempest* is "a record of Shakespeare's spiritual progress," the "culmination of a series which starts about the middle of [his] writing career and exposes to a careful analysis a remarkable coherence and significance." It is "at the same time the most perfect work of art and the most crystal act of mystic vision in our literature" (*Myth and Miracle*, reprinted in *The Crown of Life* [London: Methuen, 1948], 27, 9, 28). Later in his

career, Knight revised his position somewhat; he retained the idea of the trajectory of Shakespearean growth, but combined it with a nationalistic mythology in which, although *The Tempest* played a major role, *Henry VIII* was the culminating work (*Crown of Life*, 333–36).

6. Northrop Frye, Introduction to *The Tempest*, in *The Complete Pelican Shakespeare*, (Baltimore, 1969), 1372.

7. Ibid., 1371.

8. "Materialist" critics would add that idealizing *The Tempest* obscures the ideological role that the text and its readings have played in the definition of "English" as a discipline, which itself supports British colonialist expansionism and imperialism. See below.

9. See Terence Hawkes's witty and perceptive essay on the force of Caliban's English and its political resonances, "Swisser-Swatter: Making a Man of English Letters," in *Alternative Shakespeares*, ed. John Drakakis (London: Methuen, 1985), 26–46.

10. Chantal Zabus, "A Calibanic Tempest in Anglophone and Francophone New World Writing," *Canadian Literature* 104 (Spring 1985): 49. This important article discusses the rebellious responses to Shakespeare's play on the part of critics, poets, and novelists from Africa, the West Indies, and French Canada.

11. Clifford Williams, quoted in the program notes for the 1963 production.

12. Peter Brook, *The Empty Space* (Harmondsworth, Eng.: Penguin, 1972), 106. Brook goes on, however, to undermine his own critique by saying that the play deals with the "whole condition of man." His comments neatly reveal the gap between theatrical and allegorical ways of thinking about the play.

13. Charles Lamb, "On the Tragedies of Shakespeare," *Works*, ed. T. Hutchinson (London: Oxford University Press, 1908), 1:136.

14. A recent issue of this magazine (vol. 12, no. 4) features a manifesto that declares that "alternative approaches to literature . . . have hardened into a new orthodoxy," and argues that, among other things, "the dominant notion that language constructs reality," and the tendency to use "literary criticism to gratify, in fantasy, revolutionary desires" must be questioned. This ringing but simplistic challenge is taken up by a variety of writers and theorists, including Eagleton and several of the New Accents authors.

15. Terence Hawkes, *London Review of Books*, Nov. 21, 1985, 4. Hawkes's letter may be a bit disingenuous, however, since his own essay, cited above, is certainly "broadly-allusive, finely-tuned, widely-learned."

16. Peter Hulme and Francis Barker, "Nymphs and Reapers Heavily Vanish: The Discursive Contexts of *The Tempest*," *Alternative Shakespeares*, 191–205.

17. Ibid., 204.

18. Ibid., 195.

19. Ibid., 203–4.

20. Paul Brown, "'This Thing of Darkness I Acknowledge Mine': *The Tempest* and the Discourse of Colonialism," in *Political Shakespeare*, ed. J. Dollimore and A. Sinfield (Manchester: Manchester University Press, 1985), 66.

21. Ibid., 68.

22. Ibid., 67.

23. Richard Levin, *New Readings vs. Old Plays* (Chicago: University of Chicago Press, 1979).

24. The ironic density of the critical situation is attested to by the fact that Kermode is now more generally considered Calibanic, at least in reference to his support of "theory" and his position in the MacCabe affair at Cambridge. Further ironies may be discerned if we recall that Eagleton is a Fellow at Oxford, and Leavis was treated as an outsider at Cambridge. Prospero was once a victim too, and Calibans, if they learn the language well enough, can scale the heights.

25. "Right Thinking Critics," *PN Review* 12:4 (Fall 1985): 50.

26. Strachey, "Shakespeare's Final Period," 12.

PART II
Revaluations
Comedies

5

Fear of Farce

RUSS McDONALD

ZEUS'S SEXUAL LAPSES notwithstanding, gods are not supposed to be indecorous, and a characteristic of modern Bardolatry has been its insistence on Shakespeare's artistic dignity, particularly his attachment to the approved dramatic forms. The popular image of Shakespeare as the embodiment of high culture, the author of *Hamlet* and certain other tragedies, as well as a very few weighty comedies, is merely a version of a bias that also, if less obviously, afflicts the academy. What I am talking about is a hierarchy of modes, or, to put it another way, genre snobbery. That tragedy is more profound and significant than comedy is a prejudice that manifests itself in and out of the Shakespeare Establishment: in the impatience of undergraduates who, taking their first class in Shakespeare, regard the comedies and histories as mere appetizers to the main course, the tragedies; in Christopher Sly's equation of "a commonty" with "a Christmas gambol or a tumbling trick"; in the disdain of the tourist at the Barbican box office who, finding *Othello* sold out, refuses a ticket to *The Merry Wives of Windsor*; in the decision of that Athenian student to preserve his notes from Aristotle's lecture on tragedy but not to bother with the one on comedy.

If there is a hierarchy of modes, there is also a hierarchy within modes: *de casibus* tragedy is less exalted than Greek, for example. So it is with the kinds of comedy, and the play to which I shall address myself, *The Comedy of Errors*, rests safely in the lowest rank. Farce is at the bottom of everyone's list of forms, and yet Shakespeare is at the top of everyone's list of authors. Thus, the problem I mean to examine is generated by competing hierarchies. Most literary critics have little occasion to think about farce, and those who concern themselves chiefly with the creator of texts such as *Macbeth* and *Coriolanus* do their best to avoid the form. For many years the earliest comedies were treated unapologetically as farces and Shakespeare was praised, if mildly, for his skill at contriving such brilliant and pleasing trifles. But the need to preserve his association with higher things has led in the last three or four decades to a revision of this opinion. It seems inappropriate that the cultural monument known as Shakespeare should have anything to do with a popular entertainment that we connect with the likes of the Marx brothers (Groucho and Harpo, not Karl and Moritz). Criticism resists a Shakespeare capable of wasting his time on such a trivial form.

My purpose is to suggest that Shakespeare could be "bad," but my definition differs somewhat from those of most of the other contributors to this volume. Rather than re-examine texts that may have been over-valued or seek to locate weaknesses in dramatic technique, I shall argue that Shakespeare's taste was not invariably elevated and that certain plays are less "significant" than others (or at least that they signify different things in different ways). By addressing myself to what is and is not considered "Shakespearean," I claim an interest in one of the funda-mental issues of this collection: canonicity. A work like *The Comedy of Errors* must be deformed if it is to conform to that category known as Shakespearean comedy—as a farce it is noncanonical—and such mis-representation demands a rejoinder.

The first part of this essay surveys the evasions that critics have devised for treating Shakespeare's efforts in farce, with concentration on the dodges applied to *Errors*. The remainder, a straightforward study of that play's theatrical action, proposes to identify the playwright's strat-egies for the production of meaning in farce. In light of the concerns of this volume, to contend that *Errors* succeeds not as an early version of a romantic comedy or as an allegory of marriage but as an out-and-out farce is risky, for such an argument looks like yet another defense of the artistic experiments of a novice and thus seems to exemplify the very Bardolatry that many of these essays vigorously dispute. In fact, how-ever, my aim is to establish Shakespeare's delight in and commitment to a dramatic form that has become infra dig. To recognize such a bent is to augment our sense of Shakespeare's actual range. We whitewash our subject by refusing to admit his attraction to farce and declining to explore his talent for it.

I

Suspicion of farce has fostered two main critical maneuvers, here summarized by Barbara Freedman: "The first is represented by that group of critics who know that Shakespeare never wrote anything solely to make us laugh and so argue that Shakespeare never wrote farce at all. . . . The more popular critical approach, however, is to agree that Shakespeare wrote farce, but to consider *Errors* (as well as Shakespeare's other predominantly farcical plays) to be nonsensical *insofar* as they are farce."[1] To begin with the first group, its members are undaunted by

Shakespeare's demonstrable choice of classical or Italian farces for source material: in such cases he may be seen "transcending the farce which a lesser writer might have been satisfied to make,"[2] and thus the form is mentioned so that it can be dismissed.

The most familiar and pernicious tactic of those who would dissociate Shakespeare from the vulgar category is to discuss the early plays as precursors of the mature style, as seedbeds, that is, for ideas and methods that will flower in the later comedies and even in the tragedies. (In fact, hothouses would make a better simile, since the ideas and methods are found blooming in the early play itself by the time the critic finishes.) A. C. Hamilton, for example, asserts that *The Comedy of Errors* provides a foundation for the later comedies by revealing "their basis in the idea that life upon the order of nature has been disturbed and must be restored and renewed through the action of the play."[3] Hamilton's reticence to detect inchoate forms of particular dramatic themes from later works is not shared by Peter G. Phialas, who identifies "certain features of structure and theme, and even tone, which anticipate significant elements of Shakespeare's romantic comedies." Specifically, "*The Comedy of Errors*, though in the main concerned with the farcical mistakings of identity, touches briefly a theme of far greater significance, the ideal relationship of man and woman."[4] This anticipatory practice amounts to reading the career backward: a play is conditioned by what follows it, and its distinctive qualities may be underrated or deformed. The prophetic approach tends to manifest itself in and to merge with the second defensive strategy.

Put simply, this way of thinking involves deepening the farces, exposing their profundity. It has become the preferred means of protecting Shakespeare against his own immature tastes or the vulgar demands of his audience,[5] and it has attracted some eloquent and powerful advocates. Derek Traversi, for example, unites the two critical defenses, seeing *Errors* as both serious in itself and important in its tonal prefiguration of the later work. He emphasizes "the deliberate seriousness of the story of Aegeon, which gives the entire action a new setting of gravity, a sense of tragic overtones which, elementary though it may be in expression, is yet not without some intimation of later and finer effects."[6] In other words, the play is profound but not too profound.

That the dignifiers succeeded some time ago in making this serious position canonical is apparent in the following passage from R. A. Foakes's Introduction to the New Arden edition, published in 1962:

> These general considerations may help to illustrate the particular quality of *The Comedy of Errors*. The play has farcical comedy, and it has fantasy, but it does more than merely provoke laughter, or release us temporarily from inhibitions and custom into a world free as a child's,

affording delight and freshening us up. It also invites compassion, a measure of sympathy, and a deeper response to the disruption of social and family relationships which the action brings about. Our concern for the Antipholus twins, for Adriana and Luciana, and our sense of disorder are deepened in the context of suffering provided by the enveloping action. The comedy proves, after all, to be more than a temporary and hilarious abrogation of normality; it is, at the same time, a process in which the main characters are in some sense purged, before harmony and the responsibility of normal relationships are restored at the end. Adriana learns to overcome her jealousy, and accepts the reproof of the Abbess; her husband is punished for his anger and potential brutality by Doctor Pinch's drastic treatment; and Antipholus of Syracuse is cured of his prejudices about Ephesus. Behind them stands Egeon, a prototype of the noble sufferer or victim in later plays by Shakespeare, of Antonio in *The Merchant of Venice,* and of Pericles, central figure in a play which uses more profoundly the story on which Egeon's adventures are based.[7]

A variation of this argument is found in Harold Brooks's much-cited essay, which associates *Errors* not with a farce such as *Supposes* but with a recognition play such as the *Ion* or *The Confidential Clerk*.[8]

Those who see Shakespeare as "transcending" farce must consent to a divorce between the "serious" issues that they elect to stress and the main business of the play.[9] In other words, the critics analyze delicate sentiments while the characters knock heads. The discovery of gravity requires great emphasis on the frame story of Egeon, or Adriana's matrimonial laments, or the wooing of Luciana. Brooks candidly declares the incongruity between his emphasis and Shakespeare's: "The *Comedy* appeals first and foremost to laughter, as is obvious at any performance. I have dwelt on its serious themes and strands of romance because it is these that student and producer are prone to discount."[10] One might respond that student and producer would in this case be taking their cue from the author, who was himself prone to discount the serious themes and strands of romance at this stage of his career. We should question critical means that seek to convert the early comedies into something other than they are.

The Comedy of Errors is a superlative example of dramatic farce, a simple form of comedy designed chiefly to make an audience laugh. Freedman points out that farces are almost always characterized by an "insistence on their own meaninglessness, an insistence which by no means should be accepted at face value."[11] In other words, to regard the play as a highly developed form of farce is not to outlaw ideas. Mistaken identity is at the heart of *The Comedy of Errors,* as Antipholus of Syracuse explains in the final moments: "I see we still did meet each other's man, / And I was ta'en for him, and he for me, / And thereupon these errors have arose" (5.1.388–90).[12] This basic formula is the source of pleasure and of meaning in the farcical comedy. My goal is to increase, if only slightly, our sense of how meaning comes about in farce, and my method for doing so is to concentrate on what an audience sees and hears in the main action.[13] It seems reasonable to conclude—and worth pointing out, given the critical history of the text in question—that dramatic significance ought to proceed as much from the essential as from the ancillary features of a text.

II

To err is human, and one way of describing the imperfect condition of our experience is to say that we inhabit a state of division, of disunity, of separation from God, from nature, from one another. Lest this seem too portentous a beginning for a discussion of a farcical comedy, let me hasten to say that splitting (of ships, of families, of other human relations) is one of the most important of the play's patterns of action. In one sense, of course, the plot of *The Comedy of Errors* is founded on the natural division of twinship, for nature has split a single appearance into two persons. In the source play, Plautus exploits the confusion inherent in this division by geographically separating the Menaechmus brothers, and Shakespeare has increased the complexity of the original plot, as everyone knows, by doubling the twins.[14] What is less familiar is his tactic of making the normal avenues of reconciliation into obstacle courses laid with traps and dead ends. Virtually all comedy represents characters' attempts to overcome their isolation through marriage or reconciliation, with farce throwing the emphasis on the amusing difficulties involved in such efforts. Marriage, systems of law, commerce, language—all these are forms of communion or institutions through which people seek or give satisfaction, social instruments and (implicitly) comic means for joining human beings in a happy and fruitful relation.

And yet, for all their value, these means are naturally imperfect and likely to collapse under various pressures, either of accident or human will or their own liability to misinterpretation. When they break down, the confusion that frustrates the characters delights the audience. To a great extent, the comedy of *Errors* arises from the number of barriers Shakespeare has erected and the ingenuity with which he has done so. The greatest obstacles arise in the principal characters' relations with their servants, in the arena of commerce, and in the realm of speech itself. Shakespeare generates amusing conflict by exaggerating the forces that separate people and by weakening the media that connect them.

The presence of four men in two costumes leads first to the attenuation of the normal bonds between servant and master and between husband and wife. From the twin Sosias in Plautus's *Amphitruo*, Shakespeare creates in the Dromios a pair of agents, go-betweens who link husband to wife or customer to merchant. They are extensions of their masters' wills, instruments by which each of the Antipholuses conducts business or gets what he wants. In the farcical world of the play, however, the will is inevitably frustrated as these servants become barriers, sources of confusion, gaps in a chain of communication. For Antipholus of Syracuse, lost in a strange, forbidden seaport, his one sure connection, his "bondman," seems to fail him. This treatment of the twin servants, moreover, is representative of Shakespeare's method with other characters, including Adriana, Luciana, and the Courtesan. Although the females are often said to contribute to the play's Pauline analysis of proper marriage, their primary value is as comic troublemakers. Adriana's eloquence and Luciana's charm make the two women memorable, to be sure, but they are hardly complex. Adriana's main function is to doubt her husband, to rail against his neglect, to chase him in the streets, to enlist a conjurer to minister to him; Luciana's role is to attract Antipholus of Syracuse and thereby to fuel her sister's rage.

The disintegration of personal bonds is accompanied by the weakening of the multiple commercial connections. Although the thematic importance of debts is familiar enough,[15] it is also relevant that many of the play's amusing confrontations are grounded in thwarted commercial exchanges. Ignoring the maxim that it is best to eliminate the middleman, Shakespeare has added a host of them. Angelo the Goldsmith, Balthazar, and the First and Second Merchants are all Shakespearean inventions—businessmen, literal agents who exist to get in the way. Each functions as an additional barrier separating the twin Antipholuses, as another hedge in the maze at the center of the comedy. The Second Merchant, for instance, appears only twice and exists for no other reason than to make demands and increase the comic pressure: he has been patient since Pentecost and now needs guilders for a journey; he presses Angelo to repay the sum; Angelo must seek payment from Antipholus of Ephesus who, not having received the chain for which the money is demanded, refuses to accommodate him. In short, this importunate stranger is unnecessary: Angelo might have pursued compensation on his own initiative.

In the critical rush to find "meaning" or "tonal variety" in the addition of Luciana, Egeon, and Emilia, the structural value of the lesser auxiliary figures may be overlooked. Their untimely or mistaken demands for payment increase the confusion on the stage and damage the ties that connect them to their fellow citizens. Adriana joins the line of claimants when she tries forcibly to collect the love owed her by her husband, and her vocabulary indicates that Shakespeare has established an analogy between marital responsibilities and the cash nexus.

The setting of the comedy, as the occupations of the secondary figures remind us, is mostly the street, or "the mart," and from the beginning we observe that the business of the street is business. Most of the confrontations between characters and much of the dialogue concern the physical exchange of money or property, and other personal dealings are figured in financial terms. Egeon is a Syracusan trader unable to make the necessary financial exchange—a thousand marks for his freedom— and this fine or debt seems to have resulted from a protracted trade war. Many years before, after a period in which his "wealth increas'd / By prosperous voyages," Egeon had found himself separated from his wife by his "factor's death, / And the great care of goods at random left" (1.1.41–42). Now without family or funds, the insolvent businessman leaves the stage, whereupon Antipholus of Syracuse enters with an Ephesian merchant who tells him of the stranger's plight—"not being able to buy out his life"—and warns the young traveler to conceal his identity "lest that your goods too soon be confiscate." The citizen then returns Antipholus's bag of gold and pleads the need to pay a business call: "I am invited, sir, to certain merchants, / Of whom I hope to make much benefit" (1.2.24–25). He leaves Antipholus to his "own content, . . . the thing [he] cannot get."

This endearing soliloquy is usually said to prefigure the theme of self-understanding in the later comedies, but what is less often said is that Antipholus analyzes his dilemma in terms of self-possession: he fears that in seeking to recover his family he will "lose" himself. At the end of the same scene he frets about the loss of his treasure, worrying that Dromio "is o'er-raught of all [Antipholus's] money" and recalling the city's reputation for "cozenage," "cheaters," and "mountebanks."

The bag of gold that Antipholus gives to Dromio to deliver to the inn is the first in a list of theatrical properties that provoke farcical contention. The initial dispute occurs with the entrance of Dromio of Ephesus, to whom "the money" demanded can only be the "sixpence that I had o' Wednesday last, / To pay the saddler for my mistress' crupper"; the "charge" is not a bag of gold but a command "to fetch you from the mart"; the "thousand marks" are not coins but bruises administered by master and mistress. As Antipholus of Syracuse worries about fraud, Dromio of Ephesus reports the misunderstanding to his mistress in a speech whose opposing clauses suggest the nature of the impasse: " ''Tis dinner time,' quoth I; 'my gold,' quoth he." The metal becomes a metaphor at the end of the first scene of act 2, when Adriana speaks of reputation as a piece of enameled gold (2.1.109–15), and thus Shakespeare uses it to link the end of the scene with the beginning of the next: Antipholus of Syracuse enters puzzling over the bag of money, apparently not lost at all, whereupon his own Dromio enters, denies any knowledge of the recent dispute over the gold, and earns a beating. The pattern of confusion thus established with the thousand marks is repeated in squabbles over control of a chain, a ring, a dinner, a house, a spouse, a bag of ducats, a name, a prisoner, and a pair of strangers seeking sanctuary.

The vocabulary of these disputes is almost invariably the parlance of the marketplace: Antipholus of Ephesus and his business cronies politely debate the relative value of a warm welcome and a good meal ("I hold your dainties cheap, sir, and your welcome dear"); Nell "lays claim" to the Syracusan Dromio; to the Courtesan, "forty ducats is too much to lose"; the Officer cannot release Antipholus of Ephesus for fear that "the debt he owes will be required of me"; Antipholus of Ephesus is known to be "of very reverend reputation, . . . / Of credit infinite"; Dromio of Ephesus, declared mad and tied up, describes himself as "entered in bond" for Antipholus; and when the Abbess sees Egeon in act 5, she offers to "loose his bonds, / And gain a husband by his liberty." The great scene before Antipholus's house (3.1) becomes a dispute not just over property but over ownership of names and identity. In their efforts to get paid or to pay others back for wrongs suffered, characters often speak of "answering" each other:

> *Eph. Ant.* I answer you? Why should I answer you?
> *Angelo.* The money that you owe me for the chain.
>
> (4.1.62–63)

The merchants become enraged when their customers refuse to answer them with payment; Adriana is furious that her husband will not return a favorable answer to her requests that he come home to dinner; Antipholus of Ephesus will make his household answer for the insult of locking him out; and neither Antipholus is able to get a straight answer from either of the Dromios. This financial use of "answer" links cash to language, the most complicated and potentially ambiguous medium of all.

Exploiting the pun as the linguistic equivalent of twinship, Shakespeare creates a series of verbal equivalents for the visual duplications of the action. Initially, it seems to me, his practice is to please the audience with repeated words and images: most obviously, he develops the conflicts by ingeniously employing the language of commerce. The normal give-and-take of business activity and family life is impaired by the mistakings of the action, and when the members of the household take Antipholus of Ephesus for a troublemaker in the street, his Dromio describes him as having been "bought and sold." The "loss" of one's good name or "estimation" is risky in this world of commerce, as Balthazar explains: "For slander lives upon succession, / For ever housed where it gets possession" (3.1.105–6). Adriana's anger at her husband leads Luciana to charge her with possessiveness, and then when Antipholus of Syracuse confesses that Luciana,

> *Possessed* with such a gentle sovereign grace,
> Of such *enchanting* presence and discourse,
> Hath almost made me *traitor* to myself,
> (3.2.158–60; italics mine)

the diction of ownership ("possessions") is cleverly modulated into that of witchcraft and madness ("possession"). This ambiguity pays its most amusing dividends when Doctor Pinch attempts to exorcise the demons from Antipholus of Ephesus:

> I charge thee, Satan, hous'd within this man,
> To yield possession to my holy prayers,
> And to thy state of darkness hie thee straight;
> (4.4.52–54)

The problems of confused identity and the loss of self-control are soon compounded by the question of freedom of action. The Dromios' lives are not their own, as they reiterate in complaining that, as slaves, they are not adequately rewarded for service. These various senses of bondage—to service, to customers, to wives, to the law, to business commitments (the Second Merchant is "bound to Persia"), to a rope—reinforce each other, especially in the last two acts, as the lines of action intersect:

> *Egeon.* Most might duke, vouchsafe me speak a word.
>   Haply I see a friend will save my life,
>   And pay the sum that may deliver me.
> *Duke.* Speak freely, Syracusian, what thou wilt.
> *Egeon.* Is not your name, sir, called Antipholus?
>   And is not that your bondman Dromio?
> *Eph. Dro.* Within this hour I was his bondman, sir;
>   But he, I thank him, gnawed in two my cords.
>   Now I am Dromio, and his man, unbound.
> (5.1.283–91)

Egeon, expecting to be set at liberty, is mistaken, bound by the limitations of his senses. And here Dromio, the "freedman," steals from his master the privilege of response. As mistakes are exposed and corrected, Shakespeare relies upon the commercial vocabulary that has served him from the beginning: Antipholus of Syracuse wishes "to make good" his promises to Luciana; when Antipholus of Ephesus offers to pay his father's fine, the Duke pardons Egeon and restores his freedom and self-control ("It shall not need; thy father hath his life"); and the Abbess offers to "make full satisfaction" to the assembled company in recompense for the confusion of the day.

Words offer a way of resolving the divisions that the play explores, but at the same time they entail enormous possibilities for error. Given the present critical climate, some remarks about the unreliability of language are to be expected, but if words are included among the other media of exchange that Shakespeare has chosen to twist and complicate, then such a conclusion seems less fashionable than useful. Shakespeare almost from the beginning expands the wrangling over who owns what to include a series of battles over words and their significance. The two Dromios again offer the sharpest illustrations of such cross-purposes, usually in their interchanges with their masters. In the first meeting of Antipholus of Syracuse with Dromio of Ephesus, the shifts in meaning of "charge" and "marks" I have already cited represent the struggle for control of meaning that underlies the farcical action. Both servants are adept at shifting from the metaphorical to the literal:

> *Adr.* Say, is your tardy master now at hand?
> *Eph. Dro.* Nay, he's at two hands with me, and that my two ears can witness.
>
> (2.1.44–46)

When Antipholus of Syracuse threatens Dromio of Syracuse, "I will beat this method in your sconce," the servant resorts to linguistic subversion: "Sconce call you it? so you would leave battering, I had rather have it a head; and you use these blows long, I must get a sconce for my head, and insconce it too, or else I shall seek my wit in my shoulders" (2.2.34–39).

Yet the servants can speak highly figurative language as well: both describe the arresting officer in metaphors so elaborate that they baffle the auditors (4.2.32–40 and 4.3.12–30). Some of the verbal excursions resemble vaudeville turns, particularly the banter between the two Syracusans on baldness, and such jests represent verbal forms of what happens dramatically in the main action. In showing that "there is no time for all things," Dromio of Syracuse jestingly disproves an indisputable axiom, just as the errors of the main plot raise a challenge to the reality that everyone has accepted until now. This is more than what Brooks deprecatingly calls "elaborations of comic rhetoric."[16]

The struggle over what words signify quickens as the characters sense that reality is slipping away from them. The locking-out scene (3.1) depends for its hilarity on the stichomythic exchanges between those outside (Dromio and Antipholus of Ephesus) and those inside (Dromio of Syracuse and Luce, and later Adriana). The contestants, particularly those in the security of the house, manipulate meanings and even rhyme and other sounds as they taunt the pair trying to enter, for possession of the house is apparently an advantage in the battle of words. The Dromios' attitudes toward language are almost always playful and subversive, so that even at their masters' most frustrated moments, the servants take pleasure in twisting sound and sense, as in Dromio of Ephesus's puns on "crow" ("crow without a feather?"; "pluck a crow together"; and "iron crow").

The trickiness of language can cause characters to lose the direction of the dialogue:

> *Adr.* Why, man, what is the matter?
> *Syr. Dro.* I do not know the matter; he is 'rested on the case.
> *Adr.* What, is he arrested? tell me at whose suit?
> *Syr. Dro.* I know not at whose suit he is arrested well;
>   But is in a suit of buff which 'rested him, that can I tell.
>   Will you send him, mistress, redemption, the money in his desk?
> *Adr.* Go, fetch it, sister; this I wonder at,
>   *Exit* Luciana.
> That he unknown to me should be in debt.
> Tell me, was he arrested on a band?
> *Syr. Dro.* Not on a band, but on a stronger thing;
>   A chain, a chain, do you not hear it ring?
> *Adr.* What, the chain?
> *Syr. Dro.* No, no, the bell, 'tis time that I were gone,
>   It was two ere I left him, and now the clock strikes one.
>   (4.2.41–54)

Rhetorically, the key to this passage is antanaclasis: Dromio wrests a word from Adriana's meaning into another of its senses, as with "matter" (*trouble* and *substance*), "case" and "suit" (both meaning *case in law* and *suit of clothes*), "band" (*bond* and *ruff*). The ambiguous pronoun reference in "hear it ring" illustrates the power of words to entrap: Adriana and the audience need a moment to adjust as Dromio abruptly shifts the focus from his narrative to the present.

Just as words are apt to slip out of their familiar senses, customers or husbands or servants seem to change from moment to moment. Dialogue and stage action illustrate the limits of human control as characters try to react to these confusing turns of phrase or of event. Antipholus of Syracuse, offered a wife and a dinner, can be flexible: "I'll say as they say" (2.2.214). But words may conflict with other words and realities with other realities, as the Duke discovers in seeking the undivided truth: "You say he dined at home; the goldsmith here / Denies that

saying. Sirrah, what say you?" (5.1.274–75). Conflicts of personal identity, of contracts, of words, of stories, all make the truth seem elusive
and uncertain.

Shakespeare's strategy of breaking the integuments that bind human
beings to one another accounts for much of the mirth in *Errors* and for
much of the significance as well. By interfering with familiar and normally reliable systems of relation—master to servant, wife to husband,
customer to merchant, speaker to auditor—the dramatist achieves the
dislocation felt by the characters and the "spirit of weird fun" enjoyed by
the audience.[17] There is, moreover, an additional verbal medium that
Shakespeare has twisted to his own use, that of the play itself. The ironic
bond between playwright and spectator, that relation which Shakespeare inherited from Plautus and cultivated throughout the first four
acts and by which he assures us that we know more than the characters
know, is suddenly abrogated when the Abbess declares her identity at
the end of the fifth act: we have thought ourselves superior to the errors
and assumptions of the ignorant characters, but we too have been
deceived. Emilia's reunion with her husband and sons completes the
comic movement of the action. This is farce, so the emphasis throughout
is on the delights of disjunction; but this is also comedy, so the drama
moves toward a restoration of human ties and the formation of new
ones. Sentiment asserts itself in the final moments, of course, but Shakespeare does not overstate it, and the shift from pleasure in chaos to
pleasure in order need not jar. The confusion must end somewhere, and
it is standard practice for the farceur to relax the comic tension by
devising a mellow ending to a period of frenzy.[18]

Shakespeare attempted to write farce in *The Comedy of Errors*, and he
succeeded. Certain effects and values are missing from this kind of
drama: there is no thorough examination of characters, no great variety
of tones, no profound treatment of ideas, no deep emotional engagement. But farce gives us what other dramatic forms may lack: the production of ideas through rowdy action, the pleasures of "non-signifi-
cant" wordplay, freedom from the limits of credibility, mental exercise
induced by the rapid tempo of the action, unrestricted laughter—the
satisfactions of various kinds of extravagance.[19] Indeed, farce may be
considered the most elemental kind of theater, since the audience is
encouraged to lose itself in play. This is bad Shakespeare in the sense
that the young dramatist was content with an inherently limited mode;
the play is not *Twelfth Night*. Its value is in its theatrical complexity. And
yet the boisterous action does generate thematic issues. To admit that
Shakespeare willingly devoted himself to farce is to acknowledge a side
of his career too often neglected or misrepresented. That the author of

King Lear was capable of writing *The Comedy of Errors* should be a source of wonder, not embarrassment.

Notes

1. Barbara Freedman, "Errors in Comedy: A Psychoanalytic Theory of Farce," in *Shakespearean Comedy*, ed. Maurice Charney, *New York Literary Forum*, 5–6 (1980): 233–34.

2. R. A. Foakes, Introduction to *The Comedy of Errors*, New Arden Shakespeare (1962; reprint, London: Methuen, 1963), li.

3. A. C. Hamilton, *The Early Shakespeare* (San Marino, Cal.: Huntington Library, 1967), 107.

4. Peter G. Phialas, *Shakespeare's Romantic Comedies* (Chapel Hill: University of North Carolina Press, 1966), 3, 16. Compare the remarks of Sir Arthur Quiller-Couch in his Introduction to *The Comedy of Errors* (Cambridge: Cambridge University Press, 1922), p. xxii: "Sundry passages, even in its farcical episodes, show us the born poet, the born romancer, itching to be at his trade."

5. It would be easy enough to make merry with some of these attempts: a title such as Gwyn Williams's "*The Comedy of Errors* Rescued from Tragedy," *Review of English Literature* 5 (1964): 63–71 furnishes a sense of how far some commentators have been willing to go.

6. Derek Traversi, *Shakespeare: The Early Comedies*, Writers and Their Work 129 (London: Longmans, Green, 1960), 12.

7. Foakes, Introduction, l–li.

8. Harold Brooks, "Theme and Structure in *The Comedy of Errors*," in *Early Shakespeare*, ed. John Russell Brown and Bernard Harris (London: Edward Arnold, 1961; New York: Schocken Books, 1966), 69. Although I shall dispute the arguments of Foakes and Brooks and their less persuasive followers, I should acknowledge that this approach can be useful. In the first place, it can cast light into neglected corners of the texts. Moreover, it usually proceeds from laudable motives. Foakes, for example, recognizing the condescension often directed at comedy generally, deliberately attempts to mitigate it by underscoring the serious aspects of the work: he intends his analysis as a rejoinder to the "tradition of regarding comedy in general as inferior to 'serious' plays, and Shakespeare's comedies in particular as entertainments, plays of escape into a careless world" (p. xl).

9. The latest manifestation of this argument is Karen Newman's discussion of Antipholus of Syracuse's "inner life and realistic development" (*Shakespeare's Rhetoric of Comic Character* [London: Methuen, 1985], 84).

10. Brooks, "Theme and Structure," 69.

11. Freedman, "Errors in Comedy," 234.

12. This and all subsequent citations to *The Comedy of Errors* are to the New Arden edition. Parenthetical text references are to act, scene, and line.

13. Robert Y. Turner, *Shakespeare's Apprenticeship* (Chicago: University of Chicago Press, 1974), writes about *Errors* and its mode in a way that describes my approach: "Rather than separate the 'comic intrigue' and 'comic rhetoric' from the themes, we should ask how it is that themes, quite serious in other contexts, become the stuff of farce" (p. 167). Others who look at Shakespeare's early work in this way include G. R. Elliott, "Weirdness in *The Comedy of Errors*," *University of Toronto Quarterly* 9 (1939): 95–106, reprinted in *Shakespeare's Comedies: An Anthology of Modern Criticism*, ed. Laurence Lerner (Harmondsworth, Eng.: Penguin, 1967), 19–31, and Paul A. Jorgensen, in his Introduction to the play in *The Complete Pelican Shakespeare* (Baltimore: Penguin, 1969), 55–58. Barbara Freedman's extremely stimulating essay should be required reading for anyone interested in the play or in farce generally.

14. Two exhaustive articles by Erma Gill cover this topic: "A Comparison of the Charac-

ters in *The Comedy of Errors* with Those in the *Menaechmi*," *University of Texas Studies in English* 5 (1925): 79–95; and "The Plot-Structure of *The Comedy of Errors* in Relation to Its Source," *University of Texas Studies in English* 10 (1930): 13–65.

15. See John Russell Brown, *Shakespeare and his Comedies* (London: Methuen, 1957), 54–57, and Freedman's "Errors in Comedy," 239–40.

16. Brooks, "Theme and Structure," 69.

17. Elliott, "Weirdness," 30.

18. Francis Fergusson offers an extremely enlightening discussion of the play's ending: "All who successfully devise farce for the theatre feel the need of this final change of mood. I used to notice that the old burlesque shows at Minsky's recognized it instinctively. The travelling salesmen would be guffawing all evening at slapstick, broad jokes, and chorines with but three crucial rhinestones; but at the end the lights would soften, the music would slide from the hot, through the blue, to the frankly old-timy, and a grey-haired mamma or 'mom' would take the centre of the stage to gaze thoughtfully into the electric moonlight. So the patrons received the whole treatment, gently eased at last out of their farcical mood into something warmer, damper, and homier." Fergusson's essay is brief but satisfying: "Two Comedies: *The Comedy of Errors* and *Much Ado About Nothing*," *Sewanee Review* 62 (1954): 24–37; reprinted in Lerner, *Shakespeare's Comedies*, 32–43. The quotation is found on p. 35 of Lerner.

19. See Turner on what farce can do that other modes cannot: "Farce affords its distinctive pleasures that arise from its very limitations. It has the power to make us laugh at cuckolds, shrews, beaten servants, unpaid goldsmiths, unjust laws, even potential incest" (*Shakespeare's Apprenticeship*, 167).

6

Text, Gender, and Genre
in *The Taming of the Shrew*
PETER BEREK

WHETHER OR NOT *The Taming of the Shrew* is Shakespeare's worst play, it surely leads the canon in bad qualities. *The Shrew* has the badness of earliness—believing in artistic development, we use its faults as a foil for the accomplishments of later plays. It has a bad genre—though Frye and Barber have made comedy respectable, farce is an inferior mode. As its very title flamboyantly demonstrates, *The Taming of the Shrew* is morally bad. its patriarchal chauvinism is unalloyed with ambiguity, and its final (and most celebrated) speech unpleasantly proclaims some Renaissance commonplaces that make even our own century look good. The play even has a bad quarto.

Needless to say, critics of *The Taming of the Shrew* have not been content to let bad enough alone. No one seems to fuss much about the date, to be sure. (The New Arden editor says 1589; the Oxford editor, before 1592.[1]) But Peter Saccio has recently argued, with considerable force, for the virtues of farce as a genre.[2] The Plain Man's Sexist Reading of the play, in which Katherine's shrewishness is offensive to reason and good taste and Petruchio's humiliation of her is an occasion for celebration, has been supplanted by a variety of interpretations that try to exonerate Shakespeare's characters, or Shakespeare himself, from at least the worst excesses of sexual chauvinism.[3] There are two principal methodologies of exoneration. One is to read the play—or at least certain speeches— ironically, in the manner described by Richard Levin in *New Readings vs. Old Plays*.[4] Thus, Katherine's final speech, ostensibly a submission to Petruchio and an affirmation of the rightness of masculine dominance, is really a spoof of such arguments and meant to be perceived as such by the audience. Some critics even believe that Petruchio himself is in on the joke. And this involvement of Petruchio in the joke opens up another common strategy of exoneration. Petruchio, Marianne Novy argues, is not browbeating Katherine into submission, but teaching her how to liberate her playful spirit and join him in comic release from the duller side of Paduan society, as exemplified by Katherine's father and sister.

The stakes in these critical revisions are not trivial. No Good critic wants to ally himself or herself with a Bad remark like Sir Arthur Quiller-Couch's: "One cannot help thinking a little wistfully that the Petruchian discipline had something to say for itself."[5] It is culturally awkward to advance an interpretation of a work by an admired writer that suggests that the writer condoned unpleasant beliefs about matters that are touchstones of virtue in one's own society. Because Shakespeare's plays are "canonical," we want to associate them with our most deeply held ideals. (We have few problems with Shakespeare's monarchist ideas only because there is no serious current debate in which those ideas matter, and we have precisely analogous problems with Shakespeare's portrayals of blacks and Jews.) But it is awkward for most persons trained as literary scholars and critics to propose a revisionist reading of *The Shrew* without arguing—or at least implying—that Shakespeare himself would have given the reading his sanction. Few Shakespeareans are sufficiently deconstructed to regard their own construction of a text as superseding the author's.[6] Paradoxically, though we acknowledge that *The Taming of the Shrew* is Bad Shakespeare, we resist admitting that the play, or the playwright, is *that* bad. We want to rescue its characters, its author, and its audience from ignominy, as though we cannot bear to admit that we are continually interested in such a deplorable monument.

As much subject to these feelings about *The Shrew* as any other writer, by the end of this essay I too will be arguing that Shakespeare was less sexist than his contemporaries, though more sexist than I am, or you are. But I shall reach this Good conclusion by embracing the Bad—in particular, the badness of the bad quarto, *The Taming of a Shrew,* and the other badness of farce. I will suggest that the differences between *The Taming of the Shrew* and *The Taming of a Shrew* show that Shakespeare's ideas about the relationships of men and women were different from those of his imitators, and perhaps were misperceived by his contemporaries in ways that provide some comfort for those who (like Harold Goddard) want to argue that Shakespeare wrote a play that could be taken one way by the multitude and another way by the more sophisticated.[7] But I will also suggest that Shakespeare's choice of farce as a genre in which to dramatize the clash of gender roles reveals his fundamental uneasiness about such roles early in his theatrical career. Farce is a Good genre for exorcising Bad feelings. Shakespeare may have needed to write farce before he could write comedy.

I

The play we know as William Shakespeare's *The Taming of the Shrew* was first printed in the 1623 Folio. But in 1594 a quarto appeared called

The Taming of a Shrew. The quarto has essentially the same main plot and a similar subplot, but virtually all its language is different from the play we think of as Shakespeare's. Most of the characters in *A Shrew* have different names from those of *The Shrew*—Petruchio, for example, is called Ferando—and the setting is Athens instead of Italy. Katherine has two sisters instead of one. Like *The Shrew*, *A Shrew* begins with a prologue featuring the drunken tinker, Christopher Sly, but unlike the Folio text the 1594 quarto keeps Sly onstage throughout and gives him occasional scenes of commentary on the Katherine-Ferando action, as well as an epilogue that completes the framing structure of the play.

The plot similarities between *A Shrew* and *The Shrew* are so close as to make it certain there is some relationship between them, but the nature of that relationship has been much debated.[8] Until the 1920s most scholars thought of *A Shrew* as an earlier version of Shakespeare's play. Some saw it as a play by an earlier playwright that was later adapted and improved by Shakespeare; others thought it was Shakespeare's own early version of *The Shrew*. Some suggested that both Shakespeare and the author or authors of *A Shrew* were following a lost common source. But the most recent consensus, endorsed by both the Oxford and New Arden editors, is that *A Shrew* is some sort of bad quarto of *The Shrew*. Instead of explaining its frequently Marlovian language by suggesting that Marlowe wrote the play, they point out that theatrical pirates in the early 1590s would likely have had their heads filled with half-recollected bits of Marlowe. Such bits might then appear when they tried to cobble together dramatic verse from memory. There may be some reason to believe that the play *A Shrew* tried to copy was later revised by Shakespeare—for example, to remove the Sly epilogue. But differences between the two plays reflect either pirates' misrecollections of Shakespeare or their—or his—deliberate revisions.

Why does all this good scholarship matter to students of bad Shakespeare? Because if correct, it gives us the potential for some insight into the author's own changing attitudes toward the subject matter of *The Shrew*. If *A Shrew* is a bad imitation of a play by Shakespeare that he later revised into the Folio text, then by looking at the differences between the quarto and Folio texts we may be able to see if Shakespeare went from bad to worse, or perhaps bad to better, as he revised his own play. And indeed, there seem to be some significant differences in implied attitudes toward gender between the two versions of the play. *The Shrew* suggests more sympathy for Katherine than is found in *A Shrew,* and thereby complicates audience responses to the nastier and more violent activities of shrew taming. For example, Sander (Grumio) and Kate enter at the start of scene 11 of *A Shrew* and Kate complains of hunger: "*Sander* I prethe help me to some meate, / I am so faint that I can scarsely stande" (lines 2–3)[9]. The scene then launches into the mean-spirited taunting of

hungry Kate familiar from *The Shrew*, act 4, scene 3, and continues when
Ferando (Petruchio) enters with some meat on a dagger. (This last bit of
business, absent in the Folio text, looks like an imitation of a moment in
Peele's *Battle of Alcazar*, though Brian Morris sees a parallel to *1 Tamburlaine*, act 4, scene 4, line 40.[10])

In *The Shrew*, however, the teasing game begins with a speech that
arouses in the audience some awareness of Katherine's wounded human
dignity, not just her growling stomach:

> The more my wrong, the more his spite appears.
> What, did he marry me to famish me?
> Beggars that come unto my father's door
> Upon entreaty have a present alms;
> If not, elsewhere they meet with charity.
> But I, who never knew how to entreat,
> Nor never needed that I should entreat,
> Am starved for meat, giddy for lack of sleep,
> With oaths kept waking and with brawling fed;
> And that which spites me more than all these wants,
> He does it under name of perfect love,
> As who should say, if I should sleep or eat,
> 'Twere deadly sickness or else present death.[11]

A Shrew and *The Shrew* differ in that the Folio play makes the shrew less a
farcical figure of fun and causes the audience to be aware of the human
pain of her situation. Even allowing for the brevity of the bad quarto and
the consequent sketchiness of all its characterizations, I think it fair to
say that the Folio text complicates and enriches our sense of Katherine's
nature more than it does Ferando-Petruchio's.

But the two texts differ not just in characterization but in ideology. The
differences become clearest and most interesting in Katherine's climactic
speeches in act 5. In both plays, she submits to male domination, and in
both plays she represents her submission by placing her hands beneath
her husband's feet. But the arguments she advances for doing so are
very different from one another. Since most of us will remember Kate's
speech of submission in *The Shrew*, with its famous admission that "a
woman moved is like a fountain troubled" (5.2.142) and apologies for the
fact that "women are so simple" (5.2.161), let me begin with the less
familiar passage from *A Shrew* and quote it in full:

> Then you that live thus by your pompered wills,
> Now list to me and marke what I shall say,
> Theternall power that with his only breath,
> Shall cause this end and this beginning frame,
> Not in time, nor before time, but with time, confusd,

For all the course of yeares, of ages, moneths,
Of seasons temperate, of dayes and houres,
Are tund and stopt, by measure of his hand,
The first world was, a forme, without a forme,
A heape confusd a mixture all deformd,
A gulfe of gulfes, a body bodiles,
Where all the elements were orderles,
Before the great commander of the world,
The King of Kings the glorious God of heaven,
Who in six daies did frame his heavenly worke,
And made all things to stand in perfit course.
Then to his image did he make a man,
Olde *Adam* and from his side asleep,
A rib was taken, of which the Lord did make,
The woe of man so termd by *Adam* then,
Woman for that, by her came sinne to us,
And for her sin was *Adam* doomd to die,
As *Sara* to her husband, so should we,
Obey them, love them, keepe, and nourish them,
If they by any meanes doo want our helpes,
Laying our handes under theire feete to tread,
If that by that we, might procure there ease,
And for a president Ile first begin,
And lay my hand under my husband's feete,
    She laies her hand under her husbands feete

(18.15–44)

Kate takes the longest possible view of the reasons for female subordination, starting from God's creation of the world. God gave order to the preexisting chaos—"a forme, without a forme"—in the six days of His creation. After creating man in His own image, He takes a rib from Adam, and by that action brings sin and death into the world. The case for subordinating woman is of cosmic generality and literally damning. Woman brought death into man's world and all his woe; the least she can do for her victim is obey, love, nourish, and procure his ease. The speech is extraordinarily impersonal. Its ideas—insofar as it has any—are a muddled redaction of Genesis and have little to do with Kate, even the weakly characterized Kate of *A Shrew*. (Brian Morris describes the speech as "patched out with allusions to Du Bartas."[12]) With a few adjustments of pronouns it could just as well be spoken by a man as a woman. Clearly, it is a Bad speech in every sense of the word.

Katherine's corresponding speech in *The Shrew* looks much better, even if not positively Good. It grows out of the dramatic situation—her first remarks comment on the expressions of Bianca and the Widow whom she has just brought on stage:

Fie, fie, unknit that threatening unkind brow,
And dart not scornful glances from those eyes
To wound thy lord, thy king, thy governor.

(5.2.136–38)

When she says, "A woman moved is like a fountain troubled, / Muddy, ill-seeming, thick, bereft of beauty" (5.2.142–43), she is both noting their agitation and suggesting vanity as one reason for cultivating a sweeter disposition. The argument she then advances for hierarchy is quite down to earth, whether or not it is persuasive about Petruchio:

Thy husband is thy lord, thy life, thy keeper,
Thy head, thy sovereign: one that cares for thee,
And for thy maintenance; commits his body
To painful labor both by sea and land.

(5.2.146–49)

The issues are not theological but transactional: in return for a husband's hard work keeping his wife warm and secure, she owes her husband "love, fair looks, and true obedience" (5.2.153). Even when Kate makes larger analogies, they are specifically grounded in civil society: "Such duty as the subject owes the prince, / Even such, a woman oweth to her husband" (5.2.155–56). When Kate appeals to the orderliness of nature she does so by making an analogy between the softness of female bodies and the softness that should prevail in female minds:

Why are our bodies soft, and weak, and smooth,
Unapt to toil and trouble in the world,
But that our soft conditions, and our hearts,
Should well agree with our external parts?

(5.2.165–69)

Conventional as the ideas in the speech are—grounded in the marriage service, scripture, and the commonplaces of Elizabethan thought—it is nonetheless plausibly Katherine's, in a way the speech in A Shrew is not.

What can we make of the striking differences between these speeches—differences representative of those between A Shrew and The Shrew? If endorsing a social hierarchy in which men are superior to women is Bad, then both are Bad Shakespeare. But the sexism of The Shrew is less automatic, and thus perhaps less offensive, than that in the bad quarto. Whoever assembled A Shrew articulates an antifeminism that equates woman with sin. She is not merely a potential cause of trouble for man, but the cause of trouble. Though slack and careless, the speech nonetheless clearly casts woman in a role for which she can at best

apologize. In *The Shrew*, however, Katherine endorses patriarchal hierarchy for reasons that are more social than theological. Her acceptance of
patriarchy is as thoroughgoing in one play as in the other, but *The Shrew*
offers her more pleasures to accompany or recompense her subordinate
status. Woman can have beauty, if her fountain remains untroubled;
woman can also partake of the satisfactions of peace and order, like the
loyal subjects of a loving lord. It would distort the speech to say that it
foretells the pleasures of mutuality in a loving sexual relationship. But it
is at least possible to imagine the speaker of these words, or the husband
for whom she speaks, as taking some interest in such mutuality.

So far the speeches seem to give us some insight into the different
attitudes implied in the two texts toward the relationships between men
and women. But do they tell us anything about the beliefs of Shakespeare or his contemporaries? H. J. Oliver, the Oxford editor, argues
that the reconstructors of the bad quarto were working from a Shakespeare text different from, and earlier than, the one surviving in the
Folio. If he is right, then *A Shrew* can be taken as a point away from
which Shakespeare developed. If the theological antifeminism of Katherine's last speech was indeed Shakespeare's, he later decided to reject it.
Such a rejection does not necessarily prove that Shakespeare once believed what Katherine says to be true and later decided it was not—he
was a playwright, not a systematic philosopher, and he might just have
decided that the Folio version made better theater. But it is not unreasonable to speculate that the comparison of the two texts shows us
Shakespeare changing his mind and making a change (by our standards)
from Bad to Better, though not to Good.

But there is another possibility that seems to me equally interesting
and a bit more certain. There may not have been an earlier version of *The
Shrew* that is reflected in *A Shrew*. *A Shrew* can then tell us nothing about
whether Shakespeare changed his mind and revised his own play, but
may tell us a good deal about what some of his theatrical contemporaries
thought his play was like. Let me explain why. All theories of bad
quartos presume a profit motive. Perhaps a company of actors who had
lost their script wanted to reconstruct that script so they could perform;
perhaps actors with no right to a play decided to reconstruct a script so
they could take a London success on provincial tour; perhaps an un-
scrupulous printer recruited people, actors or others, to try to write
down a play they had seen so that he could print a book. In all cases, the
activity only makes sense if we assume that those who were assembling
a script were trying to reproduce a work that audiences admired, and
were trying to preserve as they did so those qualities of the work that the
audiences admired most. It would make no economic sense to pirate a
failure, nor would it make sense deliberately to alter a success.

Now, it is obviously the case that whoever contrived *The Taming of a Shrew* altered many things from *The Taming of the Shrew*. But most of the alterations in the main plot are verbal rather than structural—the kinds of changes one would make if one could not remember the words of a speech, but remembered what had gone on in a scene. Though the redactor comes across as something of a bungler, he does not seem to be a deliberate reviser. And it seems to me improbable that anyone pirating *The Shrew* would deliberately revise something as fundamental to the play as its attitudes toward gender. Thus, whatever attitudes toward gender we can discover in *A Shrew* are likely to be those that Elizabethan theatergoers thought they had perceived in *The Shrew*. If my line of reasoning is correct, it seems to me to follow that playgoers in the early 1590s saw *The Shrew* (and *A Shrew* as well, if they distinguished between them) as a play whose ideas were what we would now call sexist. *The Taming of a Shrew* strongly suggests that what I have called the Plain Man's Sexist Reading of *The Shrew* echoes the way Shakespeare's play appeared to Elizabethan popular taste. If this is so, then it seems to me that ironic readings of the sexism in the play have to be regarded as ahistorical. Elizabethan audiences do not seem to have perceived Kate as kidding when she thanks her husband for his support.

But the contrast between *The Shrew* and *A Shrew* may suggest something else as well. The antifeminism of the bad quarto is more rigid and less humane than that in Shakespeare's text. Shakespeare's attitudes toward women and toward gender roles, however bad they may seem to us, may nonetheless have been better than those of his audience—and correspondingly hard for that audience to perceive clearly. To argue that Shakespeare had suppler attitudes toward gender than his contemporaries—that Bad Shakespeare looks less Bad when compared with his Elizabethan contemporaries—will hardly seem like shocking news. But I take the very conventionality of the position I argue as a point in its favor, as I would argue that the unconventionality of the ironic reading of *The Shrew*, in relationship to the play's long critical history, has to count against it.

II

But what of the other badness of *The Taming of the Shrew*, the bad genre of farce? Barbara Freedman, upon whose work I propose to build, begins her discussion of Shakespearean farce by citing the *OED* definition of the genre: "a dramatic work (usually short) which has for its sole object to excite laughter."[13] The conventional assumption is that farce's bustling physical activity is matched by a corresponding lack of meaning. That which excites solely laughter need not excite scholarship or criticism.

Thus, Shakespeare critics who write about *The Shrew,* like those who write about *The Comedy of Errors* or even *The Merry Wives of Windsor,* usually either accept a low valuation of the play or devote themselves to demonstrating that the play wants to do more than make us laugh. And if it does, then it must be more than a farce.

Freedman's achievement is to point out that virtually all farces that are long and complex enough to be perceived as full-length plays do many things to audiences besides make them laugh. Such plays are striking for the way they veil their own complexity: the genre of farce does not *lack* meaning; it *denies* meaning. The conventions of farce seem to be a way of treating matters that might well be seen as highly important, such as sex, money, and power, but doing so in a way that pretends they are not important. Freedman points out that the plays' insistence on their own lack of significance should not be taken at face value. "Rather, I shall argue that a strategic denial and displacement of meaning is intrinsic to the genre and essential to the humorous acceptance of normally unacceptable agression which it allows."[14] Eric Bentley, she says, reminds us that in farce "we laugh at violence; the unacceptable becomes acceptable, even enjoyable."[15]

But Freedman goes on to describe the way in which farce is functional: "The characteristic elements of farce interact in a functional manner to enable us to enjoy the unacceptable."[16] The very absurdity of farce—its flat characterizations, its slapstick violence, which are (as Freedman says) evasions of the logic of cause and effect—function to let us take pleasure in aggressive feelings we would otherwise have to suppress.

> Were we not able to disown intent for aggression through error or dissolve remorse for its consequences through denial, the characteristic humor that ensures farce's popularity could never be achieved. On the other hand, were some initial, meaningful aggression not present to be disowned or denied, farce would lack both pleasure and humor. Like dreams, farce couples a functional denial of significance with often disturbing and highly significant content. . . . A taboo is always broken and not broken.[17]

Freedman's psychoanalytic theory of farce purports to remove the badness of the genre by making it meaningful. But the sorts of meaning she proposes inhere not so much in what characters and plot *do* as in what they avoid. Freedman shifts discussion of farce toward a discussion of the nature of the pleasure it gives audiences, and the genre becomes good because the audience enacts a complex psychological maneuver that the play itself evades.

I want to shift away from Freedman's emphasis on the audience pleasure in farce to some discussion of the satisfactions farce makes available to the maker of the joke—in this case, to Bad Shakespeare. In *Jokes and their Relation to the Unconscious*, Freud explains that jokes give pleasure to both the joker and his listener because they create "an economy in expenditure upon inhibition or suppression."[18] Freud distinguishes among play, jests, and jokes. Play, predominantly an activity of children, is "brought to an end by the strengthening of a factor that deserves to be described as the critical faculty or reasonableness."[19] Developing powers of criticism lead to the expectation that language and behavior will be meaningful. Such an expectation cuts off the growing child from the pleasures that play offered, but these pleasures can return in the form of jests. In jests, "the meaningless combination of words or the absurd putting together of thoughts must nevertheless have a meaning."[20] The surface appearance of meaning—as for example, in a pun— legitimizes a childlike pleasure in the play of sound for its own sake. The appearance of meaning in the case of the jest silences the critical faculties and makes pleasure possible. But in a joke, as opposed to a jest, meaning becomes a part of pleasure, not just a pretext for pleasure. "If what a jest says possesses substance and value, it turns into a joke."[21] However, that which has substance and value in a joke—that which has meaning— may also be that which is ordinarily inhibited or suppressed. The *form* of the joke, which Freud characterizes as being identical to the form of the jest, "bribes our powers of criticism" and enables us to take pleasure in materials that those powers of criticism would ordinarily lead us to reject. In its fully developed "tendentious" form the joke offers new sources of pleasure both to the joker and to his audience by lifting inhibitions.[22]

I want to propose an affinity between farce and jest, and a further affinity between joke and comedy. Farce is like a jest, as Freud defines the term, because the pleasures it provides are those of "repetition of what is similar, a rediscovery of what is familiar, similarity of sound, etc."—the pleasures Freud associates with childlike play, but here embodied in an action that, because it is both mimetic and verbal, implies sufficient meaning to appear legitimate to an adult mind.[23] The simplest forms of farce activity do not so much deny significance, as Barbara Freedman would have it, as evade it: the taboos broken are those against the noise and violence of childhood rather than the more focused aggressions of maturity. But as farce takes on more sexually explicit materials, it becomes more like a tendentious joke. The pleasures it provides to both its maker and its audience are those of an economy in expenditure of psychic energy upon inhibition. It is at that stage that the parallel between farce and dreams becomes most compelling; at that stage we can speak (as Freedman does) of a taboo's being simultaneously broken and not broken. But thus far the pleasures are principally those of release.

Though the pleasures of release are real and powerful, and can indeed form the basis for raising the value we place on farce, they are not the same as the pleasures of later Shakespearean comedy. Peter Saccio's terms of praise for farce in his admirable "Shrewd and Kindly Farce" are instructive. Saccio points out that the father of Katherine and Bianca has created a "distressing stalemate" by his vow that his popular younger daughter may not wed until her unpopular sister finds a husband. "Within this situation," Saccio writes, "farce celebrates the virtues of energy, ingenuity and resilience, virtues that disrupt the static dilemma and work to resolve it."[24] Saccio succeeds at his avowed task of finding positive rather than negative language to characterize what farce values. Petruchio and Katherine are indeed energetic, ingenious, and resilient; they are more than Bergsonian bouncing puppets, despite the mechanical quality of farcical play.

But the effect of their good qualities is to enable them—and us—to *accept* a distressing situation and work to resolve it essentially within its own terms. Freedman uses the idea of acceptance in her own description of farce when she speaks of "the humorous acceptance of normally unacceptable aggression which it allows."[25] Farce legitimizes the release of aggressive feelings, including feelings that are the understandable result of "distressing" situations. But to the extent that patriarchy is the cause of the distress in *The Shrew*, resilient characters such as Katherine and Petruchio find ways of adapting while accepting all of patriarchy's premises. Such an achievement should be valued—indeed, such an achievement may be essential as a first step toward attaining that capacity to survive which is the first step in achieving a capacity to question, rethink, and revalue. The achievement, I take it, is Bad Shakespeare's as well as his characters'.

But the achievement of the middle comedies—the "festive comedies"—extends beyond energy, ingenuity, and resilience even as it includes those virtues. Developing Freud's ideas, C. L. Barber spoke of the movement of comedy as being "through release to clarification."[26] By clarification, Barber means more than the release of energy suppressing a forbidden impulse. Energy is redirected, not just discharged, and that which was repressed into the unconscious is at least partially integrated into the waking, or nonjoking, life. To shift away from psychoanalytic terms, the later comedies give us heroines who are reflective. Saccio himself implicitly acknowledges the distinction when he writes, "The romantic humanization of Katherine is expressed, not in such reflective speeches as might be given to Viola, but through the resilience and energy of her co-operation with Petruchio's madcap words and actions."[27] The clarification achieved in the middle comedies enables them to produce in their audiences an effect similar to that achieved by their heroines—an effect Meredith, in his essay on the comic spirit, called "thoughtful laughter." The middle comedies have moved beyond jest and perhaps even beyond jokes, as Freud uses the term, and on into a realm where what farce and jokes both repress and release can be dealt with as matters for conscious thought.

Freud is surely right that the pleasures of a joke's audience are roughly similar to those of the maker of the joke.[28] As a maker of farces, Shakespeare creates plays that deny meaning, as Freedman suggests, or perhaps better, deny responsibility for their potential meanings. In *The Taming of the Shrew*, much of the denied meaning pertains to the emotional complexity of gender relationships. And that, I suggest, is no accident. Patriarchal structures create distress for characters that may mirror a distress felt by the maker of those characters. The play is filled with aggression and hostility, some of which may be ascribed to its author. The "earliness" of the play produces a Badness that is not the Badness of ineptitude but of unassimilated conflict. Farce is indeed an economical strategy for acknowledging and accepting hostility. But all it does is accept—it does not transform. Although the differences between *A Shrew* and *The Shrew* suggest that Shakespeare's own attitudes toward gender may have been more supple and complex than those most prevalent in the early 1590s, nonetheless the farcical mode of *The Shrew* serves more to accept than to clarify a problem.

Happily, this particular manifestation of Shakespeare's predicament is short-lived. Bad Shakespeare gets very Good indeed, especially in comparison with his contemporaries, by 1598 or 1600. But at the start of his career, whatever dissatisfaction Shakespeare may have felt with patriarchal orthodoxy gets released in explosive insults and in bombastic professions of patriarchal ideology. That we can see in this early work the potential for later and better plays should not blind us to the fact that it is not one of those better plays. But the release of badness by Bad Shakespeare in his early farce may have been a valuable, even necessary, stage in moving toward his astonishing expansion of the possibilities of gender roles, even if within patriarchal bounds, at the end of the decade.

Notes

1. *The Taming of the Shrew*, ed. Brian Morris, New Arden Shakespeare (London: Methuen, 1981), 65; *The Taming of the Shrew*, ed. H. J. Oliver (The Oxford Shakespeare, Oxford Clarendon Press, 1982), 32.

2. Peter Saccio, "Shrewd and Kindly Farce," *Shakespeare Survey* 37 (1984): 33–40.

3. Most writers on *The Shrew* since 1966 rightly point out that an excellent summary o the twentieth-century critical fortunes of the play appears in Robert B. Heilman, "The

Taming Untamed, or, The Return of the Shrew," *MLQ* 27 (1966): 147–61. I will do the same. Recent essays influenced by feminist thinking and arguing in one way or another for readings of the play that mitigate the sexism of Petruchio, Shakespeare, or both, and for a relatively positive view of Katherine, are Coppélia Kahn, "*The Taming of the Shrew:* Shakespeare's Mirror of Marriage," in *The Authority of Experience: Essays in Feminist Criticism,* ed. Arlyn Diamond and Lee R. Edwards (Amherst: University of Massachusetts Press, 1977), 84–100 (reprinted from *Modern Language Studies,* no. 5, 1 [Spring 1975]); John C. Bean, "Comic Structure and the Humanizing of Kate in *The Taming of the Shrew,*" in *The Woman's Part: Feminist Criticism of Shakespeare,* ed. Carolyn Ruth Swift Lenz, Gayle Greene, and Carol Thomas Neely (Urbana: University of Illinois Press, 1980), 65–78; Marianne L. Novy, "Patriarchy and Play in *The Taming of the Shrew,*" in *Love's Argument* (Chapel Hill: University of North Carolina Press, 1984), 45–62. A counterargument, citing Renaissance handbooks on domestic relations to demonstrate the orthodoxy of Shakespeare's views, appears in Marion D. Perret, "Petruchio: The Model Wife," *SEL* 23 (1983): 223–35.

4. Richard Levin, *New Readings vs. Old Plays* (Chicago: University of Chicago Press, 1979).

5. Introduction to the Cambridge edition, ed. Arthur Quiller-Couch and John Dover Wilson (Cambridge: Cambridge University Press, 1928, 1953), p. xxvi, cited by Heilman, "The *Taming* Untamed," 147.

6. Using contemporary theory to sidestep simple oppositions between positive and negative views of Katherine, Joel Fineman argues in "The Turn of the Shrew" that the words and actions of *The Shrew* "rehearse . . . the battle between the determinate, literal language traditionally spoken by man and the figurative, indeterminate language traditionally spoken by woman" (143). This battle prefigures that between Derrida and Lacan, between deconstruction and psychoanalysis, about the nature of sexual difference. Fineman's essay appears in *Shakespeare and the Question of Theory,* ed. Patricia Parker and Geoffrey Hartman (New York: Methuen, 1985), 138–60.

7. Harold C. Goddard, *The Meaning of Shakespeare* (Chicago: University of Chicago Press, 1951), 68.

8. The most up-to-date accounts of the controversy about the relationship between *A Shrew* and *The Shrew* can be found in the Oxford Shakespeare edition of *The Shrew,* ed. H. J. Oliver (Oxford: Clarendon Press, 1982), 13–34, and the New Arden Shakespeare edition, ed. Brian Morris (London: Methuen, 1981), 12–50. *A Shrew* is reprinted by Geoffrey Bullough in *The Narrative and Dramatic Sources of Shakespeare* (New York: Columbia University Press, 1957), 1:69–108. Bullough argues in his introduction that *A Shrew* is Shakespeare's source.

9. *The Taming of a Shrew,* in Bullough, ed., *Narrative and Dramatic Sources of Shakespeare,* vol. 1. Subsequent parenthetical citations to this edition (scene and line) will appear in my text.

10. *The Shrew,* New Arden Shakespeare, 45.

11. *The Shrew,* Oxford Shakespeare, 4.3.2–14. This and subsequent parenthetical text citations are to this edition and are to act, scene, and line.

12. *The Shrew,* New Arden, p. 48.

13. Barbara Freedman, "Errors in Comedy: A Psychoanalytic Theory of Farce," in *Shakespearean Comedy,* ed. Maurice Charney, *New York Literary Forum,* 5–6 (1980): 233–43.

14. Ibid., 234.

15. Eric Bentley, *The Life of the Drama* (New York: Atheneum, 1967), quoted from Freedman, 235.

16. Freedman, "Errors in Comedy," p. 235.

17. Ibid., 236.

18. Sigmund Freud, *Jokes and their Relation to the Unconscious,* trans. James Strachey (New York: W. W. Norton, 1960), 119.

19. Ibid., 128.

20. Ibid., 129.

21. Ibid., 130.

22. Ibid., 137–38.

23. Ibid., 128.

24. Saccio, "Shrewd and Kindly Farce," 36.

25. Freedman, "Errors in Comedy," 234.

26. C. L. Barber, *Shakespeare's Festive Comedy* (Princeton: Princeton University Press, 1959), 4.

27. Saccio, "Shrewd and Kindly Farce," 37.

28. Freud, *Jokes*, 134.

7

The Taming of the Shrew
Inside or Outside of the Joke?
SHIRLEY NELSON GARNER

IF YOU HAD GROWN UP hearing that Shakespeare is the greatest writer in the English language (or at least one of the two or three greatest) and that he is a "universal" poet, who speaks across time and national (even cultural) boundaries, you—especially if you were a woman student—would be shocked to study him in a college or university in the 1980s and to read *The Taming of the Shrew* for the first time. My own students—particularly my women students, though sometimes the men in my classes as well—often exclaim in dismay, "I can't *believe* Shakespeare wrote this!" A graduate student, rereading the play with only a faded memory of having read it before, commented that it was commonly her experience now to read something that she had once enjoyed only to find it disappointing. That was what happened when she read *Taming of the Shrew,* and it gave her a sense of loss. Reading the play from a woman's perspective, she could not help but be a "resisting reader."[1] Even if teachers of literature offer an ingenious reading of the play, their students will probably not be seduced into a very happy view of it. They will know in their hearts that—at the least—there is something wrong with the way Kate is treated. And they will be right.[2]

I am not sure that anyone except academics who have invested much—perhaps all—of their professional lives in studying Shakespeare would need to debate whether *Taming of the Shrew* is good or bad. The best that can be said for the play is just what Peter Berek concludes in his essay in this volume: that it shows Shakespeare had suppler attitudes toward gender than his contemporaries and that it "may have been a valuable, even necessary, stage in moving toward his astonishing expansion of the possibilities of gender roles." This argument makes the play *interesting,* but it does not make it *good.*

The Elizabethans probably considered the play "good." Attesting to the popularity of its main idea, numerous shrew-taming stories exist as

105

well as another version of the play, evidently, acted close to the time of Shakespeare's *Taming of the Shrew*.[3] The values that underlie the story are obviously those of a patriarchal society, in which the desirability of male dominance is unquestioned. When patriarchal attitudes are called into question, as they have been in our time, it becomes a more delicate matter to put an "uppity" woman in her "proper" place—on the stage or off—and she becomes a less easy mark for humor. *Taming of the Shrew* read straight, then, must seem less "good."

Interpretations of the play that stress its farcical elements or view the ending as ironic are often efforts, I think, to keep the play among the "good," to separate Shakespeare from its misogynist attitudes, to keep him as nearly unblemished as possible.[4] These efforts to preserve *Taming* suggest that in our time it has become one of the problematic plays in Shakespeare's canon. They demonstrate how relative to time and place are the ideas of "good" and "bad." What I wish to argue here is that no matter how you read the ending, no matter how you define the genre of the play, it is still a "bad" play. From the response of members in the seminar on "Bad Shakespeare," at which the ideas here were first presented, it is clear that some people still like the play, still count it among the "good," or "more good than bad." This fact suggests that "good" and "bad" are also relative to the pleasures of the particular members of an audience. I would also argue that whether you see the play as "good" or "bad" depends on where you see yourself in terms of the central joke. If you can somehow be "in" on it, the play will undoubtedly seem better than if you cannot be.

The central joke in *The Taming of the Shrew* is directed against a woman. The play seems written to please a misogynist audience, especially men who are gratified by sexually sadistic pleasures. Since I am outside the community for whom the joke is made and do not share its implicit values, I do not participate in its humor.[5] Because the play does not have for me what I assume to be its intended effect, that is, I do not find it funny, I do not find it as good as Shakespeare's other comedies.

The Induction makes immediately clear the assumptions about women and sexuality that are at the core of *Taming*. When a Lord, a character named only according to his rank, imagines and creates for Christopher Sly a world like his own (though more romantic), the "woman" he peoples it with suggests a sixteenth-century ideal: gentle, dutiful, utterly devoted to her husband. He directs his servingman to tell Bartholomew, his page, how to play the part of Sly's wife:

> Such duty to the drunkard let him do
> With soft low tongue and lowly courtesy,
> And say, "What is't your honor will command
> Wherein your lady and your humble wife

May show her duty and make known her love?"
And then, with kind embracements, tempting kisses,
And with declining head into his bosom,
Bid him shed tears, as being overjoyed
To see her noble lord restored to health
Who for this seven years hath esteemed him
No better than a poor and loathsome beggar.[6]

(2.114–23)

Surface manner, "With soft low tongue and lowly courtesy," defines inner character, marks the "lady" as "feminine." The importance of soft-spokenness as an essential attribute of femininity is suggested by King Lear's lament over his dead Cordelia: "Her voice was ever soft, / Gentle and low, an excellent thing in woman" (5.3.274–75). In a culture that tended to see things in opposition, to split mind and body, virgin and whore, the quiet woman represented the positive side of the opposition. The woman who spoke up or out, the angry woman, represented the negative side. At a moment when Hamlet feels the greatest contempt for himself, he mourns that he "must, like a whore, unpack . . . [his] heart with words / And fall a-cursing like a very drab" (2.2.592–93). When Bartholomew appears dressed as a lady and Christopher Sly wonders why the page addresses him as "lord" rather than "husband," Bartholomew answers:

My husband and my lord, my lord and husband,
I am your wife in all obedience.

(Ind. 2.106–7)

The male fantasy that underlies this exchange is that a wife will be subject, even subservient, to her husband in all matters.

More subtly suggested as attractive in the Induction is a notion of sexuality associated with the violent, the predatory, the sadistic. The Lord immediately directs that the drunken Christopher Sly be carried to bed in his "fairest chamber," which is to be hung round with all his "wanton pictures" (Ind. 1.46–47). After Sly is promised all the requisites for hunting, including hawks that "will soar / Above the morning lark" and greyhounds "as swift / As breathèd stags, . . . fleeter than the roe" (Ind. 2.43–48), he is offered the most desirable paintings. The movement from hunting to the predatory sexuality imaged in the pictures makes obvious the association between hunting and the sexual chase. Sly is promised by the Second Servingman:

Adonis painted by a running brook
And Cytherea all in sedges hid,

> Which seem to move and wanton with her breath
> Even as the waving sedges play with wind.

And the other men join in the game, revealing their own erotic fantasies:

> *Lord.* We'll show thee Io as she was a maid
>   And how she was beguiled and surprised,
>   As lively painted as the deed was done.
> *Third Servingman.* Or Daphne roaming through a thorny wood,
>   Scratching her legs that one shall swear she bleeds,
>   And at that sight shall sad Apollo weep,
>   So workmanly the blood and tears are drawn.
>
> (Ind. 2.50–60)

Suggestions of violence, particularly of rape, underlie all of these images. The figures the paintings depict are among the familiar ones in Ovid's *Metamorphoses:* Adonis, the beautiful, androgynous youth gored to death on a wild boar's tusks; Io, a maid Zeus transformed into a heifer in order to take her; and Daphne, who was changed into a laurel tree to prevent Apollo's raping her. The images of violence intensify, as though each character's imagination sets off a darker dream in another. Interestingly enough, the story of Adonis is drawn the least bloody though it is inherently more so. It is Daphne, the innocent virgin, who bleeds. It would seem that the most predatory and sadistic impulse calls forth the most compelling eroticism for those who participate in the shared creation of these fantasies.

It is appropriate that *The Taming of the Shrew* is acted for the male characters of the Induction, for its view of women and sexuality is attuned to their pleasure. Underlying the notion of heterosexual relationships in *Taming,* especially marriage, is that one partner must dominate. There can be no mutuality. The male fantasy that the play defends against is the fear that a man will not be able to control his woman. Unlike many of Shakespeare's comedies, *Taming* does not project the fear of cuckoldry (though perhaps it is implicit), but rather a more pervasive anxiety and need to dominate and subject. In taming Kate, Petruchio seems to give comfort to all the other men in the play. Before Hortensio marries the Widow, he goes to visit Petruchio, to see his "taming school," which Tranio describes to Bianca:

>   Petruchio is the master,
>   That teacheth tricks eleven and twenty long
>   To tame a shrew and charm her chattering tongue.
>
> (4.2.56–58)

However pleasant the idea of a "taming school" may be for men, the attitude it implies toward women is appalling.

From the outset, Kate is set up so that her "taming" will be acceptable, will not seem merely cruel. This strategy serves as a means to release the play's misogyny just as madness allows Hamlet, Othello, and Lear to castigate the women who love them—their mothers, daughters, lovers, wives—and rail against them and women in general in shocking ways. In the play's only soliloquy, Petruchio delineates his plan to subject Kate:

> Thus have I politicly begun my reign,
> And 'tis my hope to end successfully.
> My falcon now is sharp and passing empty,
> And till she stoop she must not be full gorged,
> For then she never looks upon her lure.
> Another way I have to man my haggard,
> To make her come and know her keeper's call,
> That is, to watch her as we watch these kites
> That bate and beat and will not be obedient.
> She eat no meat today, nor none shall eat.
> Last night she slept not, nor tonight she shall not.
> As with the meat, some undeserved fault
> I'll find about the making of the bed,
> And here I'll fling the pillow, there the bolster,
> This way the coverlet, another way the sheets.
> Ay, and amid this hurly I intend
> That all is done in reverent care of her,
> And in conclusion she shall watch all night.
> And if she chance to nod I'll rail and brawl
> And with the clamor keep her still awake.
> This is a way to kill a wife with kindness,
> And thus I'll curb her mad and headstrong humor.
> He that knows better how to tame a shrew,
> Now let him speak—'tis charity to show.
>
> (4.1.182–205)

Petruchio's stringent mode is just that used to tame hawks; it might well come from a manual on falconry. The notion behind this central metaphor of the play is that a shrewish woman is less than human, even less than a woman, so may be treated like an animal. Only the audience's acceptance of this premise allows them to feel the play as comic.

Critics' efforts to dismiss the play's harsh attitude toward women, to disclaim its cruelty, have led them to emphasize that *Taming* is a farce and not to be taken with the kind of seriousness that I am taking it.[7] In other words, to pay attention to its cruelty, to give credence to its misogyny, is to misread its genre. Though *Taming* does not feel to me like farce, I do not wish to argue about its genre. Accepting it for the moment as farce, I would ask rather: Could the taming of a "shrew" be considered the proper subject of farce in any but a misogynist culture? How would we feel about a play entitled *The Taming of the Jew* or *The Taming of the Black?* I think we would be embarrassed by anti-Semitism or racism in a way that many of us are not by misogyny. I do not think critics could imagine writing about those fictitious plays a sentence comparable to this written of *The Taming of the Shrew:* "Once she [Kate] was naturally and unquestionably taken to be a shrew, that is, *a type of woman widely known in life* and constantly represented in song and story [*italics mine*]."[8]

To be sure, Kate is an angry woman. She threatens violence to Hortensio; ties Bianca up and strikes her; breaks a lute over Hortensio's head when he, in disguise, is trying to teach her to play it; beats Grumio; and strikes Petruchio. Yet what is said about her makes her worse than angry. When Hortensio refers to her as "Katherine the curst," Grumio echoes him and makes clear how intolerable a "shrewish" woman is to the men in the play:

> Katherine the curst!
> A title for a maid of all titles the worst.
>
> (1.2.128–29)

Gremio refers to her at various moments as a whore (1.1.55), a "fiend of hell" (1.1.88), and a "wildcat" (1.2.196). The other men repeat his sentiments. "Shrewd," "curst," "froward," Kate is mainly noticeable for her "scolding tongue." Many of the impressions of Kate are rendered through Gremio and Hortensio, who are the most threatened by her. Gremio insists that no man would marry her, only a devil would, and asks incredulously, "Think'st thou, Hortensio, though her father be very rich, any man is so very a fool to be married to hell?" When Hortensio affirms that there are "good fellows in the world" who will marry her for enough money, Gremio replies, "I cannot tell, but I had as lief take her dowry with this condition, to be whipped at the high cross every morning" (1.1.123–34). Hortensio confesses to Petruchio that though Kate is young, beautiful, and well brought up,

> Her only fault—and that is fault enough—
> Is that she is intolerable curst!
> And shrewd and froward, so beyond all measure
> That were my state far worser than it is,
> I would not wed her for a mine of gold.
>
> (1.2.87–91)

Even Baptista accuses Kate of having a "devilish spirit" (2.1.26).

We come to understand, perhaps, that Kate does not deserve this kind of denunciation, that the male characters rail so against her because she refuses to follow patriarchal prescriptions for women's submission to men. When Bianca, so praised and desired for her "beauteous modesty" (1.2.233–34), rejects Hortensio, he immediately denounces her as a

"proud disdainful haggard" (4.2.39). This sudden reversal suggests that
the men see women only in relation to male desires and needs and
describe them accordingly. Yet we only glimpse the way their bias works.
Shakespeare does not reveal it so obviously as he does in, say, *Antony
and Cleopatra*, where the men who degrade and insult Cleopatra are
clearly threatened by her and jealous because she is able to seduce
Antony away from them.

Shakespeare also adumbrates circumstances that account for Kate's
anger. The preference of everyone around her, including her father, for a
quiet woman (in other words, a woman without any spirit) is enough to
provoke her. She undoubtedly understands the high value placed on
women's silence, which Lucentio reads, in Bianca for example, as a sign
of "maid's mild behavior and sobriety" (1.1.70–71). She, of course, understands Bianca's competitiveness with her, which is acted out with
passive aggression: "Her silence flouts me and I'll be revenged" (1.1.29).
She also chafes at her certain sense that she is men's possession, a pawn
in the patriarchal marriage game. She reproaches Baptista about Bianca:

> Now I see
> She is your treasure, she must have a husband;
> I must dance barefoot on her wedding day,
> And, for your love to her, lead apes in hell.
> Talk not to me; I will go sit and weep
> Till I can find occasion of revenge.
>
> (2.1.31–36)

Though Baptista tells Petruchio that he must obtain Kate's love before he
will give his permission for the two to marry (2.1.128–29), when it comes
down to it, Kate is simply married off, bargained over like a piece of
goods:

> *Baptista.* Faith, gentleman, now I play a merchant's part
>   And venture madly on a desperate mart.
> *Tranio.* 'Twas a commodity lay fretting by you;
>   'Twill bring you gain or perish on the seas.
> *Baptista.* The gain I seek is quiet in the match.
>
> (2.1.319–23)

She is not a woman to accommodate easily an economy that makes her a
possession of men, in which a husband can say of a wife:

> I will be master of what is mine own.
> She is my goods, my chattels; she is my house,
> My household stuff, my field, my barn,
> My horse, my ox, my ass, my anything.
>
> (3.2.229–32)

Shakespeare also allows Kate to claim her anger and gives her a moving explanation of her outspokenness:

> My tongue will tell the anger of my heart,
> Or else my heart, concealing it, will break,
> And rather than it shall I will be free
> Even to the uttermost, as I please, in words.
>
> (4.3.77–80)

Yet what is said or shown to extenuate Kate does not weigh heavily enough to balance the condemnation of her, which is an effort to prepare us to accept Petruchio's humiliation of her as a necessity, or "for her own good."

Kate and Petruchio are both strong-willed and high spirited, and one of Petruchio's admirable qualities is that he has the good sense to see Kate's passion and energy as attractive. When he hears of her tempestuous encounter with Hortensio, he exclaims:

> Now, by the world, it [sic] is a lusty wench!
> I love her ten times more than e'er I did.
> O how I long to have some chat with her!
>
> (2.1.160–62)

Presumably Petruchio puts on an act to tame Kate; he pretends to be more shrew than she (4.1.81). As one of his servants says, "He kills her in her own humor" (4.1.174). But Kate's "shrewishness" only allows Petruchio to bring to the surface and exaggerate something that is in him to begin with.[9] When we first see him, he is bullying his servant—wringing him by the ears, the stage direction tells us—so that Grumio cries, "Help, masters, help! My master is mad" (1.2.18). It surprises only a little that he later hits the priest who marries him, throws sops in the sexton's face, beats his servants, and throws the food and dishes—behaves so that Gremio can exclaim, "Why, he's a devil, a devil, a very fiend" (3.2.154). When he appears for his wedding "a very monster in apparel," we learn that his dress is not wholly out of character; Tranio tells Biondello:

> 'Tis some odd humor pricks him to this fashion,
> Yet oftentimes he goes but mean-appareled.
>
> (3.2.72–73)

The strategy of the plot allows Petruchio "shrewish" behavior; but even when it is shown as latent in his character and not a result of his effort to "tame" Kate, it is more or less acceptable. Dramatically, then, Kate and Petruchio are not treated equally.

In general, whatever is problematic in Petruchio is played down; whereas Kate's "faults" are played up. For example, we tend to forget how crassly Petruchio puts money before love at the beginning of the play since he becomes attracted to Kate for other reasons. He speaks frankly:

> I come to wive it wealthily in Padua;
> If wealthily, then happily in Padua.
>
> (1.2.4–75)

And Grumio assures Hortensio in the most negative terms that money will be Petruchio's basic requirement in a wife:

> Nay, look you sir, he tells you flatly what his mind is. Why, give him gold enough and marry him to a puppet or an aglet-baby or an old trot with ne'er a tooth in her head, though she have as many diseases as two-and-fifty horses. Why, nothing comes amiss so money comes withal.
>
> (1.2.76–81)

No one in the play speaks against this kind of materialism; indeed, it seems to be the order of the day.

Kate's humbling begins from the moment Petruchio meets her. Petruchio immediately denies a part of her *self*, her identity as an angry woman. Just as the Lord of the Induction will make Christopher Sly "no less than what we say he is" (Ind. 1.71), so Petruchio will begin to turn Kate into his notion of her. Yet because her will and spirit meet his, the absurdity of his finding Kate "passing gentle" (2.1.235–45) and his elaboration of that idea is more humorous than not. It is when Petruchio begins to give Kate ultimatums, which I know he can and will enforce, that the play begins to give me a sinking feeling:

> Setting all this chat aside,
> Thus in plain terms: your father hath consented
> That you shall be my wife, your dowry 'greed on,
> And will you, nill you, I will marry you.
> . . . .
> For I am he am born to tame you, Kate,
> And bring you from a wild Kate to a Kate
> Conformable as other household Kates.
>
> (2.1.261–71)

The reason I begin to lose heart at this point is that I am certain Kate will not be able to hold her own against Petruchio. The lack of suspense is crucial to my response. I know that an angry woman cannot survive here. When I read or see *Macbeth* or *The Merchant of Venice*, though I know the witches' prophecies will come true to defeat Macbeth and that Portia will trick Shylock out of his pound of flesh, I always feel the power of the contest. But not in *Taming*.

After Kate and Petruchio are married and go to Petruchio's house in act 4, the play loses its humor for me. The change in tone follows partly from the fact that Petruchio's control over Kate becomes mainly physical. In Padua, the pair fights mainly through language, a weapon that Kate can wield as well as Petruchio. When Kate strikes Petruchio in the city, he swears he will hit her back if she does it again (2.1.218). Though he deserves slapping in the country, she cannot risk that there. While Petruchio never strikes her, he tries to intimidate her by hitting the servants and throwing food and dishes at them. The implication is that if she does not behave, he will do the same to her. Petruchio's physical taming of Kate is objectionable in itself; it is particularly humiliating because it is "appropriate" for animals, not people. Petruchio's description of his plan to tame Kate has no humor in it; related in soliloquy, it has the sound of simple explanation.

Kate's isolation in the country among Petruchio and men who are bound to do his bidding creates an ominous atmosphere. Her aloneness is heightened by the fact that even Grumio is allowed to tease her, and her plight becomes the gossip of Petruchio's servants. Her humiliation has a sexually sadistic tinge since there is always the possibility that Petruchio will rape her, as he threatens earlier:

> For I will board her though she chide as loud
> As thunder when the clouds in autumn crack.
>
> (1.2.93–95)

Petrucho's notion of sexual relations here is worthy of Iago, who says of Othello's elopement, "Faith, he tonight hath boarded a land carack" (*Othello* 1.2.49). Grumio immediately tells Hortensio, " 'A my word and she knew him as well as I do, she would think scolding would do little good upon him. . . . I'll tell you what, sir, and she stand him but a little, he will throw a figure in her face and so disfigure her with it that she will have no more eyes to see withal than a cat" (1.2.107–14). He suggests that Petruchio can out-scold and outwit Kate, but he also implies, through particularly violent imagery, that Petruchio will use force if necessary. Petruchio even tells Baptista, "I am rough and woo not like a babe" (2.1.137).

When we hear that Petruchio is in Kate's bedroom "making a sermon of continency to her" (4.1.176), I imagine that he is obviously acting contrary (his favorite mode), preaching abstinence when he might be expected to want to consummate his marriage. I have also wondered whether we are supposed to imagine that Kate has hoped to please him by offering herself sexually. Or does she actually desire him? Is the play reinforcing the male fantasy that the more a man beats and abuses a woman the more she will fawn on him?[10] But the episode is probably related mainly to assure us that Petruchio does not rape Kate, since we have been led to think he might. A play within a play, *The Taming of the Shrew* is enacted to crown Christopher Sly's evening. I think it is intended to have the same salacious appeal as are the paintings proposed for his enjoyment.

Kate and Petruchio's accord is possible only because Kate is finally willing to give up or pretend to give up her sense of reality—which *is* reality—for Petruchio's whimsy. He will do nothing to please Kate until she becomes willing to go along with him in everything, including agreeing that the sun is the moon. When she will not, he stages a temper tantrum: "Evermore crossed and crossed, nothing but crossed!" (4.5.10). Eager to visit Padua, she gives over to him in lines that can only be rendered with weariness:

> Forward, I pray, since we have come so far,
> And be it moon or sun or what you please.
> And if you please to call it a rush-candle,
> Henceforth I vow it shall be so for me.
>
> (4.5.12–15)

What follows is one instance after another of Petruchio's testing Kate's subjection to him.

One of the most difficult aspects of the play for me is the way the women are set against each other at the end. Kate and Bianca have been enemies from the beginning, but now the Widow takes sides against Kate, calling her a "shrew" (5.2.28). Kate's famous speech on wifely duty is addressed to the widow as a reproach. The men use their wives to compete with each other:

> *Petruchio.* To her, Kate!
> *Hortensio.* To her, widow!
>
> (5.2.33–34)

Betting on whose wife is the most obedient, the men stake their masculinity on their wives' compliance. A friendly voice will be raised against this kind of wager in *Cymbeline*, but not here. Only the Widow and Bianca, who will subsequently become "shrews," demur. When Kate throws her cap under foot at Petruchio's direction, the Widow remarks, "Lord, let me never have a cause to sigh / Till I be brought to such a silly pass"; and Bianca queries, "Duty call you this?" When

Lucentio reproaches Bianca for costing him five hundred crowns, she replies, "The more fool you for laying on my duty" (5.2.123–29). Though the Widow and Bianca are hateful characters, I find myself in sympathy with them. The ending of the play simply goes awry for me.

Kate's final speech may be taken straight, as a sign that she has "reformed"; or it may be taken ironically, as though she mocks Petruchio. The happiest view of it is that Kate and Petruchio perform this final act together, to confound those around them and win the bet. Even if we accept this last interpretation, I cannot take pleasure in Kate's losing her voice. In order to prosper, she must speak patriarchal language. The Kate we saw at the beginning of the play has been silenced. In one sense, it does not matter whether she believes what she is saying, is being ironical, or is acting: her words are those that satisfy men who are bent on maintaining patriarchal power and hierarchy. For them, Kate's obedience, in Petruchio's words, bodes

> peace . . . and love, and quiet life,
> An awful rule and right supremacy;
> And . . . what not that's sweet and happy.
>
> (5.2.108–10)

For Kate, it means speaking someone else's language, losing a part of her identity. She no longer engages in the high-spirited play of wit that was characteristic of her when Petruchio first met her (2.1.182–259).

If I stand farther back from the play, it seems even less comic. It is significant that *Taming* is a play within a play: "not a comontie a Christmas gambold or a tumbling trick" or "household stuff," but "a kind of history" (Ind. 2.137–42). It seems to carry the same weight as *The Murder of Gonzago* in *Hamlet* or the rustics' dramatization of *Pyramus and Thisbe* in *A Midsummer Night's Dream*. The pithy truth that *Taming* contains implies a kind of heterosexual agony. It is noticeable that just before the play begins, the Induction calls attention to the fact that the Page, though pretending to be a woman, is actually a man. Convinced that he is a lord and that the Page is his wife, Sly wants to take his "wife" to bed. The Page begs off, claiming the physicians have said that lovemaking would be dangerous for Sly, and adds: "I hope this reason stands for my excuse." Picking up the double meaning attendant on the similarity of pronunciation between "reason" and "raising," Sly continues the phallic pun: "Ay, it stands so that I may hardly tarry so long" (Ind. 2.124–25). The source of Sly's desire is ambiguous: Is it the woman the Page pretends to be, or is it the man the Page reveals he is? Perhaps they are the same: a man in drag. In any case, the breaking of aesthetic distance here asks us to recognize that we are watching a homosexual couple watch the play. From their angle of vision, *Taming* affirms how problematic heterosexual relations are, especially marriage. The fault would seem to lie with women, who are all "shrews" at heart. If a man aspires to live in harmony with a woman, he must be like Petruchio (a comic version of Hotspur) and able to "tame" her. If he is gentle, like Lucentio, he will undoubtedly become the victim of a shrewish wife. This is not a happy view of women; it is an equally unhopeful vision of love and marriage.

Even though there may be ambiguities at the conclusion of Shakespeare's comedies, they are most joyous when couples join with the prospect of a happy marriage before them. In order for marriage to be hopeful in Shakespeare, women's power must be contained or channeled to serve and nurture men. When it is—in *As You Like It, Twelfth Night,* or *A Midsummer Night's Dream*—the comic ending is celebratory. When it is not, in *The Merchant of Venice* or *Love's Labor's Lost,* the tone of the ending is less buoyant, even discordant. In *Love's Labor Lost,* when women remain in power and set the terms of marriage, it is implied that something is not right. Berowne comments:

> Our wooing doth not end like an old play;
> Jack hath not Jill. These ladies' courtesy
> Might well have made our sport a comedy.
>
> (5.2.872–74)

When the King insists that it will end in "a twelvemonth and a day," after the men have performed the penances their ladies have stipulated, Berowne replies, "That's too long for a play." The final songs contain references to cuckoldry, and their closing note is on "greasy Joan" stirring the pot.[11] What is different about the movement toward a comic ending in *Taming* is that women are set ruthlessly against each other, Kate's spirit is repressed, and marriage is made to seem warfare or surrender at too high a price.

Taming is responsive to men's psychological needs, desires, and fantasies at the expense of women. It plays to an audience who shares its patriarchal assumptions: men and also women who internalize patriarchal values. As someone who does not share those values, I find much of the play humorless. Rather than making me laugh, it makes me sad or angry. Its intended effect is spoiled. It is not only that I do not share the play's values, but also that I respond as a woman viewer and reader and do not simply respond according to my sense of Shakespeare's intention or try to adopt an Elizabethan perspective (assuming I *could*). I stand outside of the community the joke is intended to amuse; I sympathize with those on whom the joke is played.

I understand that within the tradition of shrew stories, Shakespeare's version is more generous of spirit and more complex than other such stories. But *Taming* seems dated. I think that it is interesting historically—in tracing a tradition, in understanding sixteenth-century attitudes toward women—and that it is significant as part of Shakespeare's canon, as any work of his is. But limiting its importance this way, I imply that I find it less good than many of his comedies. And I do. If I went to see it, it would be out of curiosity, to find out how someone in our time would direct it.

Shakespeare continually depicts in comedy an infertile world in which lovers are separated; the task of the play is to restore the world by bringing lovers together. In several instances, he presents characters who are "man-haters" or "woman-haters" and unites them. Benedick and Beatrice, Hippolyta and Theseus are examples; Kate and Petruchio are forerunners of these couples. Interestingly enough, Shakespeare never again shows a woman treated so harshly as Kate except in tragedy. I think that Shakespeare either began to see the world differently or that he recognized the story of Kate and Petruchio did not quite work. Most significantly, he obviously enjoyed portraying witty women characters, and he must have seen that it was preferable to leave their spirits untamed.

Notes

1. I use Judith Fetterley's term because it so aptly names the common position of the woman reader (*The Resisting Reader: A Feminist Approach to American Fiction* [Bloomington: University of Indiana Press, 1978]).

2. Students recognizing the misogyny of *Taming* may encounter a response similar to that which, according to Leslie Fiedler, a Jewish child may meet when he confronts the anti-Semitism of *The Merchant of Venice:* "A Jewish child, even now, reading the play in a class of Gentiles, feels this [the full horror of anti-Semitism] in shame and fear, though the experts, Gentile and Jewish alike, will hasten to assure him that his responses are irrelevant, even pathological, since 'Shakespeare rarely "takes sides" and it is certainly rash to assume that he here takes an unambiguous stand "for" Antonio and "against" Shylock' " (Leslie A. Fiedler, *The Stranger In Shakespeare* [New York: Stein and Day, 1972], 98–99).

3. The other version of the play, entitled *The Taming of A Shrew,* may be by another author or a bad quarto of an earlier version of the play by Shakespeare. For a discussion of the differences between the two plays, their relationship, and the critical controversies regarding them, see Peter Berek's essay in this volume.

4. Carol Thomas Neely comments that feminist analyses of the play, including her own, emphasize "Kate's and Petruchio's mutual sexual attraction, affection, and satisfaction while deemphasizing her coerced submission to him." She provides an excellent summary of this criticism and suggests that feminist critics are responding to "conflicting impulses—to their profound abhorrence of male dominance and female submission and to their equally profound pleasure at the play's conclusion." She comments, "Feminists cannot, without ignoring altogether the play's meaning and structure, fail to rejoice at the spirit, wit, and joy with which Kate accommodates herself to her wifely role. Within the world of the play there are no preferable alternatives. But we cannot fail to note the radical asymmetry and inequality of the comic reconciliation and wish for Kate, as for ourselves, that choices were less limited, roles less rigid and unequal, accommodation more mutual and less coerced" (*Broken Nuptials in Shakespeare's Plays* [New Haven: Yale University Press, 1985], 218–19).

5. Though her reading of the play is different from mine, Linda Bamber describes a response similar to mine. Agreeing with Coppélia Kahn that "the play presents Kate's capitulation as a gesture without consequence to her soul," she comments that "it cannot seem so to a feminist reader." She adds: "The battle of the sexes as a theme for comedy is inherently sexist. The battle is only funny to those who assume that the status quo is the natural order of things and likely to prevail. To the rest of us, Kate's compromise is distressing" (*Comic Women, Tragic Men: A Study of Gender and Genre in Shakespeare* [Stanford: Stanford University Press], 35).

6. This and subsequent quotations from Shakespeare's plays are from *The Complete Signet Classic Shakespeare*, ed. Sylvan Barnet (New York: Harcourt, 1963).

7. Robert B. Heilman, Introduction to *The Taming of the Shrew* in *The Complete Signet Classic Shakespeare*, 323–27.

8. Heilman, 323.

9. Joel Fineman is either reading wishfully or perversely when he argues that Petruchio's "lunatic behavior" is "a derivative example" of Kate's shrewishness; see "The Turn of the Shrew" in *Shakespeare and the Question of Theory*, eds. Geoffrey Hartman and Patricia Parker (London: Methuen, 1986), 142.

10. Niccolò Machiavelli, *The Prince*, trans. and ed. Robert M. Adams (New York: Norton, 1977), 72.

11. Shirley Nelson Garner, "*A Midsummer's Night's Dream*: 'Jack shall have Jill / Nought shall go ill,' " *Women's Studies: An Interdisciplinary Journal* 9(1981): 47–63.

8

Conflicting Images of the Comic Heroine

DOLORA CUNNINGHAM

ALTHOUGH WE ALL KNOW that Shakespeare experimented with received ideas throughout his career, I think that in *All's Well That Ends Well* he departs radically from his own practice, especially in his treatment of the comic heroine, so that traditional and conventional materials jostle with the new and unexpected. M. C. Bradbrook thinks that "*All's Well* might have as its subtitle 'Two Plays in One' " and that Shakespeare is struggling with "the re-making of old forms." David Bevington applies the same idea to Helena, who "points back to earlier comic women in her role as engineer of the love plot, and forward to women of the late romances in her role as daughter, victim, and savior."[1]

In exploring what is new in Helena's role as engineer of the love plot, I refer to other Shakespearean comedies, especially to *The Merchant of Venice* and *Much Ado About Nothing*. In each of these three comedies, an old order is placed in purposive contrast with other attitudes, and the dramatic action turns at least in part upon opposing ideas. In comparing Shakespeare's development of these contrasts, I conclude that he transforms his models most successfully in *Much Ado* and least so in *All's Well*, and this conclusion raises important questions of evaluation. What kinds of criteria are appropriate to evaluate deliberate breaks with dramatic tradition? In what ways can one set of works be used legitimately as standards for judging others?

Portia and Helena control the final outcome of their plays as other strong Shakespearean heroines do not. Although Rosalind and Beatrice, for example, take charge of the action in various ways, they do not function directly as agents of the marvelous who remove apparently insuperable obstacles to the happy endings; nor do they act as high-powered executives or brilliant professionals. In exercising their unusual control of events, both Portia and Helena are restricted by remnants of a familiar patriarchal system. Portia's freedom of choice in marriage is limited by her father's will and the ritualistic testing of the suitors. Helena gives all credit to her father's medical skill, which she applies as a mere agent in the miraculous cure of the King, whom she sees moreover as a surrogate father arranging her marriage to Bertram.

When we first see Portia, she is protesting impatiently against the enforced passivity of her role as a prize in a guessing game:

> . . . but this reasoning is not in the fashion to choose me a husband,—
> O me the word "choose". I may neither choose who I would, nor
> refuse who I dislike, so is the will of a living daughter curb'd by the
> will of a dead father: is it not hard, Nerissa, that I cannot choose one,
> nor refuse none?
>
> (1.2.20–26)[2]

She analyzes her undesirable suitors with cool intelligence, and is "released from her static and confining role" when Bassanio answers the riddle. Although she is in a sense released into the living world, as Alexander Leggatt puts it,[3] she nevertheless at once submits her "freedom" to Bassanio and makes all his concerns her own:

> Myself, and what is mine, to you and yours
> Is now converted. But now I was the lord
> Of this fair mansion, master of my servants
> Queen o'er myself: and even now, but now,
> This house, these servants, and this same myself
> Are yours,—my lord's!
>
> (3.2.166–71)

Even in the moment of achieving freedom from the system, Portia freely chooses to rejoin it, as she substitutes her husband's will for her father's.

In some ways Helena is given more independence than Portia, but at the same time retains more elements of the long-suffering, patient model of womanhood. The question has been frequently asked, Why do such superior women go to all this trouble for these men—the rather dull Bassanio and the insufferable Bertram? If all of the heroines' talent and intelligence, their independence and high spirits, are to be submitted to the traditional bonds of marriage, then, the modern feminist critic might ask, how free are these new types of women, and where is the balance of power in the end? What do they do finally with the authority they exercise within their plays? These are questions to keep in mind as we contemplate the heroines taking charge of certain events in the developing action of *Merchant of Venice* and of *All's Well*.

Both plays point to limits on the victories their heroines win. Although all things beautiful seem to be located in Belmont—in contrast with the commerical jungle of Venice—Shakespeare makes the explicit point in act 5 that the lovers' happiness within Belmont itself is fragile, not only in contrast with Venice but also within the perspective of human history. As Lorenzo and Jessica await Portia's triumphant return, here on this wondrously fair night in peaceful Belmont, they speak, choruslike, of tragic love affairs. It is in this context that they exult in their own happiness and their narrow escape from the disorder of Venice, and proclaim the triumph over threatened tragedy.

We know at this point that we are about to celebrate the closing marriages, and so why, one might reasonably wonder, remind us of Cressida's unfaithfulness to Troilus, of Dido's betrayal by Aeneas, of Pyramus and Thisbe's sad fates, of Medea's doom?

> The moon shines bright. In such a night as this,
> When the sweet wind did gently kiss the trees,
> And they did make no noise, in such a night
> Troilus methinks mounted the Trojan walls,
> And sigh'd his soul toward the Grecian tents
> Where Cressida lay that night.
>
> (5.1.1–6)

Jessica takes up the melancholy refrain with Pyramus and Thisbe, and Lorenzo carries on with Dido's inconsolable grief:

> In such a night
> Stood Dido with a willow in her hand
> Upon the wild sea banks, and waft her love
> To come again to Carthage.
>
> (5.1.9–12)

Jessica then raises the possibility that their love might not last forever, that Lorenzo might not be true to his vows of eternal fidelity; he accuses her of slander and forgives her. It is all done lightheartedly, but the clear message is that the happiness we celebrate in Belmont is both extra-ordinary and fragile—a near thing.

The closure of *All's Well* is much more carefully qualified: Bertram says that *if* Helena can explain everything to him clearly, *then* he will love her dearly and faithfully (5.3.309–10); the King says that *if* the bitter past is ended at this point, "more welcome is the sweet" (5.3.327–28).[4] It seems a distance from the joys, however fragile, that are celebrated in *Merchant* and in other comedies—*Dream, As You Like It, Much Ado, Twelfth Night*—or, let us say, the ideal possibilities that these comedies suggest. Shakespearean comedy, even at its most romantic, is almost always sharply aware of the world as it often is, of people as they very often are, of the incongruities between any ideal of human conduct and the mixed bag we can expect. Although such awareness is, I suppose, a staple of the comic vision in general, I do not want to suggest darkly ironic readings of Shakespeare's happy endings.

There is, however, an important question of emphasis distinguishing the comic process in even a perilously balanced play such as *Merchant* from a dubiously resolved play such as *All's Well*. In the romantic Belmont part of *Merchant* (as in *Much Ado*, for example), the emphasis is upon the ordering of love in final marriages. In *All's Well*, I submit, there is an unrelenting emphasis upon the obstacles in the way of this process, and our protracted experience of intractable material seems to cast more doubt upon the outcome than in the earlier plays I have mentioned.

The matter of emphasis is also important to our view of Helena in *All's Well*. If we stress her plight and her suffering more than her exercise of control in adversity, then we move toward soap opera; or we can make Helena sound too much like Hermione in *The Winter's Tale*. I choose to stress the Helena-in-charge aspect of her role, because this emphasis helps to clarify the action and also because she is in fact given larger than usual scope. Like Portia, Helena protests women's passive role. In the opening scene as she discusses women's predicament and "the use of virginity" with Parolles, she raises Portia's argument for freedom of choice: "How might one do, sir, to lose it [virginity] to her own liking?" (1.1.147)

At the closing of the first scene, Shakespeare has Helena speak out in rhymed couplets as she sets the whole plot in motion with her firm resolve to break out of her lowly place in life and take charge of her own destiny as a free agent:

> Our remedies oft in ourselves do lie,
> Which we ascribe to heaven; the fated sky
> Gives us free scope; only doth backward pull
> Our slow designs when we ourselves are dull.
>
> . . . .
> Impossible be strange attempts to those
> That weigh their pains in sense, and do suppose
> What hath been cannot be. Who ever strove
> To show her merit that did miss her love?
> The King's disease—my project may deceive me,
> But my intents are fix'd, and will not leave me.
>
> (1.1.212–15, 220–25)

And so she goes off to court to cure the King and get the man she wants as her reward. Portia's heroism is larger than usual in the comedies preceding *Merchant*, but Helena enlarges the comic heroine's range in ways that are important to our grasp of the complexity of her play. Helena is the only heroine who does *not* at any time dress herself up as a man in order to get a hearing in the world of affairs (except for Isabella, who does not control the outcome of *Measure for Measure*). Rosalind and Celia could not escape from the evil court or travel as women; Viola, as a woman, could not even get a place to live after the shipwreck; Portia as a mere woman could not be admitted to the courtroom to plead for Antonio's life.

In this radical departure from his own usual practice, Shakespeare proceeds to a further series of innovations for the heroine of *All's Well*. As a woman, without disguise, she challenges formidable conventions, dramatic *and* social: *she* chooses the man *she* wants to marry, after getting his *mother's* blessing; *she* negotiates the marriage contract with the man's guardian (the King); *she* offers her own merit—inherited, professional, and personal—instead of the usual dowry; *she* pursues the reluctant, disdainful, scornful man, who gets the role of Lady Disdain or the scornful lady of the sonnets. It has been frequently noticed that in *All's Well* we get the taming of the shrew in reverse, as a wild young courtier is subdued to the supposedly civilized state of matrimony.

As she takes over all these functions, traditionally the exclusive territory of men, Helena pays a high price in rejection, humiliation, betrayal. It is hard to tell whether Bertram scorns Helena more for usurping these sacred male prerogatives, or for daring to speak to him from her inferior position as a mere physician's daughter. It is clear, however, that he is judged adversely within the play for both his sexism and his snobbery, and more importantly, Bertram's ethical values are judged to be false:

> . . . If she be
> All that is virtuous, save what thou dislik'st—
> A poor physician's daughter—thou dislik'st
> Of virtue for the name. But do not so.
>
> . . . .
> . . . Good alone
> Is good, without a name; vileness is so:
> The property by what it is should go,
> Not by the title. She is young, wise, fair;
> In these to nature she's immediate heir,
> And these breed honour; . . .
>
> . . . .
> . . . Here, take her hand,
> Proud, scornful boy, unworthy this good gift.
>   (2.3.121–24, 128–33, 150–51)

As the King lectures Bertram in the arranged-marriage scene, he comments directly on the nobility of Helena's character, and works out a definition of true *honor* in relation to virtue, and as opposed to Bertram's false notions of honor. To sum up briefly, the structure of this scene gives us standards for judging the dramatic situation; it also provides a context for Helena's struggle to make virtue effective in a society where false honor seems to prevail. At this point, indeed, Bertram's corrupt values seem to prevail when the marriage scene closes with his decision to go off to the wars with Parolles, and to pack Helena off to his mother's home as if she were a piece of furniture.

G. K. Hunter, in his Introduction to the New Arden edition of *All's Well*, includes a valuable discussion of the recurrent motif in the play of making women's virtue effective in the world—virtue, I would say, both in the sense of strength or power and in the sense of goodness.[5] Hunter's analysis of the rather puzzling discussion of marriage and virginity in the opening scene (1.1.110ff.) is particularly illuminating, suggesting various ways in which Helena uses her virginity in virtuous activity: to choose a husband, to suffer rejection, and finally to get Bertram to do the truly honorable thing by living up to his marriage contract. We can agree that Helena impresses herself upon the world effectively, but only up to a point. After Bertram's rejection, she not only submits her life to him beyond Portia's more or less conventional mode of submission, but also goes so far as to blame herself bitterly for Bertram's departure from his own country (3.2.102); she fears that she might be the cause of his death in war (3.2.102 16), and she repents what she calls her "ambitious love" (3.4.5). As she goes off on pilgrimage in reparation for her offense, she resolves to accept death in order to set him free:

> He is too good and fair for death and me;
> Whom I myself embrace to set him free.
>
> (3.4.16–17)

This sudden patient Griselda role has proved difficult for the justifiably realistic expectations of many audiences in different times and places. However one defines realistic, we have seen Helena as an unusually assertive type of heroine, and we have seen abolutely nothing of any goodness in Bertram. If we take Helena's self-abasement as a meaningful contrast to her unusual independence, then perhaps the repentance can serve to clarify the new image of the heroine. I do not mean to imply that the assertive and the submissive elements are reconciled to make a "consistent" character. To ignore the submissive—or to reduce it to farce—is to ask for more trouble than simply to accept apparently contradictory attitudes. Helena's repentance, moreover, reminds us of the special powers—magical and priestly—that make possible her cure of the King, and of her selfless love for Bertram. For all her independence, we are still asked to see her as an agent of the marvelous in her ritualistic quest to save Bertram.

We accept the reform of Bertram in the marriage bond, as we accept the legalistic repentance of Claudio in *Much Ado,* and yet many of us who accept the one event as part of a coherent whole remain uneasy about the situation in *All's Well.* This uneasiness has a variety of causes, but many doubts seem to focus upon the bed-trick: "Is that any way to treat a husband?"—especially for an allegedly devoted wife to treat a husband she professedly adores? One critic tells us, in a version of Bradbrook's diagnosis of remaking old forms, that *All's Well* (along with *Measure* and *Shrew*) "suffers from . . . an incoherence that comes from combining old tales with humanized women."[6] He sees Helena as being "humanized" in various ways, and specifically it is her view of sexual experience that jars with the bed-trick from an old tale. For Helena, sex is connected with the emotional and the personal, with her genuine concern for Bertram's best interests; but the bed-trick belongs to a world where sex is impersonal and women are objects; and so we are made uneasy by the collision of the mechanical and the human.

This method of resolution has also been condemned for its deceitfulness, "the confusing deception in which fornication becomes chaste love and chaste love fornication," as Charles Lyons puts it in commenting on these lines:

> . . . wicked meaning in a lawful deed,
> And lawful meaning in a lawful act,
> Where both not sin, and yet a sinful fact.
>
> (3.7.45–47)[7]

The scruple about deceit as such need not, I feel, detain us long. After all, deception and intrigue are staples of comedy that seeks to outwit falsehood, to unveil illusions, and to reveal truth. Benedick's and Beatrice's friends trick them, deceive them, into recognizing their true feelings for each other. Just so, one might say, for here we have an important difference in Helena's trick against Bertram: What truth, what feelings, are there to be revealed? We have seen nothing of a relationship of any kind, whether romantic or realistic, to be salvaged between Helena and Bertram. They have scarcely spoken to each other. We have seen no possibility of a human response from Bertram, and his response in the end seems at best perfunctory: if you can prove all this, he says, then you have won the bet against the odds. It is difficult to see a recognition of value in his pledge to love Helena in the future:

> If she, my liege, can make me know this clearly
> I'll love her dearly, ever, ever dearly.
>
> (5.3.309–10)

All's Well asks us to accept on faith a process of correcting what is obviously in need of correction and to hope that the rest will somehow correct itself. It asks us to accept not a mixture of the bitter and the sweet, but rather to accept the coexistence of puzzling contradictions between codes of behavior and attitudes toward human relations. *All's Well* makes stronger than usual demands on our acceptance; we have to struggle, with the heroine, to achieve even a precarious balance in our response to this play, and we are left with the fact that opposing elements are simply not reconciled.

If we accept *All's Well* as an open-ended work that need not give answers to all the issues it raises, we are still left to ponder critical problems that affect negatively our evaluation of the play's aesthetic unity. We continue to be troubled—in the theater and in the study, I think—by the contradictions within the heroine's role and within her relationship to the hero: the spirited independence and the abject submission; the devoted love and the crude trickery; the realistically developed heroine and a restrictive ritualistic plot that makes it practically impossible for heroine and hero to speak with each other. Setting aside for my present purposes the vexing theoretical questions about how particular works become standards for judging other works, I shall invoke *Much Ado About Nothing* as a standard for evaluating the defective aesthetic unity of *All's Well That Ends Well*. In *Much Ado* a conventionally formal and unattractive mode of courtship is represented by Claudio and Hero (who also scarcely speak to each other), and by eloquent contrast a warmly human, unconventional relationship is explored in Benedick and Beatrice. Instead of burdening his heroine with unresolved conflicts, Shakespeare has distributed some of them between two characters and two sets of lovers: a meekly submissive, humiliated, and rejected Hero is opposed to the independent, witty, and combative Beatrice who is responsible for her own choices. The stylized, legalistic Hero-Claudio affair is worked out in these terms, and the Beatrice-Benedick affair is worked out in a consistently realistic process with focus upon the struggle of two strong personalities to be free of illusions and achieve a dynamic union of mind and heart.

In the last plays, which as a group are innovative mixtures of romance, fantasy, and realism, Shakespeare continues to experiment with the heroine's role. He puts aside the assertiveness that Helena in *All's Well* brings to the action as lover-daughter-victim-savior, and instead he emphasizes a romance mode of presentation. Perdita and Hermione in their fabled roles of abandoned babe and falsely accused Queen are both innocent victims of Leontes' rage and passive agents of his redemption. Neither Perdita nor Hermione initiates any action, and they affect the final outcome only as they suffer or wait patiently for time, fortune, or providence to accomplish their benevolent designs. They are there in the end for Leontes to recognize as the good he has apparently lost. They join in an awesomely wondrous resolution, with shock waves of recognition and discovery that set it far apart from the joyless exposure of Bertram's knavery in the bleakly indeterminate end of *All's Well*.

Critics have occasionally objected to the ending of *The Winter's Tale* and have questioned the dramatic coherence of the play's structure. The editor of the New Arden edition concludes a summary of critical responses to *The Winter's Tale*: "But it *is* resolved, and the whole plot shows a pattern of life which has meaning and a clear unity in design."[8] One might wish to modify this assessment of the play's unity, but the leading women characters move consistently within romance traditions, and their relevance to the end of the whole action is clearly established in the latter part of the play.

From the perspectives I have explored, then, in *All's Well* Shakespeare has paid a price for the experiment with new materials in old forms. The conflicting images of the heroine are interesting in themselves; Helena's role is challenging and has its special relevance to important concerns of our time. The play moreover, as critics have pointed out, deals provocatively with important subjects, and it has considerable theatrical vitality, as recent performance history has shown.[9] These criteria for evaluation, however cogently applied, do not cancel the results of a test for internal coherence. The ideal of aesthetic unity, as Charles Altieri has eloquently argued, is one of the "more enduring cultural values,"[10] transcending various historical periods and special interests. If *All's Well That Ends Well*, as I have indicated, does not measure up to this standard, the play can still be appreciated as an important experiment in comic form, however it may stray from the more usual patterns of Shakespearean comedy.

Notes

1. David Bevington, "Shakespeare's Hybrid: *All's Well That Ends Well*," in *Muriel Bradbrook on Shakespeare* (Sussex: Harvester Press, 1984), 84; see also *Shakespeare: The Poet in His World* (London: Weidenfeld and Nicholson, 1978), 175; see Bevington, *The Complete Works of Shakespeare* (Glenview, Ill.: Scott, Foresman and Co., 1981), 426.

2. This and all subsequent parenthetical citations of the plays (act, scene, and line) are to the New Arden Shakespeare edition of *The Works of William Shakespeare*, general editor, Richard Proudfoot (London: Methuen and Co., 1959).

3. Alexander Leggatt, *Shakespeare's Comedy of Love* (London: Methuen, 1974), 129–34.

4. My italics. In her excellent Introduction to the New Penguin Shakespeare (p. 38), Barbara Everett comments that "Bertram's 'If' starts a chain of conditions, that lead us out of the play; so that *All's Well That Ends Well* is . . . an open-ended work indeed."

5. G. K. Hunter, Introduction to *All's Well That Ends Well*, New Arden Shakespeare (London: Methuen and Co., 1959), pp. xxxix–xliii.

6. John C. Bean, "Comic Structure and the Humanizing of Kate in *Shrew*," in *The Woman's Part: Feminist Criticism of Shakespeare*, ed. Carolyn Lenz et al. (Urbana: University of Illinois Press, 1980), 75.

7. Charles R. Lyons, *Shakespeare and the Ambiguities of Love's Triumph* (The Hague, Paris: Mouton, 1971), 121–22.

8. J. H. P. Pafford, Introduction to *The Winter's Tale,* New Arden Shakespeare (London: Methuen and Co., 1963), p. lv.

9. See John L. Styan, *Shakespeare in Performance: All's Well That Ends Well* (Manchester: Manchester University Press, 1984).

10. Charles Altieri, "An Idea and Ideal of a Literary Canon," *Critical Inquiry* 10 (September 1983): 41.

PART III

Revaluations
Tragedies and Histories

9

What's in a Good Name?

The Case of Romeo and Juliet *as a Bad Tragedy*

AVRAHAM OZ

"BAD SHAKESPEARE" is an exciting theme for a Shakespeare critic, as its application to the practice of criticism may relieve one from the often tiresome effort to justify any apparent fault in the canon in the name of Shakespeare's greatness. This application, however, is a dangerous practice, for it may lead to much-too-easy critical solutions. It is generally assumed, and not without justice, that a major function of criticism is eliminatory; namely, approaching any apparent deficiency in a given work of art from all possible angles in order to find a positive justification for it within an integrative scheme of interpretation. Only if no such justification is found, after all the positive options lying within the aesthetic confines of the given work have been exhausted, may one declare it an artistic failure. It is at this point that the evaluative function of criticism comes into the picture. One should bear in mind that this function of criticism is secondary to its analytic functions, and that the very fact of its being raised in this context may be regarded as implying an admission of failure on the part of the critic. The history of criticism is in many ways the history of shortsightedness, which explains the measure of reluctance with which we put the blame on the artist. For when we do, we seem always to leave a vulnerable spot in our argument that invites refutation on grounds of critical negligence.

The resort to evaluative criticism brings in the question of relativity. No aspect of a work by Shakespeare can be deemed faulty unless some hierarchical framework of artistic values underlies one's critical judgment. There is no consideration of "bad Shakespeare" without the knowledge of what constitutes "good Shakespeare" in a given case. Any value judgment of a Shakespearean play or any part of it must rest on some preconceived dramatic form, generic definition, or some other aesthetic principle to which the play is expected to conform. Thus

133

Shakespeare is considered bad when he fails to comply with some critical expectation, or, alternatively, the critic will overstretch his or her interpretation of the play to fit his or her preconceptions. Here bad Shakespeare will often meet its ally in bad criticism.

In some notorious cases in the history of Shakespeare criticism, critical expectations had little to do with genuine aesthetic considerations. Most of these cases belong to past centuries, but some are evident even today. Such, for instance, is the fairly popular ironic interpretation of *The Merchant of Venice*, which regards Shylock as the chiefly wronged party throughout the play and the Venetians as a bunch of devious, idle scoundrels. Now, this reading of the play bears little on any alleged deficiency in the inner consistency of the character of Shylock, when the latter is considered as the villain, or rather the comic butt, of the play. For many critics *The Merchant of Venice* is an example of "bad Shakespeare" simply because Shylock is regarded as implicating an entire race or nation ("his countrymen"). Those who wish to defend this alleged weakness in the play insist that Shakespeare's intention was just the opposite; namely, to humanize the alien and provide the revengeful victim with respectable, comprehensible motives. For several critics of the play, such motives are nothing less than tragic. And thus the play is termed deficient owing to a bad reading: its center can hardly hold tragic energies. Shylock does not bear any resemblance to the type of tragic hero who may be found in any play by Shakespeare, from his petty villainy (unlike the "noble crimes" of Othello or Macbeth) to his lowly submission at the end of the trial scene. In his element, however, Shylock is a round character, clearly related to some well-known figures from the storehouse of traditional comedy (such as Pantalone, the devil, or the Vice of medieval drama). The play as a whole is well attuned to comic models that had served Shakespeare before and were to go on serving him in his mature comedies. And if the ending of *The Merchant of Venice* involves melancholic overtones (as it surely does), it is not different in this respect from the denouement of *Much Ado about Nothing*, *As You Like It*, or *Twelfth Night*. When conceived as a romantic comedy with some gloomy notes, *The Merchant of Venice* does not stand out significantly among the mature comedies.

If tragic expectations often blur the real dramatic merits of *The Merchant of Venice*, the deficiency of the tragic patterns that are clearly inherent in *Romeo and Juliet* is sometimes ignored in the process of overpraising the play. Indeed, the vast popularity of the play with audiences in Shakespeare's time (four quarto editions before the First Folio), down to this very day, as well as some delightful poetry and tightly woven dramatic suspense, are not to be ignored. It has many moments of fine melodrama, which would not have been bad had

Shakespeare meant his play to be a melodrama. But the play seems to have aspired for more: from the very outset it raises in us overt expectations for tragic stature ("fatal loins," "star-cross'd lovers," "death-mark'd love"). These expectations, however, fail to materialize. With the unfolding of the action it becomes clear that the very foundations of tragedy, fate and human insight, are here replaced by fortuitousness and ignorance. As usual, there will always be the critic who will readily defend the play from any doubts regarding its tragic integrity:

> Does it deplete the sense of the tragic? For Aristotle, it would have, as it has for his followers. . . . I have always harbored the suspicion that such discomfiture is more a product of logical Aristotelianism than of the play. We can always revise the improbability in our imagination, but I doubt if we succeed in getting a more tragic effect. Let the message reach Romeo in time; let him rush to be present at the side of the waking Juliet; and let him meet the grieving Paris there, to be slain by Paris in the confusion of misunderstanding. We would lose much more than the occasion for some great poetry and intense pathos; we would lose the tragic connection between the value of love, the radiance and desperation of passion, and the combined joy and sorrow of man in the condition of time.[1]

This may be so, but are these lofty themes seriously reflected upon in the play as it is? The same critic, indeed, will have to admit that "for all its virtues, the play does not exhibit the power, range, and deeply probing qualities of *Hamlet, Othello, Macbeth,* or *King Lear,*"[2] to which we may add *Antony and Cleopatra,* where the aforementioned themes are widely and profoundly probed.

But it must be understood that the plot permutations or the "lack of probing abilities" are not just minor issues here. They are the very stuff the tragic in Shakespeare is made on. Shakespearean tragedy as a whole may not rigidly conform to the basic features of Aristotelian tragedy. *Romeo and Juliet* may be read against medieval theories of tragedy,[3] but even on this background it will be found lacking. What lends unity to Shakespeare's tragedies is not necessarily their correspondence with a specific historical notion of tragedy, but some common features, like the constant probing into the essence of human fate. The very quality that determines the Shakespearean tragic hero is a special prophetic insight into the world and his own nature. Lost in a universe whose fixed, Ptolemaic measures were crumbling; alienated from God, absolute values, and daily labor at once; taken prisoner by a tightly scheduled time scheme that devoured eternity, and yet injected with a new, exciting self-image as the beauty of the world and the paragon of animals, Renaissance man was constantly urged to command time and the world. It was this task to which the energies of Lear, Hamlet, Macbeth, Othello,

Antony, and Cleopatra were constantly directed. Though totally immersed in their own personal world, their human consciousness never
shuts the gates on the Renaissance universe. Any personal action has
some significance in terms of probing into the world, which constitutes,
perhaps, the real "Aristotelianism" of Shakespearean tragedy.

Without being committed to any particular theory of tragedy, Shakespeare's great tragedies are always prophetic. This sense of prophecy
may be understood on two levels: on the outer level of "the world," it
has to do with what Jacques Ellul, in his brilliant analysis of the major
myths dominating modern society, calls the myth of history.[4] As opposed to the myth of science, which presumes that any possible concept
or phenomenon already exists (though not necessarily discovered as
yet), the myth of history has to do with possible development of potentialities. All the later tragedies of Shakespeare take into account to some
degree some historical development, involving political, economic, social, or moral implications that circumscribe the individual action.

On the inner level of these individual actions, the heroes of Shakespeare's mature tragedies are always presented in one way or another
with some image of "the future in the instant," a prophetic riddle or a
task to which they are challenged to commit themselves by an act of
deliberate choice. Brutus, presented by Cassius with his image as the
noble deliverer of Rome from Caesar's presumed tyranny, wrestles in his
mind with "the ugly, broad ditch" dividing human knowledge from
reality, and his notorious "Fashion it thus" (2.1.30)[5] marks, perhaps, the
failure of his conscience to stand up against the cold verdict of his
reason. It is from this point that his tragedy unfolds. Hamlet is challenged to solve and execute a moral paradox: how not to taint his mind
and "prophetic soul" by performing a "natural" act of justice (1.5.80–85),[6]
a paradox rephrased in his mind as the simultaneous undertaking of "a
scourge and minister" (3.4.177). Othello is challenged to tell "the green-
ey'd monster" from his ironic mocker (3.3.170); Lear traps himself in the
task of making sense of Cordelia's prophetic bond:

> I love your Majesty
> According to my bond; no more nor less.
>
> (1.1.91–92)

Whereas Macbeth is challenged by the riddling prophecies of the Weird
Sisters.

The most appropriate comparison with *Romeo and Juliet* is provided, of
course, by Shakespeare's later tragedy of love, *Antony and Cleopatra*. In
the brief appearance of Portia in *Julius Caesar*, as well as Hamlet's coming
before Ophelia in her closet, Shakespeare may reject love as a refuge
from the coercive presence of the world's demands. In *Antony and*

Cleopatra, this very theme is bravely looked in the eye as the major issue at stake. When judged (by Philo) by the measures (1.1.2) of finite Rome, Antony is only himself when torn apart from Cleopatra (1.1.57–59). But there exists a higher perspective, where both Antony and Cleopatra are bound by the prophetic bond proclaimed by Antony:

> Our separation so abides and flies,
> That thou, residing here, goes yet with me;
> And I, hence fleeting, here remain with thee.
>
> (1.3.102–4)

It is a noble pledge, conscientiously accounting for a union that, when stripped of its genuine passion, may also be referred to contemptuously as:

> [he] is not more manlike
> Than Cleopatra; nor the queen of Ptolemy
> More womanly than he.
>
> (1.4.5–7)

The love of Antony and Cleopatra has to be constantly defended against the claims of the world: Fulvia's jealousy; Octavius's resentment, and Pompeius's wish to take advantage, of Antony's political and military paralysis; Agrippa's political matchmaking; and, most of all, Antony's own call of duty and political status. Antony is conscious of the contradiction between the claims of love and those of the world, and his choice is deliberate rather than fortuitous.

His own intuition is complemented by the Soothsayer's clear predictions (there is hardly a more plain-speaking prophet than that of *Antony and Cleopatra* in the entire canon), and even when he offers to play the fool of fortune, he seems less automated than choosing deliberately to "make his will / Lord of his reason" (3.13.3–4):

> Forgo
> The way which promises assurance, and
> Give up [him] self merely to chance and hazard,
> From firm security.
>
> (3.7.45–48)

Thus fortune is reminded that

> We scorn her most, when most she offers blows.
>
> (3.11.74)

When he decides to challenge Octavius to single combat, Antony is momentarily seen, indeed, as one whose judgments become "a parcel of their fortunes" (3.13.31-32); but soon enough, when Thidias[7] in the name of Octavius seriously suggests to Cleopatra that she clings to Antony not out of love but out of fear, Caesar's lack of understanding of the ways of love is balanced against Antony's deliberate immersion in love's intoxicating misguidance, which is reasserted in his last speeches to her in the monument. For those to whom Cleopatra's attitude throughout the play seems less motivated by prophetic guidance than does Antony's, but rather by "like frailties, which before / Have often sham'd [her] sex," her unmistakably prophetic dream of Antony (5.2.76–100)—if nothing else—may bridge in retrospect this gap in understanding. Her second sailing to Cydnus to meet Mark Antony (5.2.227–28) reflects on the first. And it is their adherence to their love's prophetic guidance that is, eventually, to leave "great Caesar ass, unpolicied" (5.2.306–7); the latter has to console himself in proving "too sure an augurer" (5.2.332).

By comparison, *Romeo and Juliet* proves a naive version of this mature tragic model. Unlike the later tragedies, its rather dominant sense of time is devoid of any sense of history. The effect of its being totally immersed in the myth of science is a loss of touch with "the world." Whereas the Brutuses, Hamlets, Othellos, Lears, Macbeths, or Coriolanuses of the later tragedies, all "to the manner born," struggle against the menacing tokens of a new order, there is barely an indication of such a struggle in *Romeo and Juliet*. All the characters of the play take the constant terms of the outer world for granted, and the enhanced sense of time's passage in the play only serves to stress to the full this detachment from the historical claims of "the world." Indeed, the language of Romeo and Juliet is constantly given to premonitions of disaster whose supposed source lies somewhere in the outer mystery of the world:

> I fear too early, for my mind misgives
> Some consequence yet hanging in the stars
> Shall bitterly begin his fearful date
> With this night's revels, and expire the term
> Of a despised life clos'd in my breast
> By some vile forfeit of untimely death.
>
> (1.4.106–11)

But this feeling and its phrasing is too general to be prophetic in the sense the other tragedies are. Romeo will not, and in fact cannot, take arms against this potential sea of troubles, but waits for "he that hath the steerage of [his] course" to direct his suit. Such utterances as Friar Lawrence's

> Virtue itself turns vice being misapplied,
> And vice sometime's by action dignified

> (2.3.17–18)

might be considered prophetic, if they were directed to the lovers them-selves and referred more particularly to the actual situation. His more direct warning to Romeo that

> These violent delights have violent ends
> And in their triumph die, like fire and powder,
> Which as they kiss consume.

> (2.6.9–11)

fares scarcely better, since its level of generalization remains more or less the same.

The lovers' own phrasing of their predicament suffers from a clear detachment from the contextual situation: though the world so strongly interferes with their love, the poetry of Romeo and Juliet is too harbored in convention to probe profoundly into the world. It is true that both lovers progress throughout the play from conventional attitudes toward love to more independent ones (or rather, from an explicit ideological position to a more implicit one). Nevertheless, to the very end they seem fortune's fools, responding predictably to a set of given stimuli. Unlike Antony, who tragically bears the consequence of his love's choices, Romeo's choices remind one, at best, of Wittgenstein's falling leaf, which mutters, "Now I'll go left. . . . Now I'll go right. . . ." Whereas the love of Antony and Cleopatra defeats nature, reaching cosmic levels, the love of Romeo and Juliet struggles against a local, much condemned, and seemingly avoidable feud. The lovers, immersed in their partial view of the general situation surrounding them, never seriously attempt to take issue against this contextual situation (apart from Romeo's conciliatory mood toward Tybalt who "knows him not" to be Juliet's husband, which does not differ much from his careless attitude in attending the Capulet feast), nor do they study its sources in order to try and defeat it.

Derick R. C. Marsh argues that the fact that "the play does not at any time present the lovers with the opportunity for moderation, even if, in the nature of the emotion that Shakespeare is depicting, such restraint were possible," makes the play conform "to W. B. Yeats's comment that tragedy requires a situation where no solution is possible."[8] This very argument seems to be contradicted later in Marsh's own argument, as when he says that

> The tragedy that is brought down on the lovers. . . . comes about not because of their surrender to their passion for each other, but more

directly because of Romeo's surrender to hatred, and his participation, admittedly under very great provocation, in the feud.[9]

In building Romeo's character to merit heroic stature, the play emphasizes his marked indifference to, or even contempt of, the feud. But his falling prey much too easily to the logic of feudal revenge hampers rather than strengthens his tragic stature. The fact that both lovers refrain from openly challenging, or at least probing into, the world surrounding them virtually fails to test the play against Yeats's comment.

In fact, a world to probe into is severely lacking in *Romeo and Juliet*. There is no concrete account of the contextual circumstances the lovers have to stand against, apart from some generalized features of an unexplained feud. In his *Shakespeare's Professional Skills*, Nevill Coghill praises Shakespeare for translating the generalized narration concerning the ancient feud between the two families, as it appears in Brooke's *Tragicall History of Romeus and Juliet*, into a particular stage fight.[10] This praise is justified in terms of dramatic effectiveness. But Coghill forgets to mention that in that process Shakespeare also discards whatever slight explanation Brooke provides as to the causes of the feud:

> A wonted use it is, that men of likely sorte
> (I wot not by what furye forsed) envye eche others porte.
> So these, whose egall state bred envye pale of hew,
> And then of grudging envyes roote, blacke hate and rancor grew.[11]

It is typical of the general pattern of *Romeo and Juliet* that nobody, from the servants to their masters, seems to know what the feud is all about. Has it to do with land, with social stature, or maybe with purity of blood? How deep does it go into the given premises of the actual situation? How, for instance, can Romeo court Rosaline, Capulet's cousin, undisturbed and in the open? Why is Capulet so tolerant, even laudatory, of Romeo at the feast, and why is this tolerance never explored or tested, even as a hypothetical option, when it comes to Romeo's love for Juliet (all the plot's contrivances could work the same after Capulet had a chance to express his objection to the idea)? Surely at least Friar Lawrence, who suggests that "this alliance may so happy prove / To turn [both] households' rancour to pure love" (2.3.87–88), might have considered such a move.

There is no real attempt in the play, however, to exhaust the concrete possibilities the situation offers. The lovers accept each other's name as faulty, and thus separate their love from the general issue not by choice, but by compliance. In this they become fortune's puppets, and as *A Midsummer Night's Dream*, written around the same period, may demonstrate, acting like puppets belongs to the realm of comedy. Juliet's quick wit may compare with that of Portia, Rosalind, and Viola, but it hardly transcends the realm of the comic. Like Antony and Cleopatra, both lovers here choose to die when each realizes (or seems to realize) that his or her beloved is dead. But whereas both Antony and Cleopatra choose to die while there is a world elsewhere, with its calls and duties, one does not get the feeling that Romeo or Juliet belong, even hypothetically, to any external world transcending their own relationship at the moment they choose to die.

A host of questions are left unanswered, then, throughout the play, although all of them are certainly anchored in the real world surrounding the personal tragedy of the young lovers. This is yet another token of a flawed tragedy, if not entirely "bad," since it leaves the play's (fairly manifest) claim to tragic dimensions too dependent on automatic moves (such as Romeo's reaction to Mercutio's death or Capulet's rather whimsical decision to marry his daughter to Paris immediately) or accidents (the failure in delivering Friar Lawrence's message to Romeo because of "the infectious pestilence" in Mantua).

The real test of the play's tragic power is, as usual, its stage life. Vastly popular with its audience, *Romeo and Juliet* is frequently revived, often satisfying theatergoers' rage for sensationalism on stage. When an attempt is made, however, to read its contents against an updated or topical ideological background, the play often tends to crumble. On the face of it, a stage version placing the plot in a context such as the Israeli-Palestinian conflict in the Middle East has an advantageous point of departure apt to make the play work. Such an experimental production at the Haifa Municipal Theatre, Israel[12] (in which, for instance, the balcony scene was simultaneously presented in Hebrew and Arabic by two "mixed" pairs of lovers), failed to convince primarily because the arbitrariness inherent in the Shakespearean plot rendered the entire analogy futile. The tragic potential and validity of the situation proved once again to depend more on *living* with uncompromising feudal premises rather than enclosing the entire issue within the span of the personal destiny of the star-cross'd lovers. No indication could be drawn from the original play as to the nature of the conflict itself or its possible solutions, and thus the lovers' melodrama turned in a void, unrelated to the involved (and, indeed, tragic) premises of the external conflict. The Israeli production proved once again that the age-old theme of falling in love with the enemy's daughter does not necessarily constitute a part of the ideology of peace. If any, the lesson of the production was that the topical situation might find a more appropriate reflection in the bitterness of *Troilus and Cressida* rather than in the sensationalism of *Romeo and Juliet*. Similarly, Michael Bogdanov's smoothly up-to-date 1986 Royal Shakespeare Company version of the play, full of motorbike sound and

punk fury, failed to signify any fresh meaning within the current ideological setting: the lovers' naive detachment from their surrounding
scene made little sense against the violent modern background.

Unlike the other heroes of Shakespeare's tragedies, Romeo and Juliet
are not presented at the outset, then, with any prophetic challenge to get
involved in, or at least probe into, the historical claims of the world. The
play, indeed, is a successful melodramatic masterpiece. However, those
who are too ready to defend *Romeo and Juliet*'s tragic integrity harm the
greatness of the later, more profound dramatist.

Notes

1. Douglas Cole, Introduction to *Romeo and Juliet: A Collection of Critical Essays* (Englewood Cliffs, N.J.: Prentice Hall, 1970), 16.

2. Ibid., 17.

3. See, for example, F. M. Dickey, *Not Wisely but too Well* (San Marino, Calif.: The
Huntington Library, 1957).

4. Jacques Ellul, *Propaganda: The Formation of Men's Attitudes*, trans. Konrad Kellen and
Jean Lerner (New York: Alfred Knopf, 1965). See also George H. Szanto, *Theater and
Propaganda* (Austin and London: University of Texas Press, 1978), 39ff., for an interesting, if
sometimes doctrinaire, application of Ellul's theory to the realm of propaganda theater.

5. This and all subsequent parenthetical text references to Shakespeare's plays are to
the New Arden Shakespeare editions, published by Methuen. References are to act, scene,
and line.

6. The Folio has a semicolon after "Taint not thy mind" in 1.5.85, which renders it a
separate injunction; for a detailed discussion of this point see Harold Jenkins's Introduction to *Hamlet,* New Arden Shakespeare (London and New York: Methuen, 1982), p. 457.

7. I use the Folio's version of the name. See M. R. Ridley's note in his New Arden
Shakespeare edition of the play on 3.12.31, concerning the Folio's Thidias as against most
editors' Thyreus.

8. Derick R. C. Marsh, *Passion Lends Them Power: A Study of Shakespeare's Love Tragedies*
(Manchester: Manchester University Press, 1976), 65.

9. Ibid., 71.

10. Nevill Coghill, *Shakespeare's Professional Skills* (Cambridge: Cambridge University
Press, 1964), 28.

11. Ibid., 28–29.

12. *Shakesperiment*, based on *Romeo and Juliet*, adapted and directed by Oded Kotler,
Haifa Municipal Theatre, 1981.

The Etiology of Horatio's Inconsistencies

ALEX NEWELL

WE ARE ALL AWARE that *Hamlet* has a long critical history as a problematic play. Indeed, as editor's introductions to the play invariably attest, the awareness of this fact has now become part of its critical tradition, a tradition that includes the view of *Hamlet* as a "problem" play, which may be crudely defined as a play that makes us aware of great complexity, multiplicity, and even contradictions in the possible understanding of its concerns. Because *Hamlet* stimulates so much diverse criticism, periodically an article is written that reviews and summarizes the various ways the play has been understood; similarly, there are numerous anthologies that present samples of the range of interpretation, much of it conflicting. Because the play has proven to be such a dynamic and flexible system of dramatic and aesthetic energies, it has managed both to sustain and survive what has been said about it at different times, views that have served as reflections of the cultures and periods, as well as the persons, providing the critical commentary.

A tragedy that has generated such a varied body of criticism is undoubtedly a great play but not necessarily an entirely successful or perfect work of art. On the contrary, some of the differences in understanding *Hamlet* may arise from its flaws and imperfections, whatever their cause. Given the kind of critical tradition it has acquired, there are a number of ways that the play could be examined to determine the extent to which its deficiencies have caused faulty, confused, or incomplete understandings. At one extreme, one could attempt to assess the play as a whole to check and test T. S. Eliot's view that *Hamlet* is a failure as a work of art. I dare speculate that the conclusion one might arrive at would be a kind of Eliotic paradox indicating that if *Hamlet* is indeed a failure, the very way that it fails has helped determine its popular success for centuries.

Apart from the comprehensive and debatable question raised by Eliot through his concept of the "objective correlative," there are some specific problems arising from some bad workmanship in the play. One of these concerns the strange inconsistencies in the character of Horatio, inconsistencies that have less to do with his essential attributes as a personage than with certain facts about him and the way he appears and functions at different points in the play. Although we have here an unmistakable and concrete problem that some critics have noticed, it remains nonetheless a problem that has somehow gone unexplained, surprising as it is to find that Horatio's inconsistencies have merely been recognized but not accounted for in terms of dramaturgy, text, or sources that might shed new light on Shakespeare's work.

Accordingly, the main purpose of this essay is to examine and try to explain the major inconsistencies in Horatio, especially those concerning a change in his role after the opening scene of *Hamlet*. The nature of Shakespeare's flaws in drawing this character is, however, related to a larger topic that I can do little more than specify within the narrower scope of this essay. That topic has to do with the students in *Hamlet* as part of Shakespeare's conception of the play. It is this larger topic that ultimately gives full significance to the particular problems we find in the case of Horatio.[1]

At some point or points in the uncertain history of Hamlet plays, from the earliest possible date of *Ur-Hamlet* to Shakespeare's version as we have it in Q2,[2] a host of students, singly or en masse, were enrolled in the drama: Hamlet, Horatio, Rosencrantz, Guildenstern, Polonius (who played Julius Caesar in the university), and Laertes (who is supposed to be studying music).[3] While there is no student or scholar in either the Hamlet story as Saxo Grammaticus tells it in *Historia Danica* or as Belleforest translated it in *Histoires Tragiques*, the idea to ascribe student identities to characters, especially Hamlet, could have been suggested to an Elizabethan dramatist by certain things about the Prince that are emphasized in the earliest source and its French translation: his shrewd intelligence and wisdom, his pretense of madness and the suspicion about his true condition, his melancholy (an affliction that heightens cerebral activity), and his sense of divination or intuition—matters that repeatedly draw attention to Hamlet's *mind*, the instrument of reason expected to be exercised by a student. It is not impossible that Shakespeare and the author of *Ur-Hamlet* knew Saxo's version, which had several continental editions after it was printed in Paris in 1514; however this may be, the author of *Ur-Hamlet* certainly knew Belleforest, and Shakespeare probably also knew that popular translation, which appeared in 1570 and went through numerous editions before Shakespeare wrote his version of the Hamlet story.

Since a passion for revenge defeats the force of reason in Hamlet, the idea to create him as a student with a great intellect and to embellish the play with other students figures in Shakespeare's basic dramatic thought serves to clarify the tragic outlook in the play. For if a genius like Hamlet, with his great capacity for reason (nurtured by many years at the university), can be overwhelmed by an obsessive passion, who is immune to such madness? The lofty essence of Hamlet's tragedy is well stated in Ophelia's exclamation: "O, what a noble mind is here o'erthrown!" The play amplifies this tragic idea of the mind overthrown by passion through the situation of Claudius, which is given sharp dramatic focus in his intensely reasoned (albeit shuffling) soliloquy in the Prayer Scene, and through the situation of Laertes, which parallels Hamlet's.

Since the fine mind of Hamlet, liberally educated and habitually disposed to reason, is of salient importance in Shakespeare's conception of the Prince (Frank Kermode points out that "he has been called the most intelligent figure ever represented in literature"),[4] it would be of considerable interest, in terms of how Shakespeare handled the story, to be able to determine whether he inherited or invented the student identity of Hamlet and other characters in his play. While we can conclude with certainty that Shakespeare's source play, the *Ur-Hamlet*, had a ghost that cried, "Hamlet, Revenge,"[5] we cannot conclude that there were any students in that irretrievably lost play, probably written by Thomas Kyd.

The case of Horatio as a student is especially interesting because it involves a problem in characterization that some critics have recognized but not explained. "Horatio . . . in Shakespeare's play is a somewhat chameleonic figure—a stranger or habitué of the court as the need arises," says Frank Kermode, seeing Horatio's inconsistencies in terms of his relation to the plot.[6] Harold Jenkins expresses essentially the same view in the "Problems" chapter of his book-length Introduction to *Hamlet*: "Shakespeare seems undecided whether Horatio is in Elsinore as a visitor or a denizen."[7] Of particular interest here is the inconsistency between Horatio's easy familiarity with the guards in the opening scene, as though he has been at the castle a long time, and his acceptance, in the next scene, of Hamlet's greeting him as a fellow-student just arrived from Wittenberg. Parallel to this inconsistency is Horatio's detailed knowledge (in the opening scene) of the history and current state of Denmark's relations with Norway, information one might expect of a resident of Elsinore, while a day later (in the fourth scene), he is ignorant of a Danish drinking custom, which Hamlet explains to him as though he is a visitor and not even a Dane. It is incredible that Horatio has been at Elsinore without seeing Hamlet, for there was no other reason for him to remain there after coming to the funeral of Hamlet's father, who has been dead almost two months. This matter is left in a muddle. It is equally incredible that the guards would fail to report a serious problem concerning the midnight watch to an appropriate superior officer and report it instead to a newly arrived visitor, yet Horatio suddenly appears to be just that—a visiting student—when he and the guards call on Hamlet.

The age of Horatio, especially in relation to Hamlet's age, involves still another inconsistency. Horatio would have had to have been an adult with King Hamlet to be able to confirm the identity of the Ghost by saying:

> Such was the very armor he had on
> When he the ambitious Norway combated.
> So frown'd he once when in an angry parle
> He smote the sledded Polacks on the ice.
>
> (1.1.60–63)

Yet we are given the impression that Hamlet's "fellow-student" is approximately the same age as the Prince who, if we accept the Gravedigger's word, was born the day when King Hamlet overcame Fortinbras, the "Norway" Horatio mentions in the lines quoted.[8] (In performance, to be sure, this inconsistency does not bother us or even come to mind, but it is there nonetheless and that is what may be meaningful.)

How are these inconsistencies in the characterization of Horatio to be explained? Commenting on Horatio's appearing to be a native in act 1, scene 1, and a visitor in scenes 2 and 4, Harold Jenkins says, "The play shows Shakespeare in two minds about him."[9] This observation, however, does not really address or explain the problem because it does not take into account what may be most important: Shakespeare is consistently of *one* mind in rendering Horatio as an academic. "Thou art a scholar, speak to it, Horatio," Marcellus says when the Ghost appears in the opening scene (1.1.42); "do not mock me fellow-student," Hamlet says to Horatio in the next scene (1.2.177). The common denominator, Horatio with an academic identity, is clear.

This matter brings us to the inconsistency that is most interesting and significant, just as it is most problematic: the conflict between Horatio's abrupt identity as a student in scene 2 and his special function in scene 1, a function governed by Shakespeare's dramaturgy in regulating the way Horatio appears to the audience in the opening scene. When Horatio is talking with the guards in that scene, after arriving with Marcellus for the midnight watch, an audience unfamiliar with *Hamlet* (or following a new version of a familiar story, as might have been the case with those who had seen *Ur-Hamlet*) subscribes to a certain assumption about him that serves the dramatic purpose of the play at that moment. Quite simply, this assumption is that Horatio, because he is the person who has been brought to investigate the problem, is the *appropriate* person to whom the guards should have reported the strange appearances of the Ghost. Since one would expect the guards to report a problem to their military superior if they are going to report it to anyone, the audience assumes that Horatio is such a person, for he functions like a soldier with higher rank than the others and Shakespeare introduces nothing that might make us think otherwise.

For example, at the beginning of the opening scene Bernardo formally awaits Horatio as one of the "rivals" (partners) of his watch (1.1.13), and after he arrives with Marcellus, Horatio asks the other guard to report about the Ghost: "let us hear Bernardo speak of this" (1.1.34), he says, wanting to obtain the other soldier's version of the strange events. After the Ghost appears, Horatio confirms its identity by referring (in the lines quoted above) to a time when he seems to have been in military service with King Hamlet (why else would he be at the place of a battle?). When the Ghost appears again, Marcellus asks Horatio, as though he is in charge, "Shall I strike at it with my partisan?" (1.1.143). And at the end of the scene it is Horatio who says to the guards, "Break we our watch up" (1.1.168), identifying himself formally with the watch and speaking with an officer's authority in deciding what to do. This is the crux of the playwright's strategy in managing the relation of the audience to Horatio in the opening scene of the play, where, on the one hand, the audience is not told about the friendship between Horatio and Hamlet or that Horatio is a visiting student and where, on the other hand, the audience perceives Horatio essentially as a quasi-officer figure, the easy familiarity between him and the guards seeming to convey a longstanding comradeship that has put aside formal acknowledgments of rank between officer and men.[10]

After the opening scene, however, the audience's initial assumption about Horatio, appropriate as it was, does not remain valid or intact when it is made clear that he is Hamlet's fellow student from Wittenberg, not the quasi-officer figure he appeared to be in the opening dramatic context. The audience had no difficulty in accepting an officer who is regarded as a "scholar" by the guards, who knows how to address the Ghost, and who is well-educated enough to know of the portentous conditions associated with the murder of Julius Caesar; but these academic attributes, which Shakespeare gives to the quasi-officer figure in scene 1, are not enough to make that seemingly residential military figure congruent with the visiting university student, the defining identity Shakespeare gives Horatio when he and the guards come to Hamlet late in scene 2. (As the play progresses, Horatio's identity as a visiting student seems to alter, and he appears increasingly as a courtier who resides at Elsinore because he is the friend of the Prince.) Since Horatio's role as Hamlet's friend and confidant from Wittenberg is what establishes itself as of primary importance, including Horatio as an example par excellence of the man that is not "passion's slave" (3.2.72), Shakespeare seems to have counted on the intervening court scene and the dramatic momentum of the play to obscure and leave behind Horatio's de facto function as an officer figure in the opening scene.

Even in performance the result comes "tardy" off, as Hamlet would say, and the inconsistency is a bit jarring. This miscalculation in dramaturgy, however, does not undermine the character of Horatio, because in the opening scene (and only there) Horatio merely evokes or suggests the officer figure (without ever being identified as such) and because the academic attributes of the officer figure are entirely consistent with the university man, even though the officer figure per se is not, despite Shakespeare's efforts to blur the difference. The audience, in moving along with the play, simply sheds or modifies its initial assumption, which was based only on Horatio's implicit appearance at the beginning of the play, and accepts the clarification provided by Hamlet's explicit identification of his friend, even though the new Horatio from Wittenberg cannot in fact be fully reconciled with his earlier appearance as a military man who resides at Elsinore. (The issue here, it might be noted, does not involve a question of character development through Shakespeare's technique of introducing or emphasizing new or dormant facets of a character when he appears again after being off-stage for a time, as seen in Richard II after he returns from Ireland or in Hamlet after he returns from his sea journey.)

What this faulty tack in dramaturgy suggests, through the shift in characterization, is that Shakespeare may have tried to superimpose the identity of Horatio as a student onto Horatio as an officer of the watch, if he found only the latter in the Ur-Hamlet, which is considered to be his main source for Hamlet. Or, to restate the matter, he may have tried to adapt Horatio's function as an officer of the watch in the opening scene to his main conception of Horatio as Hamlet's fellow student in the rest of the play. It is interesting to note that this hypothesis bears out Virgil K. Whitaker's view of Shakespeare's faulty workmanship in creating Horatio. Although Whitaker does not try to explain the etiology of Horatio's inconsistencies in concrete terms, he nonetheless offers a useful general explanation of their origin:

> It is customary to speak of Horatio as "plot-ridden" and to explain these inconsistencies as resulting from his function as the dramatist's mouthpiece in interpreting the play to the audience. I should prefer to say that he is "source-ridden," the victim of Shakespeare's failure to assimilate all the elements in the old play to his new design.[11]

Actually, Horatio is both plot-ridden and source-ridden, because Shakespeare had a dramatic purpose in the way he decided to change Horatio. He could have retained Horatio strictly as a military character, if that was the way he found him in the source-play, but he chose to make him a student. Whitaker's view of the problem, in any case, helps clarify the cause of Horatio's inconsistencies and enables us to understand the rationale of the misleading dramaturgy in the opening scene, especially if there was a similar scene in *Ur-Hamlet*. The imperfect merging of two distinct conceptions of Horatio—the resident military man and the visiting university man—seems to account for the kind of bifurcation we find in Shakespeare's drawing of the character. In other words, the nature of the bifurcation is probably related to what caused it.

If the hypothesis given above has merit in accounting for Horatio's main inconsistencies in *Hamlet*, there is, in addition to the internal textual and dramaturgic evidence supporting it, one important bit of external evidence which supports the notion that Horatio was indeed an officer figure in *Ur-Hamlet*. The great value of knowing the contents of that lost work, which seems never to have been published, is generally recognized. Expressing the views of many, Cyrus Hoy has affirmed that

> the effort of critics to define the dramatist's intentions in this, the most ambiguous of all his tragedies, could proceed on very much surer ground if it were possible to know which of the changes were Shakespeare's own innovation, and which had already been introduced into the earlier dramatization of the Hamlet story.[12]

Unfortunately, the only direct link we have with *Ur-Hamlet* is through *Der Bestrafte Brudermord*, that wretched, grossly debased German version of *Hamlet* which continues to tantalize and frustrate scholars with the elusive possibility that it may be able to provide useful glimpses of the lost *Ur-Hamlet*, thus leading perhaps to a clearer comprehension of Shakespeare's play.

Scholars generally agree with G. I. Duthie, who has provided us with a fine study of *Der Bestrafte Brudermord* in *The "Bad" Quarto of Hamlet*,[13] that *BB* probably came into existence originally as a composite memorial reconstruction made by a group of English actors who individually knew or had experience with several different stage versions of Hamlet plays, particularly those represented by Q1, Q2, and *Ur-Hamlet*.[14] Scholars do not agree, however, on the proportions and specifics of things derived from these sources, matters that are likely to remain unascertainable. As a collectively created acting script, *BB* was probably put together and taken to Germany sometime before Q1 and Q2 were published, in 1603 and 1604, respectively. The reasons for this view, on the basis of Duthie's findings, have to do with the peculiar inaccuracies and the hybrid mixtures of matters related to Q1 and Q2, mixtures that are best explained as having been determined by faulty recollections of Hamlet plays on the stage, not by mistakes in using the manuscripts or printed texts of Q1 and Q2.

BB exists for us only in a 1781 German publication of a manuscript (now lost) that bore the place and date: "Pretz, den 27 Oktober, 1710."[15] By 1710, over a century after its eclectic assembly in England, many alterations in the translation and the thousand natural tamperings that an acting script is heir to had encrusted this crudest of Hamlet plays with textual changes and revisions that are hopelessly beyond trustworthy detection or emendation, so that trying to make out vestiges of Ur-Hamlet through BB is like trying to see distant things through a muddied window. There would be little point in taking a limited look at BB now if there did not seem to be a hitherto unnoticed clear spot that invites a fresh effort at squinting.

Except for Hamlet, there are no students in BB. This fact, obvious as it is, has not even been so much as mentioned in any of the studies of BB that I have seen, including the work of G. I. Duthie, Virgil K. Whitaker, and, most recently, Harold Jenkins.[16] Nonetheless, this unnoticed contrast between the abundance of students in Hamlet and the dearth of students in BB is surely as concrete a matter as the well-known difference between the name "Polonius," which Shakespeare gave to his character in Q2, and "Corambis" and "Corambus," as the same character is called in Q1 and BB, respectively, whatever the reason for the difference, including the possibility that there was a Corambis in Ur-Hamlet.

Furthermore, in BB there is no problem of inconsistency in the character of Horatio. Throughout BB he is explicitly what he appears implicitly to be in only the opening scene of Shakespeare's play: an officer of the watch. He is also Hamlet's close friend throughout the play, but there is no trace of a scholar in his identity as a soldier and noble courtier who resides at Elsinore. Although Hamlet is a student, Horatio is never seen or regarded as a visiting student. His relationship to the sentinels, who call him "your worship," includes formalities, with implicit and explicit acknowledgment of rank, including a soldier identified as a corporal. In BB Horatio has not been brought by the guards to check on the Ghost; at the opening of the play he learns of the problem of the Ghost in the course of making his rounds. His function as a military man and Hamlet's view of him in that capacity are clear from the following speeches, which take place when Hamlet, who is also checking the watch, enters and is told about the Ghost (who soon appears and beckons the Prince):

Hor. Your highness, I have gone the rounds to see that every one is at
his post.

Ham. That's like an honest soldier, for on you rests the safety of the
king and kingdom.

Hor. Your highness, a strange thing has happened: regularly every
quarter of an hour a ghost appears.[17]

While Hamlet's identity as a student at Wittenberg in *BB* is clearly
traceable to the Shakespearean versions represented by Q1 and Q2,
Horatio's identity as a soldier clearly is not. As a military character he has
a non-Shakespearean source. For this reason, we can assume that the
group of actors who originally put together the *BB* script either invented
their own Horatio or, far more likely, used the one they found ready-
made in *Ur-Hamlet*, scholars agreeing that there must have been a
Horatio in that play. Since the *BB* script postdates *Hamlet*, it of course
could not have been Shakespeare's source for Horatio or anything else.
Therefore, Horatio's implicit function as an officer in the opening scene
of *Hamlet* points to a source in which he must have been a military
character, probably an officer that Shakespeare decided to meta-
morphose into Hamlet's "fellow-student." For Shakespeare, that source
could only have been the *Ur-Hamlet*, for there is no Horatio figure as
such in Belleforest.[18]

What *BB* does, through the contrast between its Horatio and Shakespeare's, is provide an explicit version of the implicit military figure that
best explains Horatio's attributes as a character and his dramatic function
in the opening scene of *Hamlet*. If *BB* and *Hamlet*, respectively, have a
common source for Horatio as a military man and Horatio with quasi-
military attributes, then the difference between the nonunified Horatio
in *Hamlet* and the unified Horatio in *BB* probably reflects the essential
difference between Horatio in *Hamlet* and Horatio in *Ur-Hamlet*. It therefore seems reasonable to think that Horatio in *BB* enables us to see a
version of Horatio in *Ur-Hamlet*, an officer character that Shakespeare
changed into a student to suit his telling of the Hamlet story.

BB is such a problem-ridden and deceiving work to try to use in a
reliable way that Harold Jenkins has reached the following extreme
conclusion about it at the end of his chapter on *BB* in his Introduction to
Hamlet:

BB . . . seems to preserve a few pre-Shakespearean strands, but for
the most part it originates in Shakespeare. . . . What it cannot reveal,
unless in some fragmentary relics of Belleforest, is what has been most
looked for in it, the content of the *Ur-Hamlet*.

This necessary conclusion is likely, I am aware, to be unwelcome.
Some scholars and sentimentalists alike will continue to hanker after a
sight of the lost *Hamlet* which served as Shakespeare's source. But the

belief that this is somehow to be seen through *BB*, with or without the help of Q1, has for far too long bedevilled the study of *Hamlet*, which will do better without the mirage.[19]

Jenkins's conclusion is hardly a logical or acceptable view of a document that provides, by his own admission, a link to Shakespeare's source-play. On the one hand, he allows that "an acting text was evolved by a group of actors whose collective memory embraced more than one version of the play," and he states unequivocally that "we must . . . accept that some vestiges of Shakespeare's source-play may have been preserved in *BB*."[20] On the other hand, apart from recognizing that "*BB* oddly corresponds with Belleforest in some details which Shakespeare omits,"[21] he virtually disallows that the vestiges of the source-play are discoverable or even worth trying to discover and concludes a priori that any sighting of *Ur-Hamlet* with the help of *BB* would be a "mirage."

It is a mistake to assume, as Jenkins implicitly does in his conclusion, that there can never be any new ideas about how *BB* might provide valuable perceptions of *Ur-Hamlet* and thus help clarify Shakespeare's handling of the Hamlet story in his play. Even though it is not possible fully to reconstruct *Ur-Hamlet* from *BB*, and even though trustworthy perceptions of *Ur-Hamlet* may be very hard to come by, this does not mean that the "pre-Shakespearean strands" and "relics" in *BB* cannot prove to be important if they can be identified with reasonable certainty and properly understood. Horatio and the other students in *Hamlet*, characters involving matters more substantial than strands or relics, provide a case in point.

In this connection, it is ironic that in the "Problems" section of his Introduction, which follows directly upon his conclusion about *BB*, the very first problem Jenkins brings up concerns Horatio's inconsistencies. Instead of examining them, he says: "These . . . are less 'problems' to be solved than local discrepancies which have to be accepted—sometimes even gratefully for the clues they give to Shakespeare's mind."[22] As I have argued here, the inconsistencies in the case of Horatio are more than "local discrepancies" that are unrelated to anything beyond the bounds of the play. Because they are best understood in terms of Shakespeare's handling of his source materials, they do indeed give a clue to the playwright's mind. Illuminating Shakespeare's idea to create a group of students in his telling of the Hamlet story, they seem to show that he changed what must have been a military character in his source, the *Ur-Hamlet*, into Horatio the university student.

BB is like a disturbed and corrupted archeological site that nonetheless constitutes an important surviving link to lost people—lost characters and their story in the case of the missing source-play. Every once in a while we hear about a surprising new find at a thoroughly explored and unpromising archeological site. In the military attributes of the character to whom the guards have reported their problem about the Ghost in the opening scene of *Hamlet*, we seem to have some remains of the Horatio in *Ur-Hamlet*. These vestiges in Shakespeare, which are not consistent with the identity of Horatio as Hamlet's fellow student, strengthen the probability that Horatio in *BB* gives us a fuller view of the lost character in *Ur-Hamlet*, just as the dearth of students in *BB* probably reflects their absence in the lost play. As this study illustrates, Jenkins's conclusion is counterproductive because it does not allow for unforeseeable new ways of comprehending what Jenkins, quoting Harry Levin, considers, "the most problematic play ever written by Shakespeare or any other playwright."[23]

The reason that scholars have not taken note of the dearth of students in *BB* and the contrasting abundance of students in *Hamlet* is probably that they have not regarded this matter as especially significant.[24] This particular contrast is of striking interest, however, to anyone who finds Hamlet's mind and his great ability to reason of singular importance in Shakespeare's conception of the character, something the playwright seems to have decided to highlight by making Hamlet an exceptionally brilliant student, giving him numerous soliloquies, and creating a cluster of other characters who are students. The critical issue involved here is quite important, both theoretically and practically, because it has a bearing on how and why a playwright sees characters as he does within his conception of a play as a whole. Shakespeare's inconsistencies in creating Horatio reveal how intent he was in changing a military man into a university man as part of his larger idea to give a strong presence to students in the play. Since critics have not perceived the thematic importance of students in *Hamlet*, Horatio as a character also has not been fully appreciated. Paradoxically, although Horatio is a minor character, that does not mean that he has minor significance.

In addition to his role as a friend devoted to Hamlet, and as a pivotal figure at the beginning and end of the play, Horatio has a muted but distinct significance in relation to the major tragic theme in the play: reason overthrown by passion within the enveloping mystery of the operation of Divine Providence. As an abstraction governing the larger design of *Hamlet*, this theme is given a beautiful loftiness by the elevated view of man's mind in the play, which celebrates it as "godlike reason." At a crucial dramatic moment in the play, when Hamlet has been stabilized by a rational scheme to test the Ghost (whose proven honesty will renew the issue of passion-driven vengeance), Horatio is set before us as a model of rational balance, with Hamlet expressing his great admiration of him as one "Whose blood and judgment are so well comeddled" and who is not "passion's slave" (3.2.69, 72). At the end of the play, it is especially appropriate that the sole surviving student, who has epitomized the stability of reason and who confronted the supernatural with rational skepticism at the beginning of the play, should be the one who will relate what the play has shown to be the inscrutable process of "heaven ordinant," to use Hamlet's phrase. Horatio, never seen as a doctrinaire disbeliever, seems to be aware both of human actions driven by passion and events governed by Divine Providence when he says, in a bitterly coarse tone explainable by his grief, that he will speak

> Of carnal, bloody, and unnatural acts,
> Of accidental judgments, casual slaughters,
> Of deaths put on by cunning and forc'd cause,
> And in this upshot, purposes mistook
> Fall'n on th' inventors' heads.
>
> (5.2.381–85)

That a man of reason is the most important survivor at Elsinore intensifies the tragedy of a man who, despite his gift of mind, could not maintain himself as a man of reason, joining other victims of passion in his death—at the very time he had arrived at a sublime understanding that "There is special providence in the fall of a sparrow" (5.2.219–20). By enabling us to see that the creation of students was a meaningful idea that Shakespeare brought to his version of the Hamlet story, the etiology of Horatio's inconsistencies helps clarify and enlarge a major universal aspect of the play. We are all sad survivors with Horatio, whom we admire because he is so superbly human, but our sadness is informed, I dare say, with a sense of awareness that in a certain set of unforeseeable circumstances we could succumb as Hamlet did. Have we not seen even Horatio give way to a passionate impulse, prevented from killing himself only because Hamlet by chance ("special providence"?) still had the strength to wrest the cup containing the poisoned drink from him? Finally, the play is ultimately uncompromising in dramatizing the idea that a passion for revenge is a desire for justice run amok, with bestial violence overwhelming rational self-control in what is essentially a form of madness.

Notes

1. An exposition of this larger topic is included in work I have in progress. This examination of Horatio's inconsistencies is part of that work, which is nearing completion.

2. The essential chronology of references to *Ur-Hamlet* may be summarized as follows: in 1589, there is Thomas Nashe's remark, in a prefatory epistle to Robert Greene's *Menaphon*, that English admirers of Seneca "will afford you whole Hamlets, . . . handfuls of Tragicall speeches"; in 1594, Philip Henslowe's diary mentions the performance of a Hamlet play, presumably but not necessarily a revival of the play alluded to by Nashe; in

1596, Thomas Lodge, in *Wit's Miserie and the World's Madness*, refers to "the ghost which cried so miserably at the Theater, like an oyster-wife *'Hamlet, Revenge.'* " *Ur-Hamlet* designates one lost play only if the few sketchy references, scattered between 1589 and 1596, are assumed to refer to the same Hamlet play. Such an assumption is entirely reasonable, but its cogency depends less on positive identification of a single play (the references *could* involve more than one Hamlet play) than on the absence of evidence identifying more than one pre-Shakespearean *Hamlet*. Some scholars believe that *Ur-Hamlet*, which may have been written by Thomas Kyd, precedes *The Spanish Tragedy* (ca. 1587). This view widens the historical time-frame and increases the possibility, albeit an unlikely one, that more than one Hamlet play existed before Shakespeare dealt with the story. Some scholars believe that Shakespeare himself wrote a Hamlet play before he reworked it in the version represented by Q2 and the Folio.

3. "Let him ply his music," Polonius instructs Reynaldo in Q2 and the Folio; and in Q1 Polonius's instructions also include, "bid him ply his learning good," indicating that those who put together Q1 saw Laertes as a student.

4. Frank Kermode, Introduction to *Hamlet*, in *The Riverside Shakespeare*, textual ed., G. Blakemore Evans (Boston: Houghton Mifflin, 1974), 1139. All subsequent references to *Hamlet* are to this edition.

5. Thomas Lodge, *Wit's Miserie* (see note 2). The Ghost's injunction seems to have become a byword. In Dekker's *Satiromastix,* for example, Tucca says to Asinius, "my name's Hamlet revenge" (4.1.150).

6. Kermode, Introduction to *Hamlet*, *The Riverside Shakespeare*, 1137.

7. Harold Jenkins, Introduction to *Hamlet*, New Arden Shakespeare (London: Methuen, 1982), 123.

8. The coincidence of two major royal events—the birth of a prince and the victory of a king—is not likely to be subject to an error in anyone's memory, not even a gravedigger's. On the contrary, each event is likely to serve as a reminder of the date of the other.

9. Jenkins, Introduction to *Hamlet*, New Arden, 447.

10. Many modern editors identify Francisco as "a soldier" and Marcellus and Bernardo as "officers," but these identifications have no authority in Q1 or Q2, which do not give a "Dramatis Personae," or in F. They appear first in the Quarto edition of 1676. Since Bernardo relieves Francisco on guard duty, he seems to have the same status as a soldier as does Marcellus, who shares the midnight watch with Bernardo.

11. Virgil K. Whitaker, *Shakespeare's Use of Learning* (San Marino: Huntington Library, 1953), 255.

12. Cyrus Hoy, Preface to *Hamlet* (New York: W. W. Norton, 1963), p. viii.

13. G. I. Duthie, *The "Bad" Quarto of Hamlet* (Cambridge: Cambridge University Press, 1941).

14. The range of possible stage versions is indicated in note 2.

15. "Note on 'Fratricide Punished,'" in *The New Variorum Hamlet*, ed. Howard H. Furness (New York: Dover, 1963), 2:117.

16. Duthie, *The "Bad" Quarto of Hamlet*, 238–71; Whitaker, *Shakespeare's Use of Learning*, 251–75, 329–47; Jenkins, Introduction to *Hamlet*, New Arden, 112–22.

17. *Fratricide Punished*, trans. H. H. Furness, in *The New Variorum Hamlet*, 2:124.

18. In Belleforest the germinal vestige of Horatio is a friendly gentleman who warns Amleth of the trick to trap him with a beautiful woman. In Saxo the friendly person who warns Amleth is his foster brother.

19. Jenkins, Introduction to *Hamlet*, New Arden, 122.

20. Ibid., 118–19, 121–22.

21. Ibid., 121.

22. Ibid., 123.

23. Ibid., 122.

24. For example, Philip Edwards, comparing Belleforest's version of Saxo's story to Shakespeare's, says: "The most important changes which appear in *Hamlet* are as follows:

1 The murder becomes secret;
2 A ghost tells Hamlet of the murder and urges revenge;
3 Laertes and young Fortinbras are introduced;
4 Ophelia's role is extended and elevated;
5 The players and their play are introduced;
6 Hamlet dies as he kills the king."

Introduction to *Hamlet,* The New Cambridge Shakespeare (Cambridge: Cambridge University Press, 1985), 2.

11

The Worst of Shakespeare in the Theater

Cuts in the Last Scene of King Lear

JOHN RUSSELL BROWN

ALTER VOLUME, tempo, pitch, rhythm, or texture; play music; introduce a crowd or the largest catastrophe that can be managed; change lighting, scenery, or costumes; ask actors to play croquet, eat apples, unfurl twenty-four umbrellas, or fire rockets; stop all action for a lengthy silence or introduce distracting business of the smallest kind such as shuffling feet or drumming fingers—in the theater there are a thousand and one ways to make bad texts less noticeable and to hold attention without much regard for what an author has written. And so it comes about that theater practice, as it is known today, can give no final verdict on what parts of Shakespeare's plays may be certified as bad. A director in command of all available resources should be able to make anything work. When a passage seems uncertain or awkward in performance, the fault will not always lie in the text, and just because Shakespeare's words are greeted with applause in a theater we cannot assume that they have contributed very much to this success.

The quality of Shakespeare's writing is given the clearest disapproval in the theater when those in charge of a number of productions of different kinds agree in refusing to stage certain parts of his text: then these words are considered so bad that they are beyond theatrical redemption. This is a yardstick that is easy to use—most promptbooks are available for consultation, and cuts are very clearly marked in them—but it leads to some surprising conclusions that are not so easy to explain.

In one respect, this summary form of judgment is reassuring. Plays that are seldom studied and rarely quoted by literary critics are found, nevertheless, to be almost entirely stageworthy and able to hold an audience from beginning to end. Productions have proved that early works, such as all three parts of *Henry the Sixth*, *Titus Andronicus*, and *The*

Two Gentlemen of Verona, must be certified as good, apart from a number of minor cuts. *Timon of Athens, Cymbeline,* and the textually imperfect *Pericles* can all be presented so that they provide authentically Shakespearean experiences—exciting, imaginative, and well-judged. None of Shakespeare's plays is considered to be so bad that it is not produced sometimes in our theaters; when their various tasks are done, directors, actors, and stagehands are apt to stand back and acknowledge, rather like Henry the Fifth after the Battle of Agincourt, that Shakespeare's hand was there, even in those scenes that have proved most troublesome or most routine.

But the critical ploy of asking what lines are considered to be unplayable is a more searching and useful question, especially when it is applied to the undoubted masterpieces. While the theater's general verdict is complacently positive, more particular judgments can be very harsh. The last scene of *King Lear,* for example, has some passages that are considered to be so bad that in the last thirty years I have never seen it performed as it was written. Always there are cuts, sometimes amounting to more than a hundred lines out of a total of three hundred and twenty-eight. Why should this be so?

Not so long ago almost any cut might be explained by the need to reduce playing time and send audiences home before 10.30 P.M., but the public has become accustomed to productions of four hours or more in length and is now summoned to the theater for an earlier start if this is considered desirable. (A marathon performance is an exceptional experience for which we are ready to leave comfortable homes and short-breathed and recordable television programs.) But even if it were imperative to shorten the text of *King Lear,* we should ask why it is not possible to remove a sufficient number of incidents from earlier in the play rather than damage its culminating moments. This does not happen, and so it is clear that the universal judgment of the theater is that the last scene of this profound and moving tragedy contains much that it is better to be without.

The Shakespeare Centre at Stratford-upon-Avon preserves promptbooks of four productions of *King Lear* staged over a period of twenty years. They can be identified by their dates and directors:

1962   Peter Brook
1968   Trevor Nunn
1972   Trevor Nunn
1982   Adrian Noble

In two successive productions, Trevor Nunn cut some lines only to restore them later, and retained others at first to cut them subsequently.

In small details his judgment changed, as if he sensed the need to take a new grip on recalcitrant material. Each of the three directors cut the last scene differently, as each had his own way with the text. But some passages, extensive, weighty, and written with obvious care, were voted out with a consistency that amounts to a unanimous motion of no confidence.

The first substantial passage that is cut in all four productions should be spoken by Edmund:

> At this time
> We sweat and bleed: the friend hath lost his friend;
> And the best quarrels, in the heat, are cursed
> By those that feel their sharpness.
>
> (55–58)[1]

Some directors remove more of this speech, before and after these lines, but this passage all reject. They are less willing than Shakespeare to spend time on being aware of time, to identify and draw attention to physical suffering, and to recognize the complexity of events. In the full text Edmund transcends his immediate concerns—he has not yet been challenged by Albany after their joint victory in battle—and may have a premonition of his own danger. As events draw to a climax in Shakespeare's text, the dramatic focus becomes confused and concentration weakens; and conventional theatrical wisdom judges that this must be bad.

The second passage to bear general disapprobation is more extensive; Edgar has told of his father's death:

> *Edmund.*　　　　　　　This speech of yours has moved me,
> And shall perchance do good: but speak you on;
> You look as you had something more to say.
> *Albany.* If there be more, more woeful, hold it in;
> For I am almost ready to dissolve,
> Hearing of this.
> *Edgar.*　　　　　This would have seemed a period
> To such as love not sorrow; but another,
> To amplify too much, would make much more,
> And top extremity.
> Whilst I was big in clamor, came there in a man,
> Who, having seen me in my worst estate,
> Shunned my abhorred society; but then, finding
> Who 'twas that so endured, with his strong arms
> He fastened on my neck, and bellowed out
> As he'd burst heaven; threw him on my father;
> Told the most piteous tale of Lear and him
> That ever ear received: which in recounting

His grief grew puissant, and the strings of life
Began to crack: twice then the trumpets sounded,
And there I left him tranced.
Albany.   But who was this?
Edgar. Kent, sir, the banished Kent; who in disguise
Followed his enemy king, and did him service
Improper for a slave.

(201–23)

The meeting of Kent with Edgar and Lear, his being left almost, if not quite, for dead, and the telling of this story can all be cut without loss to the audience's sense of what is afoot. In some ways the passage seems to have been written to the same effect as the one we have just examined: these speakers are aware of each other and of the timing of events, and so again the excitement of the onstage dramatic moment is defused. Despite Kent's subsequent reappearance in the play—which would gain in surprise if this passage were retained—there is also a premonition of his departure at the end of the play, for his "strings of life" are said to be already cracked so that he will be ready to "journey" after his "master" (323–24).

But the manner in which this narration is introduced has a larger and more immediate effect. While words emphasize the complexity and extremity of events, the first three speeches imply that these characters are divided and on the brink of silence. Shattered by what he has said already about his father, how does Edgar look as if he has "more to say"? How does an awakening of "good" change Edmund's voice and bearing? How can Albany fear to respond to yet more sorrow? What do all three do in the pause that is indicated by an uncompleted line, before "extremity" is topped? When Edgar continues his speech he seems to draw a new strength from recording the "strong arms" and "puissant" grief that followed his own first "clamor," because, although the line of thought becomes jagged, his rhythms are sustained. Perhaps the strongest effect of this passage in performance would be an impression of silent, titanic struggle, as these three men slowly begin to comprehend some great force that they are powerless to contradict or to avoid.

Directors are able to cut the play here because the words are not necessary to the unfolding of events, but in doing so they cut a manifestation of strenuous torment, both inward and outward, both individual and shared. Thus, the play becomes much simpler dynamically, and the focus is held more securely by outward behavior and spoken reactions. Directors must believe that the other elements are unnecessary or that they are more than actors or audiences can sustain. Either way, theater practice judges that the text is bad.

The last three of these five speeches were omitted from the First Folio text of 1623, so that someone else, very early in the play's history, judged that some of this passage was not worth retention. Possibly Shakespeare himself had learned that actors could not make the speeches work, or he may have been in two minds about their effectiveness. But, nevertheless, this Jacobean cut still kept the first hesitation of Edgar's together with Edmund's and Albany's contrasted responses: some loss of focus and forward drive were still implied by the text.

Twentieth-century consensus, but not the scribe or editor of the printer's copy for the Folio, is also against these further lines:

Albany.   Great thing of us forgot!
  Speak, Edmund, where's the king? and where's Cordelia?
  See'st thou this object, Kent?
              (The bodies of Goneril *and* Regan *are brought in.)*
Kent. Alack, why thus?
Edmund.   Yet Edmund was beloved!
  The one the other poisoned for my sake,
  And after slew herself.
Albany. Even so. Cover their faces.
Edmund. I pant for life: some good I mean to do,
  Despite of mine own nature. Quickly send,
  Be brief in it, to th'castle; for my writ
  Is on the life of Lear and on Cordelia:
  Nay, send in time.
Albany.   Run, run, O, run!
Edgar. To who, my lord? Who has the office? Send
  Thy token of reprieve.
Edmund. Well thought on: take my sword,
  Give it the captain.
Edgar.   Haste thee, for thy life.
              (Exit Messenger.)
Edmund. He hath commission from thy wife and me
  To hang Cordelia in the prison, and
  To lay the blame upon her own despair,
  That she fordid herself.
Albany. The gods defend her! Bear him hence awhile.
              (Edmund is borne off.)

                                                            (238–58)

Here the condemnation is not quite absolute, for sometimes Edmund's first two speeches are retained, at least in part. But not one of the directors in this group keeps all the short phrases that give an impression of a shared and dazed urgency—the brief questions, imperatives, affirmations, and exclamations, each one wrung out of need and forceful as an attempt to cope with and hold back disaster. With this verbal activity will go physical changes and gestures, not least when without immediate warning the dead bodies of Lear's daughters are brought silently on stage, a piece of business that could involve eight bearers and very different reactions from each of the four people chiefly concerned.

In practical terms, the whole of this passage is unnecessary. We have seen already that Edmund sent an executioner after Lear and Cordelia, we know that Goneril and Regan are dead, and we shall hear later, from the king himself, how Cordelia was hanged. We know all the essentials except Albany's prayer—which is never answered—and Edmund's intention to do good—which comes too late. (In the absence of his earlier confession that he was moved in hearing of his father's death so that he felt the stirrings of an impulse toward "good," Edmund's last-minute reformation in "despite" of his "own nature" may be such a new development that the actor would have difficulty in making it credible.) This time the strongest defense of Shakespeare's full text would be to argue that a confused and urgent sense of crisis should be established before the king enters with Cordelia in his arms; men should be seen to be doing their ineffectual best. And again Shakespeare seems to have found means to accentuate the passage of time and the increase of complexity. The entry of dead bodies and the bearing off of Edmund, who is not quite dead but panting for life, provide a slow visual augmentation of what urgent words might deal with too quickly for full comprehension.

Elsewhere in the scene, directors have cut other short phrases as if they have found that these also were too busy or irrelevant to the main action. At least two of these directors cut each of the following:

> About it; and write happy when th'hast done.
>
> (36)

> Draw thy sword,
> That if my speech offend a noble heart,
> Thy arm may do thee justice: here is mine.
>
> (127–29)

> Hold, sir;
>
> (157)

> Methought thy very gait did prophesy
> A royal nobleness: I must embrace thee:
>
> (177–78)

> Worthy prince,
> I know't.
>
> (179–80)

> List a brief tale;
> And when 'tis told,
>
> (183–84)

What kind of help? . . . Speak, man.

(224)

'Tis hot, it smokes;

(225)

Produce the bodies, be they alive or dead.

(232)

O, is this he?

(234)

Very bootless.

(296)

Bear them from hence. Our present business
Is general woe.

(320–21)

Together with brief phrases in the longer passages already considered, these cuts show that, for modern theater practice, Shakespeare's provision of orders and information is supererogatory, almost pedantic in such a charged situation. Directors believe that it is bad to clog the scene with individual concerns and ineffective assertions, bad to provide contrast to the strong-willed domination of the king, bad to take any more time than is absolutely necessary except for presenting the heart of the matter, the suffering of Lear.

This last consideration led all three directors to snip off small pieces from some longer speeches that they could not totally remove. Edgar and Edmund lose most, including some powerful images that draw on a deeper consciousness than that concerned with their immediate response to events. Edgar is likely to forego any or all of the following:

thy victor sword and fire-new fortune . . . the descent and dust below thy foot . . . most toad-spotted traitor. . . . exchange charity. . . . my heart would burst. . . . semblance / That very dogs disdained. . . . Told him our pilgrimage. . . .

(134–200)

From Edmund may be taken:

pluck the common bosom on his side . . . turn our impressed lances in our eyes. . . . thy tongue some say of breeding breathes. . . . Back do I toss these treasons to thy head . . . With the hell-hated lie o'erwhelm thy heart. . . .

(50–149)

Shakespeare has not provided the concentrated attention on a single consciousness or on present business that directors believe is right for the conclusion of a tragedy.

One theme in particular recurs in the text more frequently than is acceptable. The full script requires characters to be conscious repeatedly of other times, even as they relinquish their control over what is about to happen next. Eloquent lines may be cut to avoid this reiteration, and even a few famous ones. Here is a further tally from the Stratford promptbooks beyond those already quoted:

> and we'll wear out,
> In a walled prison, packs and sects of great ones
> That ebb and flow by th' moon.
>
> (17–19)

> I'll make it on thy heart,
> Ere I taste bread,
>
> (94–95)

> Let sorrow split my heart, if ever I
> Did hate thee or thy father!
>
> (179–80)

> O, our lives' sweetness,
> That we the pain of death would hourly die
> Rather than die at once!
>
> (186–88)

The general indictment of Shakespeare implied in all the cuts that are made in this last scene of *King Lear* is that he unnecessarily and willfully complicated the drama. He was too concerned with how all his characters grappled, even if unsuccessfully, with immediate concerns and how they remained watchful of each other and conscious of other times and other situations. Again and again he held back the powerful forward surge of plot and action to explore the interdependence of all those who are closely involved. To his central character he gave only sixty-four lines in the entire scene (some of them half lines), which means only one line in five; most theater directors will change this proportion to give Lear one out of four or three and a half. Shakespeare did not keep the focus tight enough or the tension firm enough. At times, in the full and authoritative text, action seems to stall, like an aircraft losing height as well as forward momentum.

Other questions are implied in this conclusion. First must be whether these are accidental features of this particular play or vices endemic in the whole of Shakespeare's work. The further question is whether a new style of Shakespeare production might arise that could thrive on those very elements of his dramaturgy that are now dismissed as unnecessary, disadvantageous, or just plain bad. While theater practice can prove little about Shakespeare's plays, I would like to see a production that dared to risk a loss of tension in act 5 of *King Lear* in order to present all the remaining characters grappling with a changing situation, imperfect understanding, and all the "long-ingafted conditions" of their own lives. An audience might then sense that everything is at risk, even the coherence of the play and the power of fate to draw all to its conclusion. Each character might seem to struggle as if everything depended on his own efforts, mental, physical, and emotional. While the last act, in such a performance, would be even more painful to witness, or at least more generally so, its ending might seem to be more the result of individual and collaborative human effort, than of ineluctable fate or the half-crazed actions of a hero-king. Perhaps the passages that are ordinarily cut in our theater hold clues to reaches of Shakespeare's imagination where directors, actors, and critics have not yet followed.

Note

1. This and all subsequent quotations are from *King Lear*, ed. Russell Fraser (New York: New American Library, 1963). Parenthetical text references are to line(s) in act 5, scene 3.

12

Wormwood in the Wood Outside Athens

Timon *and the Problem for the Audience*

NINIAN MELLAMPHY

IN THE 1960s and throughout the greater part of the 1970s one of the problems that faced the instructor who wished to discuss *Measure for Measure* before or with an undergraduate audience was how to elicit from that audience some sympathetic appreciation of Isabella's response to Angelo's "most pernicious"[1] proposition. Product of the new morality, champion of sexual permissiveness, that fabulous being, The Typical Undergraduate of the Time, found it difficult to understand Isabella's dilemma: the choice between head and maidenhead, between life and virginity, was not really so difficult. Isabella's scrupulous concern about her hymen was, after all, much ado about next to nothing. Like the Hamlet who is unnecessarily dilatory when all he has to do is kill a king, Isabella was unnecessarily finicky, when all she had to do was come across. Indeed, it was perhaps easier to win from the student an imaginative realization of the awfulness of regicide than of the viciousness of the choice imposed on Isabella. The instructor of the 1980s faces different difficulties, but not the one described above. Today's undergraduate, acutely conscious of the enormity of the crime of rape, is not likely to see the question as one of new morality. In this respect at least, *Measure for Measure* has improved immeasurably in a short few years; it is, let us say, more relevant than ever it was in the Age of Relevance.

The point of this misleading introduction—to a discussion that is not primarily about *Measure for Measure*—is to suggest that the success or failure of a play, its aesthetic and dramatic goodness or badness, cannot be reliably assessed with reference to the niceties of taste or thought of any individual group or period, because particular preferences and prejudices cause at times whole or partial blindness to essential elements of the play. The assessment should at least depend upon how well and how often the play has positively impressed those exposed to it throughout history. The assessment should also depend not only on the play's capacity to approximate, in whatever way, the unfailingly powerful impact of the never complete *Murder of Gonzago*, but upon its appeal, too, to Hamlet's elitist judges of the caviar of drama.[2]

To appeal to the judiciousness of aesthetic appreciation so prized by Hamlet is not to deny that a drama may be limitless in its suggestiveness; nor is it to deny the validity of whatever response the work of art may evoke in a particular society or audience or individual as it shows each "age and body of the time his form and pressure"; it is, rather, to insist upon the necessity for nonfinite response. Just as a royalist come to see *Julius Caesar* at the Globe in 1599 was challenged to become open to the values of republicanism, the modern playgoer is challenged to be as sensitive to the quandary of Isabella as a Miss Anne Hathaway or a Father Henry Garnet would have been. In its relevance to its audiences a play is a chameleon, infinite, or nearly so, in its variety. But, like a chameleon, it has essential shape as well as accidental shades: the audience that ignores (in the French as well as the English sense of the word) certain historical assumptions embodied in *Measure for Measure* is in Hamlet's sense barren and unskillful, as well as unappreciative of caviar. An important part of the function of our representative instructor is to reveal to those in the classroom the shape of the play and to bring them to an openness to its design that is, in Holofernes' words, generous and humble.[3]

The argument so far depends upon an implicit distinction between play and performance. It associates "play" with that primary artifact, the text or script that is imitated and interpreted in the theater—the performance being a work of art of a different kind. This distinction is necessary to the extent that the play is a literary construct independent of any performance of it: it is the distinction we make when we term a performance of a play delightful or disappointing. The play as text is distinct from whatever production results from the use of the text as scenario.

Once the distinction between play and performance is acknowledged in this way, the student of literature can examine a theatrical performance in the light of its respect for the objective reality of the text. The expression "objective reality of the text" may seem to betray a desire for an absolute interpretation or a standard reading, but it does not necessarily do so. It reflects, instead, the desire to differentiate between the play as something that speaks *to* us and the play as something that speaks *for* us, or for some of us at least. The difference might be indicated by referring to three productions of *Measure for Measure* in three different decades, one directed by Peter Brook in Stratford-upon-Avon in 1950, another by Peter Zadek in Bremen in 1967, and the third by Robin Phillips in Stratford, Ontario, in 1976.

Brook saw the play through the moral philosopher's interpretative lens, emphasizing the centrality of the theme of mercy and giving us a Duke of Vienna benevolent in intention and beneficent in effect.[4] Phillips, taking a far more cynical position, revealed a far less reassuring Vincentio, an unmistakable Duke of Dark Corners.[5] Different as they were, each of these renditions sought to reveal, not remake, the form of the play in a responsible interpretation,[6] one finding its inspiration in the scriptural resonance of the title, the other in the suggestive commentary of Lucio. Each heard the text speak to us differently but in the sense advocated above, each listened respectfully.

Zadek, on the contrary, neither heard nor listened, nor did he wish to. Taking outrageous liberties with the text to express his dissatisfaction with Shakespeare's handling of justice,[7] he accorded himself the rights of *nuovo fabbro*, in Eliot's sense, if not *miglior,* respecting neither poetry nor plot.[8] He gave to Isabella the language of the streets (of his own Bremen, not of her Vienna), to Mistress Overdone the dispensation of ironic justice (though that is hardly the word for it), and to Angelo the fate that he himself invites when he offers to let his own judgment pattern out his death (1.4.29–30). In contrast with Brook and Phillips and in a different sense unlike that devious interpolator Hamlet, Zadek did not imitate or interpret the play; he designedly abused it, thereby effectively making two statements: first, the declaration that Shakespeare's play is not worth our attention because it disagrees with our values; second, the indirect articulation of the principles, as well as the direct parody of the practices, of those who fail or refuse to allow the text to address us, and who see it, anyway, as ours rather than Shakespeare's.

An appeal for a theatrical performance that reflects a proper respect for the objective reality of the text would be naive if it were based on an assumption about the text as monolithic, unchanging, perfected. One does not need to be reminded of how markedly *Lear* challenges the textual critic, not to mention the editor or director, to recognize the innocence of such an assumption. There is no Shakespearean text that is not problematic. The evidence of revision in *Love's Labor Lost* alone[9] should convince us that Shakespeare, as a man of the theater, may have had habits similar to those of our contemporary Simon Gray, whose norm, if it exists, appears to be a commitment to rewriting for production, not a striving toward an ideally stabilized text.[10]

There is a difference, however, between the demand for the impossible, an unavailable perfected text, and the demand for the possible, an honest imitation on the stage of as good a text as scholarship in our day can make available. A demand for the latter can hardly be unreasonable at a time when the Shakespeare industry is thriving in part because people get to know the plays in the study and in the classroom and, often, attend a theatrical presentation in order to witness a fresh reading of a familiar text. The same demand can be defended also on the grounds that our "honest" representation of the text may alert us to dramatic deficiencies in the primary work of art that are so essential as to present perennial problems to the interpreter on the stage and in the study.

What are we to say of a play that consistently undermines the best efforts of the actor and consistently disappoints the expectations of the audience? Let us suppose an audience patient and educated, with what I have termed a desirable openness to the play's informing assumptions; let us also suppose a production that is an ideal one in the sense that it provides a full and intelligent translation of page to stage by skillful and skillfully directed actors; then let us suppose that the audience is to some extent unmoved, displeased, even bored. In such a case, might we not conclude that the failure may lie in the very form of the play, not in the audience or the interpretation? If an appeal to the history of the performance of the play—including performances of texts submitted to the pruning or grafting of various theatrical gardeners—results in evidence of inevitable failure, then ought we not to conclude that the failure must lie in the text? In such a case it should be possible to discover and identify an aesthetic or dramatic flaw that constitutes the failure in design. Such a flaw, were it to exist in a Shakespearean text, would be the reality that justifies the term "bad Shakespeare."

Thoughts about "bad Shakespeare" must occur to the audience of *Timon of Athens*, whether or not the production approximates to a great degree the ideal rendition we have imagined. They must have occurred often throughout the centuries.[11] They certainly occurred to playgoers such as myself when the Grand Theatre Company of London, Ontario, opened its repertory season in September 1983 with a critically acclaimed rendition of the play, one that won from its admirers praise for the achievement of the players rather than of the playwright, praise for the daring of the director, not the good judgment.

If it were true that, as one opening night critic put it, *Timon of Athens* is that kind of "Shakespeare that no one in their right mind would handle,"[12] it would be well to identify the source of the difficulty. Without making any claims for an ideal rendition or an ideal audience, it must be acknowledged that the director, Robin Phillips, and a goodly number of the company, including William Hutt, who played Timon, had already accumulated a wealth of experience in staging Shakespeare at the Stratford Festival and elsewhere. The audience could accurately enough be

described as Stratford regulars, hence, people capable of responding to a
difficult, even demanding, play without manifesting the fickleness of
Timon's fair-weather friends. Even so, the program notes to this con-
fessedly "strangely atypical"[13] play subtly invited patience, referring to
Timon as puzzling for scholars, pointing to the sketchiness of the Alcibiades story, mentioning several scenes that are short and seemingly
hastily drawn, and implicitly lamenting a well-nigh Cyclopean intensity
of focus in Shakespeare's concentration on the hero's mounting disillusionment. But this pleading may have had as much of the muted boast as
the overt apologia about it, for everything about the production suggested a confidence in it as an interpretation of *Timon* that had solved
many problems.

   Phillips, perhaps not surprisingly, set the scene in the Edwardian
period (he had done the same for *Measure for Measure*)—a decision that
underlined Shakespeare's "ability to speak to us across the centuries,"[14]
that gave to the Athenians the myopic self-confidence of a lavish, dec-
adent, and doomed pre-War Europe, and that provided for a display of
imperial opulence that spectacularly exploited the period suggestiveness
of a restored century-old proscenium arch stage. Here was an Athens
where Timon first appeared in velvet smoking jacket and through which
Alcibiades strutted in jodhpurs. Here white-tie banquets were lavish
with silver and crystal, giving ironic suggestiveness to Cenacolo-group-
ings of diners entertained by fin de siècle trollop and finocchio in a
cavorting banquet of sense. Here, in the primping and pummeling
comfort of a men's-club steam room, sycophants-turned-creditors talked
of the embarrassment of a strapped Timon. Here Apemantus appeared
as a tweedy photographer whose candid snapshots told of more than
painter-poet dialogue ever touches. The setting for the second act of this
production (4.3 and 5.1 in the text) was a stark and white waste, fea-
tureless but for a grim tree and the trapdoor pit in which Misanthropos
dug and railed. This echoed not only with the sound of fife and drum at
Alcibiades' approach, but with that of hunting horn—suggested by the
beagle and beast of prey images and allusions—and so recalled another
hunting scene in another wood outside another Athens where hope and
blessing and restoration were not so remote as here.

   Whatever compromises with the text this extravagantly visual production may have made in costuming and setting, it made few others.
Phillips decided to have confidence in the poetry, even if this meant an
offering of no quarter to the audience: we were exposed to the undiluted
acidity of all that is negative and brutal in the play. One effect of that
decision was to reveal that certain inconsistencies and irregularities of
this not quite complete and not quite uncorrupt text are not problematic
for the audience. The problem in the first three acts of "five" or "fifty" or

"five hundred" or merely "so many" talents faded in a world of uncertain opinion and report. The irregular prose, rhyme, and blank-verse sequence of Apemantus in act 1, scene 2 seemed part of the infinite variety of a for-the-nonce Menippean satirist. The problems in lineation in act 3, scene 5 were dealt with as a rude-am-I-in-my-speech limitation of an Alcibiades, who, unused to suing, cannot but speak "like a captain" (3.5.41), and those of Flavius's farewell speech in act 4, scene 2, as the vocal irregularities that occur when the spontaneities of deep feeling jostle with the banalities of formal utterance. In short, what seems an artistic defect in the study did not necessarily appear one in the theater. This was especially true of Hutt's passionate rendering of the "All's obliquy" tirade (4.3), where the handling of syllabic irregularity and truncated lines gave no hint that the verse cries out for a reviser's hand. Finally, even the problem of the contradictory epitaphs explained itself away when the line "our captain hath in every figure skill" (5.3.7) became the suggestive basis for a second reading of the epitaph (5.4.70): the new version could conceivably have been the result of editorial intervention by "our captain."

Two other defects apparent to editors of school texts became unimportant, one the question of tragic vision—Is Timon truly tragic?—the other the question of design—Is the Alcibiades story too incomplete to be satisfactory, the relationship of Alcibiades to Timon too unclear?

Hutt's Timon appeared from the start as the absolutist whose intemperate optimism and immoderate generosity betray an obliviousness to his own creaturehood and an attendant presumption of godly transcendence of the limitations of creaturehood. The naiveté of Timon, thus interpreted, is no more improbable than Lear's and no more risible than Othello's; it has in it an idealism and confidence, the underside of whose coin is the stubbornness and pride of the egomaniac: unwisely *and* ignobly hath he given, alas. The exposure of the invalidity of his hubristic certainties causes titanic resentment whose basis is the terror of unaccustomed doubt and the shock of undermined pride. The Brobdingnagian energy of Timon's rejection of "detested parasites" in the second banquet scene most clearly echoed that (3.6.88–105). One saw that the protagonist's incapacity for compromise and consequent resentment at a world of circumstance that defies, denies, and mocks his expectations is the very stuff of the tragic, the stuff that makes for endurance to the utterance. In a world whose faithful (and rejected) Flavius is nothing in comparison with a rediscovered Cordelia, a vindicated Desdemona, or a reassuring "special providence," Hutt's Timon penetrated to the heart of darkness and found only darkness.

The sketchiness of the Alcibiades action did not seem to constitute a problem either. As played by Maurice Good, Alcibiades represented the heroic option unavailable to Timon. This Alcibiades, polo player as well as womanizer, had about him the charismatic dash of a Hotspur and the intellectual depth of a Fortinbras, but, finally, something of the good sense of a Hal.

According to such an interpretation, Alcibiades knows no world of absolutes, no realm of angst: sensualist, pragmatist, civil not servile, man of deeds rather than of gestures, rationalist rather than idealist, he answers betrayal with swords, not words, makes honor his chief good and thus escapes the disillusionment that senatorial ingratitude might have wrought. Inhabitant of a world whose reality is Aristotelian and whose virtue too is Aristotelian, he can effect that compromise that saves Athens not only from his own vindictive destruction but from the idea of Athens that loomed so large and so absolute in the mind of crazed and cursing Timon.

This was a production that recognized in the formalized discussion of poet and painter a key to the ritual of a play whose grand design seems complete. In this production, as so often in others, Phillips's blocking had in it much of the liturgical and much stately formality and restraint, especially in act 1, scene 1 and act 4, scene 3. In these, the introductory scenes of the two major movements, the structural principle is a succession of formal dialogues between a constant figure and others who interact seriatim with him. Watching them, one had the sense of pageantry more than drama, of thematic explication more than the buildup of action to a crisis. By revealing the implicit principle, this production may also have revealed an explicit problem.

The successes of that 1983 production have been stressed for two reasons: first, to suggest that minor problems, while they may be problems, do not necessarily make for bad theater, since the actor's craft can provide an elision of defect, if there is defect; second, to suggest that although a play can be informed, in part or whole, by an erroneous assumption of theatrical viability, such an assumption may be so erroneous that no felicitous inventions of director and player can remedy the text while honestly interpreting it. This may be the reason why—to return to the audience at The Grand Theatre—the history of Timon's popularity during the 1983 repertory season was the history of declining numbers—so shrunken ultimately that seats in the balcony and side aisles were, by the cunning of the computer, made out of bounds, so that the poor devils on the stage might have some sense of a crowd to play to. What is more, even a Bardolater could not regret the absence of those who stayed away, for they were, wittingly or not, avoiding the theater of frustration. Phillips's pageantry caught only too well the deliberate style of the play; one had to conclude, sadly, that the production exposed the play's defects even as it embodied the play's vision.

Though the design of the first three acts of *Timon of Athens* is clear and well-realized, that part of the play fails to move us. The prime cause of failure may be this: that the ideal that Timon relies on and the failure or denial of that ideal lack the essential, familiar symbols (flesh-and-blood correlatives to the ideal) that Shakespeare provides in other tragedies—for example, the Hyperion of Hamlet's prelapsarian perfection, the predictable daughters of Lear's untroubled past, the meek and just kinsman-king of Macbeth's "Duncan" days, and the Desdemona in whom Othello finds and loses and rediscovers the real embodiment of his ideal assumption. Timon is the unavailing, resentful defender of an indefensibly romantic thesis that has no close human symbol. We respond more intellectually than feelingly to his predicament: we sympathize, paradoxically, with an abstraction.

If one major flaw in the design of *Timon and Athens* is thematic abstraction that too seldom is feelingly realized, another is its tone, in fact its monotony. Act 4, scene 3, with its more than five hundred lines, provides a good example. There Timon in cursing monologue and cursing dialogue rails against defective nature, relying invectively and repetitively on images of materialism, animality, disease, and license, directing his barbs at the too generalized target of ungrateful man (4.3.188). He lacks, and we need, a localized and vital symbol worthy of opprobrium. Neither Alcibiades nor the whores have done him wrong. Here we find no adulterous Gertrude or painted Ophelia, no fiendish Goneril or Regan, no triple-turned whore as incarnation of the idea of betrayal, corruption, and loss. The unrelenting intensity of the rhetoric, the extremism of the despair, and the predictability of Timon's attitude, utterance, and tone to all his visitors have in them that little more than a little that is by much too much—and we may well wonder whether the shocked response of the banditti (4.3.451–53) might not be, like Miranda's little snooze, a device to syphon off, and yet validate, the resentment or the boredom of the theatergoer exposed to too much "exceptless rashness" (4.3.495). Admittedly, the encounter with and rejection of the "singly honest" steward (4.3.523) can deeply affect us, but Flavius's sentiments are a long-awaited respite from unflagging satiric excess. Timon has too long been too constant in his obsession, too savage in his tone, too unchanging.

If *Timon of Athens* provides significant, unusual evidence of fallibility on the part of Shakespeare, it does so by revealing that if a scene is designed to be expository and the ideas presented in it are borne by but not embodied in dramatis personae, then the scene fails dramatically: however effectively it may enlighten us intellectually, it does not affect us at the visceral level. Prospero's recital of the background to the action of *The Tempest* (1.2) provides an obvious example, though there the use of narrative compounds the dramatic problem. Act 4, scene 3 of *Timon* is a simpler instance. In that scene, Timon's visitors are no more than wan exempla of evil, especially for those of us who find the idea of evil compelling when it takes the individualized form of a fratricidal Claudius, an insinuating Iago, a memory-banishing Macbeth, or even a conspiratorial Antonio. *Timon of Athens* provides no dearth of evidence of what could be considered imperfect dramatic decision making, evidence that Shakespeare may occasionally nod. However vehemently the Bardolater may refuse to acknowledge the defect, this play proves one thing at least: that scenes dramatizing a stasis of conviction, as opposed to the dynamism of growth, can—if they are extensive, especially—lull the audience into an indifference that has nothing to do with whatever Aristotle meant by catharsis.

Notes

1. *Measure for Measure* 2.4.150, in *The Riverside Shakespeare*, ed. G. Blakemore Evans (Boston: Houghton Mifflin, 1974). All subsequent references to this play and others are to the Riverside edition and are to act and scene, or act, scene, and line, as appropriate.

2. *Hamlet* 2.2.435–45 and 3.2.22–24. It must be acknowledged that in Hamlet's "the play's the thing" (2.2.604) there is no such fine distinction as I make later on between text and theater. The performance of a scenario, complete with interpolations, is to move Claudius. Hamlet's purposes are those of detective; he abuses the text accordingly.

3. *Love's Labour's Lost* 5.2.629.

4. Peter Brook in *The Empty Space* (Harmondsworth, Eng.: Penguin Books, 1972), 100, gives the impression that the 1950 production was indebted to G. Wilson Knight's "*Measure for Measure* and the Gospels." Interestingly, a new edition of *The Wheel of Fire* had appeared in 1949. Phillips may have been influenced by Anne Barton's preface in *The Riverside Shakespeare* (545–49), which had been published shortly before his production.

5. An example of this: in act 4, scene 1, the text was not disturbed, but shared chuckles and shared sherry were interpretive additions that led the audience to wonder what, beyond giving "advice," the "man of comfort" may have done to still Mariana's "brawling discontent."

6. See Richard David, *Shakespeare in the Theatre* (Cambridge: Cambridge University Press, 1978). There Brook is praised for having "the inventiveness (without the irresponsibility) of Guthrie" in his seeking "to penetrate the innermost intention of the dramatist" (65).

7. This account is indebted to Wilhelm Hortmann's discussion of iconoclastic Shakespeare productions at the "Shakespeare in Germany" session of The World Shakespeare Congress, Berlin, April 1986.

8. Zadek's outrageous liberties are nothing new, of course. Gamini Salgado notes that adaptations by Davenant and Gildon held the stage from the Restoration until Mrs. Siddons played Isabella in 1738. See his *Eyewitnesses of Shakespeare: First Hand Accounts of Performances 1590–1890* (London: Sussex University Press, 1975), 216. See also George C. D. Odell, *Shakespeare from Betterton to Irving* (New York: Charles Scribner's Sons, 1920), both volumes.

9. For example, Berowne's apologia for vow breaking, 4.3.285–362.

10. The differences between the text of *The Common Pursuit* (London and New York: Methuen, 1984), published to coincide with the Hammersmith premiere, and the as yet

unpublished text for the 1986 Broadway production provide interesting evidence of the relativity of the Gray text to its performance context.

11. *Timon* has a remarkable history of disappointing performances. See Gary Jay Williams, "Stage History, 1816–1978," published as an appendix in Rolf Soellner's *Timon of Athens: Shakespeare's Pessimistic Tragedy* (Columbus: Ohio State University Press, 1979), 161–85.

12. Ray Conlogue, the Toronto *Globe and Mail*, 26 September 1983.

13. *"Timon of Athens:* The Story," in The Grand Theatre Company, program, vol. 1, no. 4.

14. Ibid.

"To Reform and Make Fitt"

Henry VIII *and the Making of "Bad" Shakespeare*

ISKA ALTER

THE NOTION THAT there exists "bad" Shakespeare is a valuable conceit for numerous reasons. Not only does it deflate the sentimentalized, unthinking Bardolatry that remains a cultural legacy from past centuries; not only does it challenge the belief in a permanent judgmental hierarchy that neatly defines and places the great man's work as each theatrical and scholarly generation necessarily reconsiders the critical sureties of its predecessors; but it also, and finally, undermines the concept of canonical acceptability by forcing those connected with the Shakespeare industry back to the text and its theatrical representations in order to understand both how and if any given play works. It is especially appropriate to remember this implicit interrogatory function in any examination of *Henry VIII,* Shakespeare's last, equivocal effort in what was surely a dying genre.

Although *Henry VIII* was performed and revived with surprising frequency throughout the eighteenth and nineteenth centuries, the play's reputation becomes increasingly tarnished throughout this period, resulting, by the late twentieth century, in the somewhat cavalier dismissal of the work's critical significance and theatrical effectiveness. What accounts for its relative rarity in performance as well as in scholarly discussion, compared with other late plays such as *The Winter's Tale* and *The Tempest*?[1] The "badness" of *Henry VIII* grows out of the confluence of several troublesome factors: the complex interpretive problems of a history play so nearly contemporaneous with its audience's experience; the question of authorship; the changing assumptions of what constitutes valid dramatic action; a problematic definition of the historical process; and a restrictive generic definition of the form itself.

I

Unlike the earlier tetralogies, *Henry VIII* does not focus on the violent politics of legitimacy or on the disruptive pressures of external threat.

From Norfolk's gilded description of Henry and Francis clinging "In their embracement, as they grew together" (1.1.10–11) on the Field of the Cloth of Gold to Cranmer's projective golden age of individual self-sufficiency, the play seems to operate in the realm of redemptive history. But although these selected actions and events of Henry's reign are directed toward the creation of a visionary utopian conclusion, the audience is constantly reminded that England is still a kingdom riddled with betrayal, greed, ambition, deceit, and the arbitrary exercise of authority. Unlike the earlier tetralogies, *Henry VIII* possesses no clear-cut heroes or obvious villains, thereby dispersing dramatic energy throughout the play rather than concentrating attention on singular controlling figures or on a primary dyadic conflict. Unlike the earlier tetralogies, *Henry VIII* is concerned with the details of internal governance (hardly the most vivid matter for performance) rather than with the grand or grandiose posturings of battle.

These uncomfortable, seemingly distracting, perhaps even disintegrative tensions within a work presumably dedicated to peace, continuity, and regenerative power (or so most critics have maintained)[2] produce a play more ambiguous in its impressions and more intricate in its effects than heretofore realized. Much of this recovered complexity would appear to be the result of the interaction among the text as presented by Shakespeare (and his possible collaborators), the relative contemporaneity of the depicted historical situation, and the consequential awareness possessed by the playwright(s) and audience alike. Indeed, the questions of interpretation that transform *Henry VIII* from a disappointment (that is, "bad" Shakespeare) to a challenge (possibly "better" Shakespeare) reach into the generic heart of the history play.

1. How can historical villainy be defined and then portrayed, if there is to be such a force operating in the play? Is Wolsey a wicked counterfoil to Henry's legitimate apprehensions about the kingdom or is he a curious kind of scapegoat for those actions that are actually Henry's wrongdoings? The Cardinal is accused by Katherine of being responsible for her disgrace; yet his own fall is partially attributed to his reluctance to prosecute the required divorce. Wolsey is the vauntingly ambitious and exploiting son of an Ipswich butcher greedy for wealth as well as secular power who embraces his fall. It is ironic and poignant that only in death can his virtues be described and extolled by Griffiths, and even grudgingly acknowledged by the dying Katherine.

2. What should be the response to Katherine of Aragon? Is it possible to remain sympathetic to her position as fallen queen (as the audience is surely meant to be), while accepting the fact that if England's Golden Age is to occur with Elizabeth's birth, Katherine must be treated with a

harshness amounting to cruelty in a way that seems justified and/or dramatically sound?

3. How should Anne Bullen be presented? That she is Elizabeth's mother demands that she be depicted as a circumspect woman of purpose, beauty, and honor, although the audience would have known her for the morally ambiguous figure history has proven her to be.

4. How does one create an effective portrait of Henry, the play's presumed center of power, a king who must be appropriately regal, but who cannot be too aggressive, lest he lose the sympathy of the audience in his treatment of Katherine and their respect in his pursuit of Anne Bullen, and who is finally left on stage to be remembered only as Elizabeth's father? The audience's familiarity with the equivocal nature of the king's later reign would have made such a portrait problematic.

5. How should Cranmer's resonant prophesy be regarded? The audience would have lived through the anxious years before Elizabeth's death, an experience that might have darkened their appreciation of all promised utopias. And would the audience have seen the disjuncture between Cranmer's words, Elizabeth's administration, and James's rule?

In its radically different exploration of historical processes, in its manipulation of the audience's educated anticipation of what is to come, *Henry VIII* is, at the very least, a more interesting play than criticism has allowed. But factors other than critical interpretation and appraisal have determined the status of this play.

II

Doubts about authorship began in the mid–eighteenth century with the suspicions of Roderick, Johnson, and Farmer[3] (perhaps as one of the consequences of the developing Shakespeare Bardolatry). The doubts became assertions in the nineteenth-century claims of Spedding, Hickson, and Dowden, among others.[4] They find further validation in the "scientific" investigations of Partridge, Farnham, Waith, and Mincoff,[5] until Cyrus Hoy's good sense seems to settle the matter.

> The truth about Fletcher's share in *Henry VIII* is to be found where truth generally is: midway between the extreme views that have traditionally been held regarding it. Those who would deny his presence in the play altogether are wrong to do so, for he is assuredly there. Those who award him ten and one-half of the play's sixteen scenes (the usual ascription) claim too much.[6]

However, I am not especially interested in once again rehashing the old arguments about who is responsible for what in *Henry VIII*. Certainly the scholarly energy that has been expended in the attempt to solve this particular problem has often obscured the questions of meaning, character, and genre that the play does, in fact, raise. But I am concerned with the context within which Spedding, Hickson, and Dowden worked as they tried to demonstrate that Shakespeare was not "the onlie begetter" of this, his last history play. For it is this context of justification that proves to be one of the major determinants in creating the "bad" play of *Henry VIII*.

By 1850 adoration of the Bard had become very much a part of English culture. Just as Shakespeare was viewed as the paradigmatic artist, so too was his work perceived to be the very model of aesthetic achievement. Not surprisingly, what constituted the perfection of his art was defined by Victorian literary standards, and what shaped dramatic response was Victorian theatrical convention. Given the values that Shakespeare was believed to embody for nineteenth-century English society in all its verities, it is no wonder that Spedding saw in *Henry VIII* imperfection, incoherence, and inconsistency:

> The effect of the play *as a whole* is weak and disappointing. The truth is that the interest instead of rising towards the end, falls away utterly, and leaves us in the last act among persons whom we scarcely know and events for which we do not care. The strongest sympathies which have been awakened in us run opposite to the course of the action.[7]

Accepting the play as flawed, unwilling or unable to examine the premises underlying its assumed discontinuities, Spedding, like numerous Victorian scholar-critics, chooses the idea of dual authorship to interpret the play's seeming anomalies. Rather two authors, one of whom is clearly less able, than a deficient or inadequate Shakespeare. By acknowledging two (or perhaps three) contributors to the making of *Henry VIII*, Spedding can therefore reject those portions of the work that he deems unnecessary or irrelevant to carry out the dramatic possibilities, as does Dowden—"The fifth act, for one who has been deeply interested in the story of the Cardinal, is an artistic impertinence"[8]—and even Odell:

> The trouble with *Henry VIII* is that it is impossible to maintain interest in its story after the fall of Wolsey and the death of Katherine; the bits about the christening of Elizabeth and the trial of Cranmer are actually glued on the first part in order to eke out the necessary five acts. Irving and Tree realised this fact, and cut away most of the unnecessary appendages.[9]

It is suitably ironic, of course, that the rationalization of stage adaption provided by this scholarly concept of dual authorship creates precisely

the kind of fragmented, disorderly, and unfocused play condemned by
these very same scholars.

In addition to serving as justification for a slash-and-burn definition of
the editorial process, the Victorian notion of theatrical collaboration,
which carried well into twentieth-century judgments about *Henry VIII*,
presupposes that multiple authors are unable to contrive unified drama.
Says Dowden of the play he believes written by Shakespeare and
Fletcher: "It has . . . no dramatic centre; no ascent, no culmination, no
subsidence. The tragedy of Buckingham is succeeded by the tragedy of
Wolsey, and this by the tragedy of Queen Katherine; then the play closes
with triumph and rejoicings."[10] As Dowden's narrow view of dramatic
unity indicates, the Victorians had little comprehension, and even less
sympathy, with what Jonas Barish sees to be the essential nature of
Renaissance theatrical experience:

> Through repetition, through simultaneity, through its insistence on
> doing everything at once, it tried to keep us in touch not with a limited
> and local reality but with the totality—with everything that is, every-
> thing that has been, and everything that can be imagined to be all at
> one and the same time.[11]

It is this culturally qualified understanding of the ways in which
Elizabethan and Jacobean theater practice manipulated the explosive and
manifold dramatic energies of the period that so predisposes the nineteenth-century scholar-critic toward the formulation of a disintegration
theory of collaboration. Such a theory, along with a concurrent belief in
tragic providentiality as the sole constituent of the generic history play,
become the means (or the excuse) for denouncing *Henry VIII* as a failure,
without confronting the necessity of actually examining the strategies
used in making the play.

III

Although there can be no doubt that the efforts of the Victorian
scholar-critics have been crucial in establishing the criteria by which we
may misjudge the play, the stage history of *Henry VIII* has been an
equally important force in conditioning our responses. An examination
of that history as well as of the performance practices associated with the
work throughout the late eighteenth, nineteenth, and even twentieth
centuries reveals the extent to which they not only reinforce certain of
the negative critical judgments but also offer new grounds upon which
to perpetuate what I believe to be a wrongful assessment of the drama.

Given the infrequency with which *Henry VIII* is performed in our
century, its relative popularity in earlier periods seems unexpected to

say the least, raising inevitable questions about what factors ultimately determine the ongoing theatrical vitality of plays within the canon. In the first half of the eighteenth century, surely a low point in the history of Shakespeare production, *Henry VIII* was the tenth most popular Shakespearean play to be staged in London, exceeding in favor such stalwarts as *Romeo and Juliet* (believe it or not), *As You Like It*, and *Henry V*.[12] By 1751–1800, it had dropped to thirteenth, but it still remained more popular than *Twelfth Night*, *A Midsummer Night's Dream*, and *Julius Caesar*, among some surprising others.[13] Throughout the nineteenth century, it was often revived to serve as a major vehicle for every prominent actor and actress from Macready and Edmond Kean (whose singularly unsuccessful Wolsey netted only £60) to Irving and Beer-bohm-Tree, and from Sarah Siddons to Ellen Terry. Charles Kean's revival in midcentury ran for 100 performances,[14] the first Shakespeare play to do so, while Irving's costly, extravagant *Henry VIII* (1892) continued for 172 performances[15] (an astonishing figure considering the usual length of a Shakespearean run during most times, including ours).

The continued viability of *Henry VIII* as an effective theater property, even when its underlying design was becoming increasingly incomprehensible to the nineteenth-century critic, scholar, and audience, can be attributed to two features: the opportunity the play gives for festive ceremony and the availability of two powerful acting roles. These elements are invariably strengthened by almost all adaptations prepared for the stage, distorting text, structure, and meaning.

Beginning with the play's first reappearance on the stage after the Restoration under the aegis of William Davenant (and we all know with what care he treated the Shakespearean script), most productions of *Henry VIII* have been occasions for lavish pageantry; indeed, the purpose seems to be defined by this celebratory function. Of this production, Pepys, superior to the material as usual, observes, "Though I went with resolution to like it, it is so simple a thing made up of a great many patches, that, besides the shows and the processions in it, there is nothing in the world good or well done."[16] Mrs. Katharine Philips, in a letter of 22 January 1664, criticizes the effects of these shows and processions: "They say Harry the 8th and some later ones are little better than puppet plays and will therefore be likely to please the citizen's wives."[17]

Colley Cibber appeared in a version of *Henry VIII* commemorating the coronation of George II that was filled (perhaps overfilled) with additional spectacle in order to crowd the theater:

> *Henry VIII* owed its success primarily to the pantomime coronation ceremony in Act IV, which was made to resemble as closely as possible the real ceremony which had just taken place in Westminster Abbey, and indeed the imitation seems to have been scarcely less impressive

than the original. Choir boys and privy councillors, aldermen and knights of the garter, earls, dukes, and bishops followed one another over the stage, and finally in regal robes the queen herself. . . . the play proved so popular that the managers were soon encouraged to provide it with "additional decorations" and to add a second interlude in pantomime—"The Ceremony of the Champion in Westminster Hall," for which it is said, they borrowed armor from the Tower.[18]

Garrick's *Henry* was "selected as a vehicle for costly expenditure";[19] Kemble's, containing a banquet scene of such elegance that it was reviewed as "the most dazzling stage exhibition . . . ever seen";[20] Kean's, infused with "much greater . . . pomp and pageantry, an increased gorgeousness of detail";[21] Irving's exhibition, costing £11,879 1s. 10d.[22]— each revival more prodigal in its expenditure than its predecessor. Even the twentieth-century presentations of the play emphasize the spectacular, whether it be the richness of Lewis Casson's debt to Holbein or the eccentric splendor of Terence Gray's avant-garde vision:

> *Henry VIII*, which was . . . the most satisfactory of all his Shakespearean productions, was played on a set of great beauty and dignity consisting simply of a tremendous aluminium ramp rising steeply in a great curve until it vanished out of sight high above the stage. The actors, dressed in formalised costumes suggesting the court figures in a pack of cards, made their entrance from above, down the ramp. The constantly changing lighting, glowing on the aluminium, was of extraordinary beauty and effectiveness, heightening the different moods of the play like an accompaniment of incidental music.[23]

And in the 1930s, Margaret Webster directed an elaborate amateur pageant-production of the work with the entire cast of 800 present at the concluding baptism.[24]

No one would deny the relevance of pageantry to the play's significance. But it is neither the central concern nor the complete context fashioning the dramatic action. Nor should it be, whatever the performance tradition might demand. Scenes illustrating the public forms of royal power mingle with more private, less open scenes of political intrigue, individuated emotion, personal decline, and spiritual renewal. This complex interaction of public and private behavioral realms often undercuts the apparent control exercised by figures of authority, creating a version of history (and the history play) that effectively mitigates against the role of villainy as a permanent force in the historical process. However, when the various adaptations of the text used for theatrical production insist upon excessive display, as they so often do, while eliminating the representation of alternative events and modes of conduct, it becomes virtually impossible to see and understand the "good" play of *Henry VIII*.

IV

R. A. Foakes, in his introduction to the New Arden edition of *Henry VIII*, rightly notes that critics have focused their attention on the superb acting roles of Katherine and Wolsey at the expense of a more thorough examination of other aspects of the play.[25] But I wonder if this observation, accurate though it is, does not put the critical cart before the theatrical horse. This emphasis, effectively simplifying both the content and the context of the drama, seems as much a result of choices made in the theater for the purposes of performance by actors, managers, and the editors of stage adaptations as it is of scholarly study. Such choices are further reinforced and justified by a theory of acting as a series of star turns, by a vision of the history play as providential tragedy concerned with the moral and spiritual consequences of the fall of the eminent, and by a concept of history as a process shaped by the conduct of great men.

That the political dimensions of *Henry VIII* should have proved attractive to the unsentimental audiences of the post-Restoration period can hardly seem surprising. Actors such as Betterton, Booth, and Quin were drawn to the role of Henry, a monarch who learns the value, power, and necessity of intrigue during the course of the play that bears his name, not to the emotional melodrama that is inherent in Wolsey's fall. Indeed, the preferred image of the Cardinal is that of a scheming politician, as Colley Cibber remarks:

> The Solicitude of the Spiritual Minister, in filching from his Master the Grace, and Merit of a good Action, and dressing up himself in it, while himself had been Author of the Evil complain'd of, was so easy a Stroke of his Temporal Conscience, that it seem'd to raise the King into something more than a Smile, whenever that Play came before him.[26]

However, beginning in the 1730s (when a Dublin edition of the text was entitled *King Henry VIII. A TRAGEDY.*),[27] each successive adaptation down through Irving's version strips away any language that might suggest the complexity of behavior, of motive, and of interaction that this revisionary history does, in fact, possess. This consistent pattern of editing radically diminishes the importance of Henry, and forces audiences increasingly susceptible to sentimentality to suffer the pathos of the play's multiple falls. By the nineteenth century, when tragedy had become the highest form of dramatic experience, the play belonged to Wolsey and Katharine and the actors who played those roles, notwithstanding the fact that Henry, the Cardinal, and the Queen have approximately the same number of lines.[28] The fifth act, whose troublesome politics is both incomprehensible and irrelevant to Victorian notions of theatrical decorum and historical acceptability, was frequently reduced to the ennobling pageantry of Elizabeth's christening in productions from Kemble's to Beerbohm-Tree's. There even exists a three-act truncation, apparently acted, that ends with Wolsey's fall.[29] As Odell asserts with bland but infuriating arrogance:

> Shakespeare's historical plays . . . sadly lack unity; the Elizabethans felt that they must honestly pack in every episode of importance in the life of the King who gave the title to the play. Henry VIII suffers particularly under this weakness, and he would be a rash purist who would insist on the preservation on the stage of all the material of the last two acts. Undoubtedly the dramatic interest ceases with the death of Queen Katharine.[30]

With the reconsideration of the playwright's last plays and a reawakened interest in the content and generic design of the histories—facts of twentieth-century Shakespeare studies—the "bad" *Henry VIII* has given way to a more measured consideration of the work's merits. Nevertheless, there continues to operate among numerous scholars and critics a not unexpected presumption that the problems that have conditioned the responses to the play are embedded in the problematics of a written, collaborative text: questions related to characters, structure, and language. I contend that many of the difficulties that we have come to regard as inherent are, rather, theatrical constructs, created by the requirements of an older, culturally determined idea about what constituted effective and appropriate dramatic action. It is worth noting that when *Henry VIII* is reconceived for a medium such as television that by its very nature controls the scope of the spectacular and constrains the excesses of the star performance, as in the recent BBC version, the play can be seen "new." It challenges and provokes, as good theater must, reminding us that it is "a play for genuine teamwork, demanding a number of first-rate players, not rival stars and still less 'one bright star' . . . not an historical adaptation with a strict eye to the main theatrical chance."[32] This essay then becomes a plea for the further exploration of the extent to which theatrical tradition and performance history shape what we have previously assumed to be the intrinsic meanings of a particular play.

Notes

1. In the last ten years or so, *Henry VIII* has been subject to increasing scrutiny. Among the more provocative essays are Lee Bliss, "The Wheel of Fortune and the Maiden Phoenix of Shakespeare's *King Henry the Eighth*," *ELH* 42 (1975): 1–25; Frederick O. Waage, Jr., "*Henry VIII* and the Crisis of the English History Play," *Shakespeare Studies* 8 (1975): 297–309; Frank V. Cespedes, " 'We are one in fortunes': The Sense of History in *Henry VIII*," *English Literary Renaissance* 10 (1980): 413–38; and Alexander Leggatt, "*Henry VIII* and the Ideal England," *Shakespeare Survey* 38 (1985): 131–43.

2. Among the most eloquent and articulate presentations of the redemptive idea in *Henry VIII* are G. Wilson Knight, *"Henry VIII* and the Poetry of Conversion," in *The Crown of Life: Essays in Interpretation of Shakespeare's Final Plays* (1947; reprint, New York: Barnes & Noble, 1965); and Frank Kermode, "What Is Shakespeare's *Henry VIII* About?" in *Shakespeare: The Histories*, ed. Eugene M. Waith (Englewood Cliffs, N.J.: Prentice-Hall, 1965), 168–175; originally published in 1948.

3. For an excellent summary of the scholarship down through Cyrus Hoy's work, see the annotated bibliography in *Evidence for Authorship: Essays on the Problems of Authorship*, ed. David V. Erdman and Ephim G. Fogel (Ithaca, N.Y.: Cornell University Press, 1966), 457–78. Information on the attitudes of eighteenth-century scholars and critics appears on 458–60. R. A. Foakes's Introduction to the New Arden edition of *Henry VIII* (London: Methuen, 1964), pp. xv–xxviii, also contains much material on the problems of authorship.

4. Erdman and Fogel, *Evidence for Authorship*, 460–66.

5. Ibid., 467–78.

6. Quoted by Foakes, Introduction, pp. xxvii–xxviii.

7. J. Spedding, "Who Wrote Shakespeare's *Henry VIII?" Gentleman's Magazine* 178 (Aug.–Oct. 1850): 116.

8. Quoted by C. K. Pooler in his Introduction to the 1915 Arden edition of *Henry VIII*, pp. xix–xx.

9. G. C. D. Odell, *Shakespeare from Betterton to Irving*, 2 vols. (New York: Scribner's, 1920; London: Constable, 1963), 2:43–44.

10. Quoted by Pooler, Introduction, p. xix.

11. Jonas Barish, "The Uniqueness of Elizabethan Drama," in *Drama in the Renaissance: Comparative and Critical Essays*, ed. Clifford Davidson, C. J. Gianakaris, and John H. Stroupe (New York: AMS Press, 1986), 9; originally published in 1977.

12. These statistics appear in Charles Beecher Hogan, *Shakespeare in the Theatre, 1701–1800* (Oxford: Clarendon Press, 1952), 1:459–60.

13. Ibid., 2:715–19.

14. John William Cole, *The Life and Theatrical Times of Charles Kean, F.S.A.* (London: Richard Bentley, 1859), 140.

15. William Winter, *Shakespeare on the Stage*, First Series, 1911; reprint (New York: Benjamin Blom, 1969), 546.

16. Quoted by Hazelton Spencer, *Shakespeare Improved: The Restoration Versions In Quarto and On the Stage* (1927; reprint, New York: Frederick Ungar, 1963), 76.

17. Ibid., 105.

18. Richard Hindry Barker, *Mr. Cibber of Drury Lane* (New York: Columbia University Press, 1939; reprint, New York: AMS Press, 1966), 140.

19. Cole, *Charles Kean*, 141.

20. Odell, *Shakespeare from Betterton to Irving*, 2:102.

21. Cole, *Charles Kean*, 138.

22. Odell, *Shakespeare from Betterton to Irving*, 2:445.

23. Norman Marshall, *The Other Theatre* (London: John Lehmann, 1947), 66.

24. Margaret Webster, *The Same Only Different: Five Generations of a Great Theatre Family* (New York: Alfred A. Knopf, 1969), 368.

25. Foakes, Introduction, p. xlvii.

26. Colley Cibber, *An Apology for the Life of Colley Cibber*, ed. B. R. S. Fone (Ann Arbor: University of Michigan Press, 1968), 299.

27. William Shakespeare, *King Henry VIII. A Tragedy* (1734; reprint, London: Cornmarket Press, 1969).

28. The rough count taken from the Norton Facsimile edition of *Henry VIII* is King Henry, 461 lines; Queen Katherine, 382 lines; Wolsey, 403 lines. This disposition of speeches and dialogue seems to indicate that the original intention of the playwright(s) (if

such a thing really can be determined) was to create a kind of theatrical equality among these three characters and to emphasize the ensemble nature of the production.

29. Shirley S. Allen, *Samuel Phelps and Sadler's Wells Theatre* (Middletown, Conn.: Wesleyan University Press, 1971), 224.

30. Odell, *Shakespeare from Betterton to Irving*, 2:289–90.

31. Muriel St. Clare Byrne, "A Stratford Production: *Henry VIII*," *Shakespeare Survey* 3 (1950): 127.

PART IV

Questions of Text

14

Good News about "Bad" Quartos

STEVEN URKOWITZ

> *Val[entine]*. My eares are stopt, & cannot hear good newes,
>   So much of bad already hath possest them.
> *Pro[teus]*. Then in dumbe silence will I bury mine,
>   For they are harsh, un-tuneable, and bad.
>   (*Two Gentlemen of Verona*, TLN 1274–77; 3.1.206–9)

THE EARLIEST printed texts of *Hamlet, The Merry Wives of Windsor, Henry V, Richard III, Romeo and Juliet, Henry VI*, parts 2 and 3, and, until quite recently, *King Lear* have been called "bad" by modern editors, and they have been kept buried, out of sight and out of mind of modern readers, scholars, and performers of Shakespearean drama.[1] They were first printed in quarto or octavo formats and are collectively referred to as "bad quartos." These earliest texts are very different from later printed versions of the same plays: the overall length, the arrangement of scenes, the names and speech mannerisms of characters, stage properties and movement called for by dialogue and formal stage directions, entrances and exits, and literary style and diction appear radically altered when earlier and later texts are compared.

Some early printed quartos of other Shakespearean plays differ very little from later printings; these are called "good quartos," and they include the texts of *Titus Andronicus, Richard II, Henry IV*, parts 1 and 2, and others. When they brought out the 1623 Folio edition of Shakespeare's plays, his fellow players John Heminge and William Condell referred to *all* previously printed texts as "stolne, and surreptitious copies, maimed, and deformed by the frauds and stealthes of injurious impostors, that expos'd them." Modern editors have selectively applied these censures to only the "bad" quartos, and they have kept what they feel are stealthy frauds safely quarantined and out of common circulation. But Heminge and Condell included their blanket condemnation of the pre-Folio texts as part of a lighthearted, tongue-in-cheek appeal to potential buyers of the massive, expensive volume they had assembled:

To the great Variety of Readers.

From the most able, to him that can but spell: There you are number'd. We had rather you were weighd. Especially, when the fate of all Bookes depends upon your capacities: and not of your heads alone, but of your purses. Well! It is now publique, & you wil stand for your priviledges wee know: to read, and censure. Do so, but buy it first. That doth best commend a Booke, the Stationer saies. Then, how odde soever your braines be, or your wisedomes, make your licence the same, and spare not. Judge your sixe-pen'orth, your shillings worth, your five shillings worth at a time, or higher, so you rise to the just rates, and welcome. But, whatever you do, Buy. Censure will not drive a Trade, or make the Jacke go.

"Well! . . . read, and censure. Do so, but buy it first." Displaying the boldness and wit often ascribed to players, this appeal is scarcely a firm basis for dismissing the possible interest of the earliest printed texts. And indeed until the twentieth century many critics and editors read the earliest texts as authorial or theatrical documents showing the development of Shakespeare's plays as working drafts or as performing scripts for Elizabethan acting companies. The major problem in our current textual turmoil over Shakespeare's plays arises from the outright rejection by modern textual critics of the earliest or "bad" quarto scripts as having any worth for modern students of the plays. Their usually unstated hypothesis is that Shakespeare composed only a single, full-length version of each play, that he took no important part in theatrical revision or adaptation of his own scripts, and that the providers of the "stolne, and surreptitious copies" were ignorant, incompetent, and insensitive to the drama and poetry of Shakespeare's "perfect" originals.

To get some idea of the dimensions of the problem, a specific example might prove helpful. The 1603 First Quarto text of *Hamlet*, a "bad" quarto, includes a king's adviser named Corambis. The 1605 Second Quarto edition of *Hamlet*, a "good" quarto, contains about twice as many lines as the 1603 version, radically varies the First Quarto's ordering of the plot, the arrangement of scenes, and the themes of characterization such as Hamlet's sexuality and the King's generosity, and the King's counselor is named as we know him, Polonius. After Ophelia reports to her father the apparently traumatic effect that her rejection of Hamlet's affections has had upon him, the Second Quarto has Polonius say,

> come, goe we to the King,
> This must be knowne, which beeing kept close, might move
> More griefe to hide, then hate to utter love,
> Come.

(E2v; 2.1.114–17)

The counselor sees only two grim alternatives, grief or hatred.

The equivalent moment in the "bad" First Quarto instead shows Corambis offering Ophelia hope for her love:

> Let's to the King, this madnesse may proove,
> Though wilde a while, yet more true to thy love.
>
> (D3; 2.1.114–17)

Father Corambis holds out the expectation of eventual success or recovery, a significantly different vision than appears in the later printed text. This is one of a score of similar variations between Corambis in Q1 and Polonius in Q2, and it is typical of the theatrical alternatives in the roles of virtually every speaking character. The 1623 First Folio text of *Hamlet* introduces even more changes, primarily in wording, in stage action, and in the characterization of Queen Gertrude.[2]

Explaining the sources of the multiple texts and differences such as those in the three *Hamlet* texts brings Shakespearean textual scholars into conflict. Is the First Quarto of *Hamlet* Shakespeare's first surviving version of the play, or is it a corrupt product of other hands who pirated Shakespeare's work as best they could and peddled their "stolne and surreptitious copy" as if it were authentic? Did Shakespeare revise his plays, writing one version and then another, or did he compose in a single effort and then leave a unique script to the vagaries of theatrical revisers and adapters who then became our varying witnesses to the lost original? Is there one Shakespearean *Hamlet* distorted by transmission into three alternative texts, or are there three Shakespearean *Hamlet*s representing stages of the playwright's revising process?

In the late 1920s, one group of scholars seemed to establish a firm and orthodox procedure for analyzing and editing Shakespeare's plays—including both the single-text plays and also those with alternative texts. Led by A. W. Pollard, R. B. McKerrow, and W. W. Greg, these scholars concentrated on the quartos and Folio as manufactured objects, the products of the book trade. They learned about the changes that typesetters and printers imposed on the manuscript copy that they had to work from, and they showed that some characteristics of Shakespearean printed texts derived from the printing process itself rather than from the author's manuscripts. For example, they demonstrated conclusively that many spelling practices were peculiar to the individual compositors who typeset the plays, and that spelling was liable to change when a different man was at the type case. Their analytic program came to be known as the New Bibliography, and its elegance and rigor led its practitioners to the head of textual scholarship in England and America during the early decades of the twentieth century.

If changes were imposed upon an author's manuscript by the printing process, an editor could sometimes recover details of a lost original manuscript by comparing the changes found in successive editions of a book, and the editor could also discover which of several alternative printings was closest to the author's manuscript. These same New Bibliographic techniques could seriously distort an investigator's perceptions, however, if any of the textual changes between editions had been generated not by a worker in the printing house but, rather, by the author revising the copy underlying the variant texts. If an author were responsible for alternative readings, then an editor's task would shift radically. Rather than clearing up the printer's changes and restoring the author's words, the job of the editor of a text with authorial revisions involves an embarrassment of riches. Should an editor print the earliest text, or the latest, or the most aesthetically pleasing? Or should the editor or a team of editors find a way to print separately *all* the versions for the reader? Or should the editor assemble a composite text, drawing eclectically from the extant versions?

When they came to edit Shakespeare's multiple-text plays, the major figures of the New Bibliography concluded that the multiple versions resulted from problems of transmission rather than from authorial revision. The radically variant texts, the bibliographers argued, took their different forms primarily because nonauthorial agents, such as theatrical adapters, theatrical pirates, and revising actors, distorted Shakespeare's unique originals.

Before the New Bibliographers achieved their prominence, editors had vigorously disputed the question of authorial revision versus playhouse contamination or illicit transcription. Many highly reputable editors felt that Shakespeare was a revising artist responsible for many of the variants in his multiple-text plays. But, until the recent debates over the texts of *King Lear,* for the half century after the New Bibliographers took over the field no major editors and very few critics championed the theory that Shakespeare was responsible for the radically variant "bad" quarto texts.

The current revolution in Shakespearean textual studies attempts to be more bibliographically conservative than the twentieth-century hegemony of the New Bibliographers. While editors following Greg attempt to recover or re-create a single Shakespearean "original" script for each play, I and others are trying to encourage scholars to consider the possibility that each of the multiple texts may represent a different stage in Shakespeare's and his acting company's composing and revising process, and then to read variant texts simultaneously, learning their distinctions firsthand rather than accepting an editor's representation of them.[3] But before expecting anyone to follow such a suggestion, I intend to show that the conventional approach to Shakespeare's multiple-text plays may be inadequate. To do so, I offer an assessment of the traditional theoretical and practical foundations of one important aspect of the editorial tradition. I will survey some of the major arguments for a theory of "memorial reconstruction," the principal justification for our contemporary editorial practices.

*   *   *

In the eighteenth and nineteenth centuries, some editors argued that texts such as the First Quarto of *King Lear* and *Henry V* were printed from illicit manuscripts. They suggested that during performances someone with a good memory, or a journeyman actor who played small roles in a production, would memorize or transcribe the dialogue as recited by the actors and then sell this reported version to a printer. This hypothesized process came to be known as "memorial reconstruction." In the twentieth century, Greg presented a major and influential analysis of memorial reconstruction as the explanation of the bibliographic problems of a Shakespearean multiple-text play in his 1910 edition of the First Quarto of *The Merry Wives of Windsor.* According to Greg we have one relatively authentic and one extremely spurious text of *Merry Wives:* for Greg the Folio represents Shakespeare's intentions after parts of the last act were revised by another hand and then garbled slightly by production and press. And, in Greg's opinion, the Quarto records a shifting spectrum of variants generated by many different agents—a playhouse adapter, who may have cut scenes and characters for the company; a reviser other than Shakespeare responsible for some of the variants where both the Quarto and the Folio differ from a hypothetical, lost Shakespearean original; Shakespeare's fellow actors, who distorted the script in performance; and over all, a memorizing reporter or "playhouse thief":

> Of his presence there can be no manner of doubt. . . . The most cursory examination of the text shows that there is everywhere gross corruption, constant mutilation, meaningless inversion and clumsy transposition. . . . The playhouse thief reveals himself in every scene, corrupting, mutilating, rewriting.[4]

But how does Greg know that the Quarto is not an authorial version, a rough draft indicating the author's own difficulties with rapid composition and the weaving of different stories into a single dramatic fabric? If he had compared the two *Merry Wives* texts with extant authorially revised versions of works by Sheridan, or Keats, or Dickens, or Ben Jonson, or George Bernard Shaw, Greg would have found in their writings all the signs ascribed to "memorially reconstructed" texts: transpositions, anticipations, recollections, substitutions, as well as similar changes in characters' names and motives, actions and lines of plot, quirks of expression, and moral themes. Given these similarities, a simpler hypothesis would have been that the early printing of *Merry Wives* represented an authorial draft. We know for certain, however, that Greg did not compare the two *Merry Wives* texts with any confirmed instances of "memorially reconstructed" Renaissance plays because no such texts exist. Instead, Greg offers a charming anecdote about how he convinced himself that the Quarto was written by an illicit reporter:

> A very few visits to the theatre would have enabled a pirate of even moderate parts or experiences to vamp up such a text as the quarto in general supplies. In making this assertion I am not speaking without book, for I have tried the experiment myself. It happened that after four visits to *John Bull's Other Island* I was called upon to give some account of the piece for strictly private entertainment, and I found that I was able to reproduce all the material parts of the dialogue sufficiently accurately to convey an idea of the play which was not seriously modified by subsequent reading. . . . After I had seen the play five or six times I tried the further experiment of writing out from memory the passage of Act IV from the departure of Barney Doran and his gang to the exit of Aunt Judy (pp. 86–92 of the printed text). . . . I still possess this reconstruction of mine and have since collated it with the printed text. I think it will compare favourably with any scene of the quarto which can reasonably be paralleled with it in extent. *John Bull's Other Island* is considerably longer than the full text of the *Merry Wives,* and I had no previous experience whatever in the art of dramatic piracy.[5]

Greg never printed his own "reported text" of *John Bull's Other Island* by George Bernard Shaw, so we cannot learn if the differences between it and Shaw's were at all like those between the hypothetical pirate's "bad" quarto and the "genuine" *Merry Wives* of the Folio. Greg insists that we trust his judgment about the most basic proposition of his hypothesis, a risky condition to impose upon any scholarly dispute. Reduced to its simplest terms, Greg's argument might be paraphrased, "I say that I memorized a new play at performances of it and then wrote out its text; believe me, my reconstruction looks just like the 'bad' quarto of *The Merry Wives of Windsor;* so therefore I have demonstrated that *The Merry Wives* 'bad' quarto is a memorial reconstruction." Aside from not providing any sample of his own "reconstruction," Greg neglects to mention that Elizabethan plays were presented in a season of "rolling repertory"; except in extraordinary cases, a play would be given only a half dozen to a dozen times during a whole season. A "pirate" could not return night after night as Greg did to *John Bull's Other Island.* Further, Greg fails to consider seriously that Shakespeare himself could have been responsible for many systematic or purposeful variations in plot, in characterizations, and in literary style found between the *Merry Wives* Quarto and

Folio. He claims that the Quarto is "corrupt," but it may simply be tentative and exploratory, like almost any author's first drafts. We find patterns of variation between the Quarto and Folio versions of *Merry Wives* that resemble similar patterns found in other variant Shakespearean texts.[6] And we find expressions in the Quarto different from those in the Folio but just as linguistically inventive and delightful as those in Shakespeare's other "authentic" writings.

One example appears when Falstaff reports to Mr. Ford his dismal experience wooing his wife. Both Quarto and Folio texts have him refer to the ordeal as three "deaths"; the Quarto reads:

> Ile tell you M. Brooke, by the Lord for your sake
> I suffered *three egregious deaths:* [1] First to be
> Crammed like a good bilbo, in the circomference
> Of a pack, Hilt to point, heele to head: and [2] then to
> Be stewed in my owne grease like a Dutch dish:
> A man of my kidney; by the Lord it was a marvell I
> Escaped suffication; and [3] in the heat of all this,
> To be throwne into Thames like a horshoo hot:
> Maister Brooke, thinke of that hissing heate, Maister
> Brooke.
>> (E3v; 3.5.107–22. Italics and bracketed numbers added.)

In the Folio Falstaff talks of "three several deaths" rather than the "three egregious deaths" of the Quarto. But then, oddly, the Folio goes on to list *four* traumas. The first in the Folio has no equivalent in the Quarto, the second in the Folio corresponds with the first in the Quarto; and the third and fourth of the Folio present the same events as the Quarto's second and third deaths, but here they are woven into a very different but equally seamless verbal fabric:

> But marke the sequell
> (Master Broome) *I suffered the pangs of three severall deaths:* [1] First, an intollerable fright, to be detected with a jealious rotten Bell-weather: [2] Next to be compass'd like a good Bilbo in the circumference of a Pecke, hilt to point, heele to head. And then [3] to be stopt in like a strong distillation with stinking Cloathes, that fretted in their owne grease: thinke of that, a man of my Kidney; thinke of that, that am as subject to heate as butter; a man of continuall dissolution, and thaw: it was a miracle to scape suffocation. And in the height of this Bath (when I was more than halfe stew'd in grease (like a Dutch-dish) to be [4] throwne into the Thames, and coold, glowing-hot, in that serge like a Horse-shoo; thinke of that; hissing hot: thinke of that (Master Broome.)
>> (TLN 1773–89; 3.5.107–22. Italics and bracketed numbers added.)

The Quarto includes what Greg would call clumsy repetitions of Falstaff's exclamations, "By the Lord" and "Master Brook." But the Folio text has its own repetitions of "think of that" and "Master Broome." I would propose an alternative hypothesis in opposition to Greg's piracy theory: perhaps Shakespeare in an early draft experimented with various patterns of repetition, trying out two *by the Lord*s and three *Master Brook*s in the version underlying the Quarto, then later settling on two *Master Broom*s and four *think of that*s in the manuscript forming the basis of the Folio.

Greg, who seems to deny Shakespeare any significant contribution to the details of the Quarto, tacitly fails to deal with the problem of how the "mutilating" reporter could also come up with the expression, only in the "bad" text, "By the Lord for your sake I suffered *three egregious deaths*," where the Folio has "I suffered the pangs of *three several deaths*." (Greg rhetorically asks: "How many speeches are there which could be ascribed to [Shakespeare] in the form in which they appear in the quarto?"[7] Even one, and I believe that here at least is one that could be ascribed to Shakespeare, should be sufficient to encourage scholars and students of Renaissance drama to look closely and imaginatively at all the speeches in the Quarto text.)

Greg's arguments work convincingly only so long as they are not checked against alternative explanations of the same data. Although Greg's story about his own memorial reconstruction is charming, it remains simply a forceful testament of Greg's own belief that Shakespeare could not compose by a process of rough drafting and subsequent polishing. More important, Greg's analysis of *The Merry Wives of Windsor* in no way resembles the careful bibliographic study of printed books and manuscripts upon which his extraordinary and merited reputation depends.

Thirteen years after publication of his edition of the Quarto of *Merry Wives*, another influential study by Greg of the problem of variant versions of Elizabethan playscripts, *Two Elizabethan Stage Abridgements* (1923),[8] was published. Again his personal opinions of theatrical evidence, rather than any bibliographic arguments, support a theory of memorial reconstruction in the extent texts of *Orlando Furioso* and *The Battle of Alcazar*. Greg's work on these plays has been accepted for more than sixty years. But recently theatrical and textual critics have been reexamining the fundamental premises of his opinions. For example, in any essay forthcoming in a festschrift for F. S. Johnson, the late Bernard Beckerman concluded that Greg's interpretations of the relationships between dramatic plots and promptbooks on which he based his theories were "illusory" and ultimately "unconvincing." My own findings, based on thorough checking of Greg's evidence and reasoning, lead me to concur with Beckerman that Greg's work in this area is speculative rather than reliable. Because Greg misconstrues the fluid potentialities for the writing and revising of scripts on the Shakespearean stage, his work has been misleading and his theories harmful to our understanding of variant texts of Elizabethan and Jacobean playscripts.

* * *

Another form of the memorial reconstruction argument was developed by Peter Alexander in *Shakespeare's Henry VI and Richard III* (1929). Alexander's primary contribution was to recover the Folio versions of these plays as whole units of Shakespeare's writing; most critics at the time were ascribing major portions of these plays to other playwrights. Once he turned to analyze the variants between the Quarto and Folio texts, however, Alexander fell into serious problems of his own.

Like Greg with *Merry Wives*, Alexander argues that the earliest texts of *Henry VI*, parts 2 and 3, and *Richard III* were pirated "memorial reconstructions." Alexander begins by offering as an analogy the case of pirated versions of plays of Richard Brinsley Sheridan printed in England almost two hundred years after the Shakespearean texts he is discussing. Sheridan's play *The Duenna* indeed was memorially reconstructed by a player who had performed in the London cast, and Alexander gives samples of both the authorial form of the play and the pirated reconstruction.[9] However, discovered and published at roughly the same time that Alexander was presenting his suggestive analogies, we also happen to have Sheridan's own early versions of his plays and his later revisions.[10] When we compare Sheridan's early text and Sheridan's later text we find that they contain the kinds of changes noticed between the Quarto and the Folio versions of *Henry VI*, parts 2 and 3, and *Richard III*. But the pirated text of *The Duenna* and the author's published text do not look at all like the alternative authorial forms of either Sheridan's plays or the Shakespearean texts in question. Work on the Sheridan piracies and the Sheridan authorial revisions proceeded through the 1930s, but Alexander's erroneously drawn analogies were not and have not yet been corrected by later editors of the texts of Shakespeare's plays.

Like Greg, Alexander gets caught up in highly subjective literary analyses of his variant texts. He must demonstrate that one version is "good" and "authorial" while the other is "bad" and "pirated." Looking at the "bad" quarto version of the end of *Henry VI*, part 2, Alexander says, "In the last two scenes, for example, there are twenty lines which are very similar to the corresponding parts in the Folio, the rest is rubbish."[11] But if we pick through the Quarto's "rubbish" we find dramatic action as vivid (and as Shakespearean) as is found in the Folio.

Sometimes we have essentially the same action indicated differently in the two texts, and sometimes we find entirely different actions. A fight scene between York and Clifford, for example, appears in two radically incompatible forms. In the earliest text, the two men are mutually vituperative, politically simplistic, and unrelievedly bitter.

> *Yorke.* Now Clifford, since we are singled here alone,
>   Be this the day of doome to one of us,
>   For now my heart hath sworne immortall hate
>   To thee and all the house of Lancaster.
> *Cliffood.* [*sic*] And here I stand, and pitch my foot to thine,
>   Vowing never to stir, till thou or I be slaine.
>   For never shall my heart be safe at rest,
>   Till I have spoyld the hatefull house of Yorke.
>   *Alarmes, and they fight, and Yorke kils Clifford.*
> *Yorke.* Now Lancaster sit sure, thy sinowes shrinke,
>   Come fearefull Henry grovelling on thy face,
>   Yeeld up thy Crowne unto the Prince of Yorke.
>   (H2v–H3; 5.2.19–30)

In contrast to this feral exchange, in the later text York pauses silently before closing to fight against Clifford. He seems to grasp the poignancy of their conflict and to appreciate the tragic nobility of his opponent. Both men share the highest values of their chivalric code.

> *Clif.* What seest thou in me Yorke?
>   Why dost thou pause?
> *Yorke.* With thy brave bearing should I be in love,
>   But that thou art so fast mine enemie.
> *Clif.* Nor should thy prowesse want praise & esteeme,
>   But that 'tis shewne ignobly, and in Treason.
> *Yorke.* So let it helpe me now against thy sword,
>   As I in justice, and true right expresse it.
> *Clif.* My soule and bodie on the action both.
> *Yor.* A dreadfull lay, addresse thee instantly.
> *Clif. La fia Corrone les eumenes.*
> *Yor.* Thus Warre hath given thee peace, for [thou] art still,
>   Peace with his soule, heaven, if it be thy will.
>   (TLN 3232–51; 5.2.19–30)

While the Quarto shows a political order destroyed by men already reduced to primitive fury and tribal bloodletting, the Folio shows the same order being destroyed by men still exquisitely sensitive to nobility and grace. The Quarto certainly is simpler, but its theatrical syntax nevertheless seems to be drawn from the same fountain of theatrical invention that we label "Shakespearean" in the Folio. Alexander can call the Quarto version "rubbish" only because he fails to examine the theatrical values of either text. Alexander's case for "memorial reconstruction," like Greg's, uses none of the disciplined and verifiable methodologies of the New Bibliography. Nonetheless, it remains the primary basis for textual discussion of the *Henry VI* plays.

* * *

Another influential contribution to the memorial reconstruction argument, Alfred Hart's *Stolne and Surreptitious Copies* (1942), attempts to ground the "memorial reconstruction" theory on a comparative analysis of word lists drawn from variant texts such as the First and Second *Romeo and Juliet* Quartos and from different, unrelated play texts. Hart concludes that Shakespeare could not have revised the Quarto text of *King Lear* into the Folio version, for example, because Shakespeare's *Lear* uses only 40 percent of the vocabulary found in its source, the old chronicle history *Leir*, while the Folio contains more than 90 percent of the vocabulary found in the Quarto: "I find it impossible to believe that Shakespeare almost simultaneously used two widely divergent and mutually exclusive methods of rewriting source plays. . . . That the mature Shakespeare should have employed these two self-contradictory methods of rewriting . . . seems to me as incredible as absurd."[12] The illusory contradiction in authorial method Hart finds unacceptable arises because he refuses to consider that Shakespeare could return to his own manuscript and make detailed, consistent changes in it: "Certainly the poet who, his fellows said, 'never blotted out [a] line' does not fit the picture of dull and patient drudgery which such line-by-line revision suggests."[13] Hart's strident rhetoric masks the simple alternatives to his assertions, that, indeed, Shakespeare could revise his work painstakingly, line by line. And Shakespeare could just as well have first adapted a draft of *King Lear*, roughly, from source material like *The Chronicle History of King Leir*, to produce a text such as is found in the 1608 Quarto of *King Lear*, and then Shakespeare could have fine-tuned a later version for performance, leaving something like the Folio text of *King Lear*.

Hart refers to the original actors of Shakespeare's plays as "ignorant, ill-educated mummers [unable] to pronounce the unusual words used by the company's poet."[14] He further asserts that Shakespeare's "original versions," as found in the longer "good" texts, were *always* cut down in performance to about 2,000 lines, or "two hours traffic." Although most plays could be performed in two hours, surviving promptbooks from the period demonstrate that plays of more than 3,000 lines were not cut to reduce playing time, and indeed none of the extant playhouse documents give any evidence of concern for a play's length.

Examining the variant forms of commands that initiate exits, Hart imagines that the "good" versions were prompted by Shakespeare's recognition of a general dramatic incompetence of Elizabethan actors, while the "bad" equivalents represent those same bad actors' efforts at simplifying Shakespeare's stagecraft:

> Shakespeare knew that the dull actor always found it difficult to make a natural exit at the end of a scene, and devised many ingenious methods and varied forms of words to help him get "within" gracefully. In a surreptitious quarto such as *Contention* [the "bad" version of *Henry VI*, part 2] the actors reduced his diversity of formulas to two, viz., "and so farewell" and "come lets go," and variants of these. Wherever one of these two occurs in the last line of a scene, corruption may be suspected. . . . One humorous incident occurs at the end of the sixth scene of *Contention*. The Duke of York has invited the Earl of Salisbury and his son, the Earl of Warwick, to sup with him at the ducal palace. . . . [At the scene's end] York thanks them, and closes the scene with the words, "come lets goe"! These stupid mummers did not understand that during this scene the stage represents the palace of a prince and that by using the words "come lets goe" their host was asking his important guests to leave his house. Shakespeare's dramatic ingenuity [in the Folio] had provided for the difficulty of getting the nobles off the stage. Six lines before the end Salisbury rises from his seat and says (2.2.77) to York: "My Lord, breake we off; we know your minde at full." All rise and as they walk to the stage door, Warwick promises his help; and the Duke of York concludes the scene, as they leave the stage together, with a promise (2.2.81–2): "to make the Earle of Warwick / The greatest man in England, but the King."[15]

Hart ingenuously fails to notice that the two texts offer completely different actions prior to the exit from the scene. Here is the Quarto version—in it the Earl of Warwick encourages the Duke of York to claim the throne of England and offers to support his coup d'état with ten thousand soldiers.

> *Yorke.* I thanke you both. But Lords I am not your King, until this
>   sword be sheathed even in the hart blood of the house of Lancaster.
> *War.* Then Yorke advise thy selfe and take thy time,
>   Claime thou the Crowne, and set thy standard up,
>   And in the same advance the milke-white Rose,
>   And then to gard it, will I rouse the Beare,
>   Inviron'd with ten thousand Ragged-staves
>   To aide and helpe thee for to win thy right,
>   Maugre the proudest Lord of Henries blood,
>   That dares deny the right and claime of Yorke,
>   For why my minde presageth I shall live
>   To see the noble Duke of Yorke to be a King.
> *Yorke.* Thanks noble Warwicke, and Yorke doth hope to see,

> The Earle of Warwicke live, to be the greatest man in England,
> but the King. Come lets goe.   *Exet omnes.*
>   (C4v–31; 2.2.64–83)

York's final command seems like an important assertion of his tenuous control over Warwick, potentially "the greatest man in England, but the King," and his "ten thousand Ragged-staves." The simple exit tag is also a powerful social code showing who takes precedence within the group, who issues commands and who obeys. The alternative in the Folio presents a different series of actions. Rather than acceding to a plan offered by Warwick, York instead designs his own Machiavellian strategy—an exercise in *Realpolitik* rather than *forte main.*

> *Yorke.* We thanke you Lords:
>   But I am not your King, till I be Crown'd,
>   And that my Sword be stayn'd
>   With heart-blood of the House of Lancaster:
>   And that's not suddenly to be perform'd,
>   But with advice and silent secrecie.
>   Doe you as I doe in these dangerous dayes,
>   Winke at the Duke of Suffolkes insolence,
>   At Beaufords Pride, at Somersets Ambition,
>   At Buckingham, and all the Crew of them,
>   Till they have snar'd the Shepheard of the Flock,
>   That vertuous Prince, the good Duke Humfrey:
>   'Tis that they seeke; and they, in seeking that,
>   Shall find their deaths, if Yorke can prophecie.
> *Salisb.* My Lord, breake we off; we know your minde at full.
> *Warw.* My heart assures me, that the Earle of Warwick
>   Shall one day make the Duke of Yorke a King.
> *Yorke.* And Nevill, this I doe assure my selfe,
>   Richard shall live to make the Earle of Warwick
>   The greatest man in England, but the King.
>   *Exeunt.*
>   (TLN 1029–50; 2.2.64–83)

The secondary character Salisbury initiates the idea for the exit, and then first Warwick and next York both stand pat, unmoved by Salisbury's suggestion, until they each get in their last words.

Neither version looks as if it were designed to accommodate a "dull actor" in the troupe with which Shakespeare performed, and a "stupid mummer" able to create the coherent but different Quarto text is a theatrical craftsman of remarkable accomplishment. Indeed, when seen in a context larger than the brief snippets presented by Hart, the alternatives look like authorial revisions, the earlier printed text resembling an author's early draft, the later text of the Folio resembling a later version composes afresh by the same artistic sensibility weaving into his text more complex issues of loyalty and subversion. The rich variety of these alternatives resembles the recasting of the combat between York and Clifford at the end of the same play, discussed earlier.

Hart's bellicose attacks against Shakespeare's actors epitomize the argumentative methods found in the major contentions for "memorial reconstruction" and other destructive interventions that attempt to explain away variants that would otherwise be considered typical authorial changes in theatrical scripts. Although it stands on demonstrably false (if not absurd) prejudices and misinterpretations of evidence, Hart's work has been cited as a conclusive proof of the "memorial reconstruction" hypothesis by Harold Jenkins in the New Arden *Hamlet* (1982), Brian Gibbons in the New Arden *Romeo and Juliet* (1980), and Gary Taylor in *Three Studies in the Text of "Henry V"* (1979).

* * *

Corollary hypotheses that grow out of the "memorial reconstruction" theory frequently catch the imagination of Shakespearean scholars. For example, any reader of the textual notes on *Hamlet* in almost any modern edition will learn that the "pirate" who "memorially reconstructed" the 1603 Quarto of *Hamlet* was the actor who played the role of Marcellus, or perhaps he was the one who played the ambassador Voltemand, or perhaps he doubled these parts. To discover the culprit we need only apply an elementary technique of deduction easily adapted from twentieth-century detective fiction. If a larcenous player wished to memorize and then sell a play in which he was performing, the hypothetical villain would have a head start because he would know his own speeches. Not only would they have been memorized, but he would have been given his cues and his speeches written down for study. Find the role or roles with no differences between the "bad" and the later "good" text and there you have him. Marcellus was first fingered by W. H. Widgery in 1880, and again in 1913 Henry David Gray enthusiastically announced the same discovery.[16] Today almost all editions report to us that Marcellus and/or Voltemand pirated the Q1 *Hamlet*.[17]

But Frank G. Hubbard in 1918 went back to check Gray's data.[18] Hubbard showed that both Widgery and Gray seriously misrepresent the "goodness" of Marcellus's part in the "bad" quarto. The hypothetical pirate who played Marcellus made twenty-ódd significant errors in the wording of his own very small part; he also managed to forget entire speeches that he was supposed to say according to the "good" Second Quarto script. Further, Marcellus remembered himself delivering a speech given to Hamlet in the "genuine" text, and he padded Horatio's part by transferring to him a speech that he, Marcellus, was supposed to say. A suspect because he is supposed to be so good at his own part, indeed because he would have had his own part available in writing, Marcellus blundered fatally. Hubbard showed that Widgery and Gray's detective fantasies about Marcellus as a pirate fail to fit the data.

Hubbard subsequently brought out an edition of the Q1 *Hamlet* in which he offered further challenges to the prevailing memorial reconstruction hypothesis.[19] Hubbard argued instead that the Q1 *Hamlet* has many of the qualities one would expect to find in an authorial draft. Henry David Gray responded to Hubbard's challenge seven years later simply by announcing confidently that his own earlier article was correct and by indicating that J. Dover Wilson had arrived independently at a similar memorial reconstruction hypothesis.[20] Neither Gray nor Wilson addressed any of Hubbard's arguments.

Now, one would expect any survey of the textual criticism of *Hamlet* to record the existence of this interesting debate. None does. Instead, Gray's pseudo-scientific detection entered the folklore of Shakespearean textual studies and is cited repeatedly, while Hubbard's devastating challenge to Gray is mentioned nowhere. Hubbard's valuable edition of the Q1 *Hamlet* is also missing from all bibliographic surveys of Shakespearean scholarship likely to be consulted by students and scholars. Arguments raised in opposition to the prevailing "memorial reconstruction" hypothesis were first ignored and then effectively buried by omission from the surveys and guides prepared by editors for readers of their popular and scholarly texts of *Hamlet*.

Let us look further at other instances of this phenomenon. Back in 1877 P. A. Daniel claimed that the First Quarto of *Henry V* was a "memorial reconstruction" of the "genuine" authorial text of the Folio. Two years later, in 1879, Brinsley Nicholson questioned each point in Daniel's argument. Nicholson showed that Daniel's case depended solely upon personal literary taste rather than upon convincing analogies, forceful logic, or bibliographic evidence.[21] But only Daniel's work has been remembered, and it is today cited as if it were unimpeachable (or at least unimpeached). Nicholson's powerful rebuttal disappeared; it is not listed in bibliographic surveys or mentioned by subsequent scholars.

In another more recent instance of the same phenomenon, Harold Jenkins argued in 1960 that the Folio text of *Hamlet* contained "actors' interpolations," and so it was untrustworthy in many of the ways that the "bad" quartos were also supposed to be. Jenkins's opinion was vigorously contested by Terence Hawkes in 1977 and again by Maurice Charney in 1978.[22] But in his 1984 New Arden edition of *Hamlet*, Jenkins repeats his own earlier position as if it had never been questioned. The problem is not that an objection to a hypothesis necessarily refutes it, but rather that repeatedly in Shakespearean scholarship concerned with the issue of "memorial reconstruction" we have neither simple acknowledgment nor responsible evaluation of alternative theories.

* * *

In the past, editors and bibliographers argued that their primary task was to present a "best possible" Shakespearean script, one for each play. I am arguing instead that we all would learn more about Shakespeare's plays if we could look at the actual raw material, the variant quarto and Folio versions. Even if I am wrong about the source of these variants, and all these changes were corrupt alternatives introduced by pirates or players, at least those pirates or players stood through repeated performances of Elizabethan plays in Elizabethan playhouses. W. W. Greg did not. If the playhouse scribe or an "ignorant mummer" changed the characterizations of York, Clifford, Warwick, and Salisbury in two scenes from *Henry VI*, or that of Polonius-Corambis throughout *Hamlet*, then scholars, teachers, students, and actors should be encouraged to see what else that unknown agent or those hypothetical agents happened to change.

Where does this survey finally lead? First, I believe that we must reexamine the current status of the "memorial construction" hypothesis, whatever its ultimate validity, because (perhaps inadvertently) it seems to have prevented close examination of the fundamental documents of our literary-dramatic tradition by its practitioners, teachers of literature and performers of plays. Labeling certain texts as "bad" quartos has removed them from the normal discourse in which such documents would otherwise be included. A student can find a thirty-page extract of Brooke's *Romeus and Juliet* printed with the inexpensive Arden or New Cambridge *Romeo and Juliet* because it is a "good" source of the "genuine" play, but the same student has available only the costly and unwieldy Allen and Muir volume if he or she wishes to consult the "bad" though equally interesting First Quarto of *Romeo and Juliet*.

Second, I believe that we must reexamine the basic questions asked and procedures followed in discussions of when the earliest printed texts of Shakespeare's plays were composed or compiled. In the so-called bad quartos, patterns of imagery, poetic devices (particularly repetitions), meaningful uses of stage action, dramatic characterization, development of themes, and the rest—the entire repertory of theatrical art—should be studied for what they are, in and of themselves, rather than solely as pernicious desecrations of Shakespeare's iconic originals.

Third, I believe that, as a consequence of close study of these variant texts, future teachers, editors, students, and performers of Shakespeare's plays will be more conscious of the pervasive distortions of specifically theatrical values that appear in virtually all editions currently in use.

Fourth, I believe that we should encourage theatrical productions of these earliest Shakespearean playscripts to explore the theatrical phenomena they encode. A step in this direction appears in David Richman's brief report of a production of the 1608 "bad" text of *King Lear*, which overturns 90 percent of the denigrating commentary on the Quarto's theatricality offered by editors and textual critics during the past eighty years.[23]

Fifth, I believe that we should reject the implicit and explicit Bardolatry that tries imaginatively to remove Shakespeare from his active, craftsmanlike, and proprietary involvement in the day-to-day operations of his commercially successful acting troupe. The opportunities for further study of these variant dramatic scripts are unprecedented. The rewards promise to be great.

Notes

1. Quotations of the Folio referenced parenthetically in the text are from *The Norton Facsimile: The First Folio of Shakespeare*, ed. Charlton Hinman (New York: W. W. Norton, 1968); quotations of the quarto texts are from *Shakespeare's Plays in Quarto*, ed. Michael J. B. Allen and Kenneth Muir (Berkeley: University of California Press, 1981). Through Line Numbers (TLN) are from the Hinman facsimile, and modern act, scene, and line numbers are from *The Riverside Shakespeare*, ed. G. Blakemore Evans (Boston: Houghton Mifflin, 1974). In all quotations, *u* and *v*, *i* and *j*, *s* and long *s*, as well as typographical ligatures, have been normalized to modern conventions; italicized proper nouns in the dialogue of the originals are here printed in roman type, and the few stage directions set in roman in the originals are here put in italic.

2. See Steven Urkowitz, " 'Well-sayd olde Mole': Burying Three *Hamlets* in Modern Editions," in *Shakespeare Study Today*, ed. Georgianna Ziegler (1986), 37–70.

3. See Michael J. Warren, "Textual Problems, Editorial Assertions in Editions of Shakespeare," in Jerome J. McGann, ed. *Textual Criticism and Literary Interpretation* (Chicago: University of Chicago Press, 1985), 23–37.

4. W. W. Greg, ed. *Shakespeare's Merry Wives of Windsor* (Oxford: Clarendon, Press, 1910), xxvi–xxvii.

5. Ibid., xxvii–xxviii.

6. See Steven Urkowitz, "Five Women Eleven Ways," in the forthcoming *Images of Shakespeare: Proceedings of the Third Congress of the International Shakespeare Association, 1986* (Newark: University of Delaware Press, 1988).

7. Greg, *Shakespeare's Merry Wives*, xxvi. Greg's detailed notes blandly comment on several glaring contradictions between his theory and his data. For example: "*Have I caught my heavenlie Jewel?* The folio gives this line in the form: 'Have I caught thee, my heavenly Jewel?' It is a quotation from Sidney's *Astrophel and Stella* (second song . . .), and it is to be remarked that the quarto gives the line correctly" (p. 74). To fit into his theory, either Greg's pirate, or the actor playing Falstaff, or the playhouse adapter "corrected" Shakespeare's misquote in this spot. Or does the quarto here represent an early draft, closer to sources than subsequent rewritings?

8. W. W. Greg, ed. *Two Elizabethan Stage Abridgements* (London: Oxford University Press, 1923).

9. Peter Alexander, *Shakespeare's Henry VI and Richard III* (Cambridge: Cambridge University Press, 1929), 51–55.

10. See R. Crompton Rhodes, "Some Aspects of Sheridan Bibliography," *The Library,* 4th ser., 9 (1928): 233–61, and Richard Little Purdy, ed., *The Rivals, a Comedy, as It Was First Acted at the Theatre-Royal in Covent Garden* (Oxford: Clarendon Press, 1935).

11. Alexander, *Shakespeare's Henry VI,* 74–75.

12. Alfred Hart, *Stolne and Surreptitious Copies: A Comparative Study of Shakespeare's Bad Quartos* (Melbourne: Melbourne University Press; London: Oxford University Press, 1942), 37.

13. Ibid., 27.

14. Ibid., 36–37.

15. Ibid., 409.

16. W. H. Widgery and C. H. Herford, *The First Quarto Edition of Hamlet, 1603: Two Essays to which the Harness Prize Was Awarded* (London: Smith, Elder, 1880); Henry David Gray, "The First Quarto *Hamlet,*" *Modern Language Review* 10 (1913): 171–80. See especially Gray's note on 176–77.

17. See Philip Edwards, ed., *Hamlet,* New Cambridge ed. (1985), 24n, and Harold Jenkins, ed., *Hamlet,* New Arden Shakespeare ed. (1982), 20n.2, 21n.1.

18. "The 'Marcellus' Theory and the First Quarto *Hamlet,*" *Modern Language Notes* 33 (1918): 73–79.

19. *The First Quarto Edition of Shakespeare's Hamlet,* University of Wisconsin Studies in Language and Literature, vol. 8 (1920).

20. "Thomas Kyd and the First Quarto of *Hamlet,*" *PMLA* 42 (1927): 721–35.

21. P. A. Daniel, Introduction, in B[rinsley] Nicholson, ed., *King Henry V: Parallel Texts of the First Quarto (1600) and First Folio (1623) Editions* (London: N. Trübner, for the New Shakespere Society, 1877).

22. Harold Jenkins, "Playhouse Interpolations in the Folio Text of *Hamlet,*" *Studies in Bibliography* 13 (1960): 31–47; Terence Hawkes, "That Shakespeherian Rag," in *Essays and Studies,* ed. W. Moelwyn Merchant (1977), 22–38; Maurice Charney, "Hamlet's O-Groans and Textual Criticism," *Renaissance Drama,* n.s., 9 (1978): 109–19.

23. David Richman, "The *King Lear* Quarto in Rehearsal and Performance," *Shakespeare Quarterly* 37 (1986): 374–82.

Contributors

Iska Alter, Assistant Professor of English at Hofstra University, is the author of *The Good Man's Dilemma: Social Criticism in the Fiction of Bernard Malamud* (1981) and of articles on modern drama and on Shakespeare. She is currently working on a book on Shakespeare's *Henry VIII*.

Peter Berek is Morris Professor of Rhetoric and Special Assistant to the President at Williams College. He has written on Shakespeare, Renaissance drama, and Renaissance poetry, and has recently completed a book, *From* Tamburlaine *to* Hamlet: *Realism and Meaning in the 1590s*.

John Russell Brown is Director of Graduate Studies at the Theatre Department of the University of Michigan; he is also an Associate of the National Theatre of Great Britain. He has directed numerous plays by Shakespeare, the most recent being *Richard II* for a touring workshop presentation by the National Theatre. His many books include *Discovering Shakespeare, Theatre Language,* and editions of plays by Shakespeare and Webster.

Maurice Charney is Distinguished Professor of English at Rutgers University and currently President of the Shakespeare Association of America. He has written widely on Shakespeare and modern drama, including *Shakespeare's Roman Plays, Style in Hamlet, How to Read Shakespeare, Joe Orton,* and the forthcoming *Hamlet's Fictions*.

Dolora Cunningham is Professor of English at San Francisco State University, sometime director of the Shakespeare Institute of the Oregon Shakespeare Festival, and a founding Trustee of the Shakespeare Association of America. She has published various articles on Shakespeare and Jonson.

Anthony B. Dawson, Associate Professor of English at the University of British Columbia in Vancouver, is the author of *Indirections: Shakespeare and the Art of Illusion* and *Watching Shakespeare: A Playgoers' Guide*. He is currently working on a series of essays that focus on issues of power, gender, madness, and theatricality in Elizabethan and Jacobean drama.

SHIRLEY NELSON GARNER, Professor of English at the University of Minnesota, is an editor (with Claire Kahane and Madelon Sprengnether) of *The (M)other Tongue: Essays in Feminist Psychoanalytic Interpretation*. She has published articles on Shakespeare and various women writers and is a founder of *Hurricane Alice: A Feminist Quarterly*.

TERENCE HAWKES is a Professor of English at the University of Cardiff in Wales and editor of *Textual Practise* and the New Accents series at Methuen. Among his many books are *Shakespeare and the Reason, Shakespeare's Talking Animals, Metaphor*, and, most recently, *That Shakespeherian Rag*.

HARRIETT HAWKINS, Senior Research Fellow at Linacre College, Oxford, is currently Visiting Professor of English at Emory University. Her publications include *The Devil's Party: Critical Counter-Interpretations of Shakespearian Drama, Poetic Freedom and Poetic Truth*, and *Likenesses of Truth in Elizabethan and Restoration Drama*. In press is a critical introduction to *Measure for Measure*.

RICHARD LEVIN, Professor of English at the State University of New York at Stony Brook, is the author of *The Multiple Plot in English Renaissance Drama* and *New Readings vs. Old Plays: Recent Trends in the Reinterpretation of English Renaissance Drama*. He is currently at the National Humanities Center.

RUSS MCDONALD is Associate Professor of English at the University of Rochester. He is the author of *Shakespeare and Jonson/Jonson and Shakespeare*, as well as essays on other Renaissance playwrights, Flannery O'Connor, and opera.

NINIAN MELLAMPHY is Associate Professor of English at the University of Western Ontario. He has published articles on Shakespeare, Irish literature, and the theory of fiction.

ALEX NEWELL is a Professor of English at Concordia University in Montreal and is completing a book on *Hamlet*. He adapted *Yesterday the Children Were Dancing*, Gratien Gélinas's play about French-English conflict in Quebec, into *White Clouds, Black Dreams*, a drama about racial conflict in the United States.

AVRAHAM OZ is a former chairman of the Department of Theatre of the University of Tel Aviv in Israel, and a director of the Cameri Theatre in Tel Aviv. He has translated Shakespeare's *Merchant of Venice* and other plays into Hebrew.

STEVEN URKOWITZ is Associate Professor of English at the City College of New York and the City University Graduate Center. He is the author of *Shakespeare's Revision of King Lear* and articles on Shakespeare's multiple-text plays. He has directed medieval and Renaissance plays and coached the Western Wind Vocal Ensemble.

Index

211

ALVERNO COLLEGE LIBRARY
"Bad" Shakespeare
822.33G1b

2 5050 00701921 5

179048

822.33
G 1b

REMOVED FROM THE
ALVERNO COLLEGE LIBRARY

Alverno College
Library Media Center
Milwaukee, Wisconsin

DEMCO